Chinese Link

中 文 天 地

Zhōng   Wén   Tiān   Dì

Elementary Chinese

Level 1	Part 1

吴素美   于月明   张燕辉   田维忠

Sue-mei Wu   Yueming Yu   Yanhui Zhang   Weizhong Tian

Carnegie Mellon University

PEARSON
Prentice Hall

woRLd
Languages

Upper Saddle River, New Jersey 07458

Library of Congress Cataloging-in-Publication Data

Chinese link : Zhong wen tian di : elementary Chinese / Sue-mei Wu ... [et al]—Simplified
   character version.
     p. cm.
   ISBN 0-13-156442-0 (alk. paper)
   1. Chinese language—Textbooks for foreign speakers—English. I. Title: Elementary
Chinese. II. Wu, Sue-mei, 1968–

   PL1129.E5C418 2006
   495.1'82421—dc22

                                                      2005050939

Acquisitions Editor: Rachel McCoy
Publishing Coordinator: Claudia Fernandes
Executive Director of Market Development: Kristine Suárez
Director of Editorial Development: Julia Caballero
Production Supervision: Nancy Stevenson
Project Manager: Margaret Chan, Graphicraft
Assistant Director of Production: Mary Rottino
Supplements Editor: Meriel Martínez Moctezuma
Media Editor: Samantha Alducin
Media Production Manager: Roberto Fernandez
Prepress and Manufacturing Buyer: Brian Mackey
Prepress and Manufacturing Manager: Nick Sklitsis
Interior and Cover Design: Wanda España/Wee Design Group
Director, Image Resource Center: Melinda Reo
Interior Image Specialist: Beth Boyd Brenzel
Manager, Rights & Permissions IRC: Zina Arabia
Senior Marketing Manager: Jacquelyn Zautner
Marketing Assistant: William J. Bliss
Publisher: Phil Miller
Cover image: Jerry Darvin

This book was set in 12/15 Sabon by Graphicraft Ltd., Hong Kong, and was printed
and bound by Courier – Westford. The cover was printed by Phoenix Color Corp.

© 2007 by Pearson Education, Inc.
Upper Saddle River, NJ 07458

Printed in the United States of America
10 9 8 7

ISBN 0-13-156442-0

Pearson Education Ltd., *London*
Pearson Education Australia Pty, Limited, *Sydney*
Pearson Education Singapore Pte. Ltd.
Pearson Education North Asia Ltd., *Hong Kong*
Pearson Education Canada, Ltd., *Toronto*
Pearson Educación de México, S.A. de C.V.
Pearson Education – Japan, *Tokyo*
Pearson Education Malaysia Pte. Ltd.
Pearson Education, *Upper Saddle River,* New Jersey

目录 CONTENTS

范围和顺序 Scope and Sequence

Foundation

Lessons & Topics	Objectives & Communications	Grammar	Culture Link
1 Hello! 你好! *p. 1*	■ Conduct simple greetings in Chinese ■ Ask simple yes/no questions ■ Answer simple yes/no questions ■ Discuss other people	1. Chinese Sentences 2. The Pronouns 我, 你 and 他 3. The Interrogative Particle 吗 4. The Modal Particle 呢 5. 是 Sentences 6. The Adverb 也	**Culture Notes:** Basic Chinese Greetings 问候语 **Fun With Chinese:** Motto: 学而时习之。 **Let's Go:** Sign: Service Stand 服务台
2 What's Your Surname? 您贵姓? *p. 13*	■ Exchange names ■ Get to know each other ■ Find out who someone else is	1. 您 2. 您贵姓 3. The Interrogative Pronouns 什么, 谁 4. The Particle 的	**Culture Notes:** Chinese Names 中文姓名 **Fun With Chinese:** Idiom: 同名同姓 **Let's Go:** ID Card 身份证
3 Which Country Are You From? 你是哪国人? *p. 29*	■ Find out someone's nationality ■ Ask which language they speak ■ Talk about each others' nationalities and languages	1. 哪(哪国人) Which Nationality? 2. 国名和国人 Country Names and People 3. 说 and 语言 4. 一点儿 5. Conjunction 和	**Culture Notes:** Chinese Concept of "Native Town" 中国人的家乡观念 **Fun With Chinese:** Idiom: 说来话长 **Let's Go:** On-line Language Tutoring Center 网上语言家教中心

Lessons & Topics	Objectives & Communications	Grammar	Culture Link
4 What Do You Study? 你学什么？ *p. 43*	■ Ask what something is ■ Explain what something is ■ Ask about majors in school ■ Talk about courses	1. Demonstrative Pronouns 这，那 2. 量词 (Measure Word/Classifier) (1): 本 3. Adverb 很 4. Suffix 们(我们，你们，他们) 5. Grammar Summary 语法小结	**Culture Notes:** The Chinese Educational System 中国的教育制度 **Fun With Chinese:** Proverb: 书中自有黄金屋，书中自有颜如玉。 **Let's Go:** After-school Learning Center 补习班
5 This Is My Friend 这是我朋友 *p. 63*	■ Introduce people ■ Make small talk ■ Find out what someone owns	1. 有 Sentences (没有) 2. Question Word 几 3. Adverb 都 4. 都 With 不 5. 都 With 也 6. Location of Adverbs 也都常很 (Summary of 也都常很)	**Culture Notes:** Chinese Forms of Address 中国的称谓文化 **Fun With Chinese:** Motto: 有朋自远方来，不亦乐乎？ **Let's Go:** Marriage and Friendship Social Center 婚友联谊中心
6 My Family 我的家 *p. 77*	■ Introduce yourself ■ Talk about your family	1. 是 ... 的 Construction 2. 在 3. 量词 (2) 个，辆，只，本. Questions: 几个，几辆，几只，几本	**Culture Notes:** Chinese Families 中国家庭 **Fun With Chinese:** Idiom: 爱屋及乌 **Let's Go:** Propaganda Posters 宣传标语

Lessons & Topics	Objectives & Communications	Grammar	Culture Link
7 Where Do You Live? 你住哪儿？ *p. 95*	■ Ask someone's address ■ Tell them your address ■ Describe a place ■ Ask/give phone numbers	1. 住 2. 住址的写法 Word Order for Addresses 3. Topic-Comment Sentences 4. 多少 and 几	**Culture Notes:** Traditional Chinese Houses — Si He Yuan 中国传统住房—四合院 **Fun With Chinese:** Motto: 远亲不如近邻。 **Let's Go:** Handle with Care 小心轻放
8 Do You Know Him? 你认识不认识他？ *p. 111*	■ More yes and no questions ■ Make and respond to a plan	1. Affirmative-Negative Questions ("A 不 A" Pattern) 2. Tag Question	**Culture Notes:** Business Cards in China 中国的名片文化 **Fun With Chinese:** Idiom: 一见钟情 **Let's Go:** Important Figures on Currency 钞票上的大人物
9 He Is Making a Phone Call 他正在打电话 *p. 125*	■ Make a phone call ■ Handle various phone situations ■ Ask what someone is doing ■ Explain what you are doing	1. The Progressive Aspect of an Action 在/正在 2. Summary: Ways of Asking Questions	**Culture Notes:** Cell Phones in China 手机在中国 **Fun With Chinese:** Slang: 不管三七二十一 **Let's Go:** Telephone Card 电话卡

Lessons & Topics	Objectives & Communications	Grammar	Culture Link
10 I Get Up at 7:30 Every Day 我每天七点半起床 *p. 145*	■ Give times and dates in Chinese ■ Describe your daily schedule ■ Write letters in Chinese	1. How to Tell the Time 2. Adverbs 就 and 才 3. Grammar Summary 语法小结	**Culture Notes:** University Life in China 中国的大学生活 **Fun With Chinese:** Slang: 开夜车 **Let's Go:** TV Programming Schedule 电视节目时间表
11 Do You Want Black Tea or Green Tea? 你要红茶还是绿茶? *p. 169*	■ Order food at a restaurant ■ Present/choose from alternatives ■ Ask what someone wants ■ Tell someone what you want	1. 还是 2. 量词 (Measure Words/Classifiers) (3)	**Culture Notes:** Chinese Food 中国菜系介绍 **Fun With Chinese:** Slang: 饭后百步走，活到九十九。 **Let's Go:** Chinese Snacks 小吃

Appendices

Recognizing that the world is becoming increasingly interlinked and globalized, the goal of the **CHINESE LINK: Zhongwen Tiandi 中文天地** (Elementary Chinese) project has been to integrate the "5Cs" principles of the National Standards for Foreign Language Education — Communication, Cultures, Comparisons, Connections, and Communities — throughout the program in order to provide a new approach for the teaching and learning of Chinese language in the 21st century. The program aims to help beginners develop their communicative competence in the four basic skills of listening, speaking, reading, and writing, while gaining competence in Chinese culture, exercising their ability to compare aspects of different cultures, making connections to their daily life, and building links among communities.

A language curriculum should be attractive to both students and instructors, therefore the authors provide a practical, learner-centered, and enjoyable language and culture learning experience for beginning students of Chinese, as well as an efficient and comprehensive teaching resource for instructors.

Proficiency in a language involves knowing both the structural forms of the language and their appropriate use in different cultural contexts. Care has been taken to introduce and explain grammar points clearly and systematically, yet not in a fashion that would be overwhelming to beginners. In keeping with the communicative focus of the text, grammar points are related to communicative, task-oriented content.

Each version of the text (Traditional and Simplified) presents both traditional and simplified versions of Chinese characters, since it is likely that students will encounter both forms. Similarly, care has been taken to present both Taiwan and Mainland China usage where they differ, and to incorporate new vocabulary items, such as "Internet," "cell phone," and "VCD." Culture notes at the end of each lesson are designed to catch the interest of the beginning learner and to explain important features of Chinese culture. Photographs and drawings are provided to make the text vivid and eye-catching, and to provide visual cues to aid in communicative exercises and activities.

Features of CHINESE LINK: Zhongwen Tiandi 中文天地　(Elementary Chinese)

- A clear and organized **Scope and Sequence** of the textbook is presented that provides an overview of the entire textbook, listing each lesson and its objectives, as well as the contents of the lesson's subsections. The **Scope and Sequence** lists the contents of four major sub-sections of each lesson: Grammar, Culture Notes, Fun with Chinese, and Let's Go!

- The 5Cs (**National Standards**) are blended consistently throughout the content and exercises in the program.

- The **Foundation** unit introduces important background information on Chinese language, useful classroom expressions, and a complete introduction to Pinyin and pronunciation.

- From the beginning of the text, we help students build from words and phrases to sentences and cohesive passages and then to application in **communicative tasks**.

- The textbook contains many **drawings** and **authentic photographs**, and utilizes a clear, attractive layout.

- **Grammar** points are introduced systematically and with a writing style that attempts to avoid excessive linguistic jargon. Grammar points include many examples.
- **Pronunciation and Pinyin** exercises are consistently emphasized throughout the entire text.
- **Both Traditional and Simplified character forms** are listed for every **vocabulary** item. When students see the two forms side by side it helps them to make an association between the two.
- **In-class exercises** are included in the main text as handy teaching aids and guidelines for instructors.
- Each lesson consists of **four types of exercises**: Pinyin, character, grammar, and communicative tasks. The exercises progress from drills and practice to content-based communicative tasks.
- Differences in usage between **Mainland China and Taiwan** are consistently identified.
- Interesting **cultural notes** are included in each lesson and supplemented with authentic photographs from Mainland China, Taiwan, and Hong Kong.

Organization of the Textbook

The textbook is divided into three main parts: **Foundation, core lessons,** and **Appendices.** The flexible design of the text allows instructors to use it in varying ways, depending on the number of contact hours per week and whether a school is on the semester or quarter system. Sample syllabi are available in the Instructor's Resource Manual.

Foundation:

The **Foundation** module provides fundamental knowledge about Chinese and learning Chinese that is useful for beginning students. It contains linguistic as well as cultural background material. Following are the major sections of the **Foundation** unit:

- **Introduction to Chinese:** This section briefly introduces some characteristics of Chinese language such as tones, the importance of word order, pictographic characters and its history and development.
- **Pinyin Foundation and Exercises:** Pinyin is the most widely used phonetic transliteration system to be introduced as a tool for representing the sounds of Chinese. This section introduces the Pinyin system as well as the structural components of Chinese syllables: initials, finals, and tones. There are many Pinyin exercises. Tongue twisters are introduced to show different aspects of rhythm and rhyme and the sounds of Chinese.
- **The Chinese Writing System:** This section discusses the formation of Chinese characters. It introduces the common components, radicals, and the structure of Chinese characters. Exercises are included.
- **Classroom Expressions and Exercises:** This section introduces the most useful and common phrases encountered in the Chinese classroom. Introducing these phrases early helps the instructors to limit use of English in the classroom. It also allows students to learn some phrases that they can make use of right away.

- **Abbreviations of Parts of Speech:** This section lists the abbreviations used later in the grammar notes and vocabulary sections.

Core Lessons:

The content of the 22 lessons is selected to meet the practical needs and interests of students. The focus of the content begins with individual, family, and school activities, then gradually expands to include wider social occasions and societal contact. Great care has been taken to clearly and systematically present and practice the core vocabulary and grammatical expressions of elementary Chinese.

The major sections of each lesson are described below:

- **Core Vocabulary:** Core vocabulary terms, which appear in the **Language Link** section, are introduced here. For each vocabulary item, traditional and simplified character forms are presented along with Pinyin pronunciation, grammatical function, and English meaning. This section also points out differences between Mainland China and Taiwan usage.

- **Language Link:** This section contains situations that incorporate the lesson's core vocabulary and grammar points. It is accompanied by an art program that adds context and makes the lesson more interesting. **Language Link** serves as a model of the correct usage of the vocabulary and grammar points introduced in the lesson. Notes are provided to further explain the text. For most of the lessons, **Language Link** includes dialogues; for some selections it includes essays, diaries, e-mail, and letters. The length of **Language Link** is carefully controlled, and gradually increases to provide pedagogical sufficiency and challenge.

- **Grammar:** Core grammar points from **Language Link** are explained in this section. We adopt the pedagogical grammar approach to better fit with the communicative approach to language learning. Grammar explanations are supplemented with examples that use vocabulary items previously covered in the textbook. We have tried to avoid linguistics jargon, with the exception of such commonly used terms as *syntax, sentence, clause, subject, predicate, object, modifier,* etc. For review and consolidation, the communicative exercises of each lesson are designed to elicit the use of grammatical structures introduced in the lesson.

- **Supplementary Practice:** Each lesson has a **Supplementary Practice** section with themes, vocabulary, and grammar similar to those found in **Language Link**. This allows students to practice immediately what they have learned from their study of the main text. Care has been taken to use a different format from that found in **Language Link**. For example, if **Language Link** contains a dialogue, **Supplementary Practice** will include a prose format, and vice versa. The pedagogical purpose is to help students learn to use vocabulary and grammar structures in varying forms of communication.

- **Activities:** This section is designed primarily for classroom use. Listening, character, grammar, and communicative exercises are included throughout the text. Care has been taken to provide balance between structural drills and real-life communicative tasks. The exercises integrate with the grammar points to provide a systematic extension of usage skills from vocabulary-item level to sentence level and on to discourse-level narration and description. Since these exercises are for class meeting time, they are designed to be dynamic and interactive. Most involve interaction between instructor and students, student and student, or group and group. Communicative activities are based on situations designed to elicit the grammar points and vocabulary students have learned in the lesson and in prior lessons. Visual aids are provided to help set the context for the communicative activities. Our goal in providing classroom exercises is to help save instructor time, which makes the text convenient and efficient for instructors to use.

- **Culture Link:** This section contains three components:
  - **Culture Notes:** The topics of the **Culture Notes** are carefully chosen to relate to those of the core lessons. It is hoped that the **Culture Notes** will help students to better understand Chinese societies, as well as how language reflects culture. Authentic photos are provided to create a vivid and interesting learning experience. The discussion questions are designed to encourage students to discuss and compare cultural differences by helping them to be aware of the features of their own culture and to be more understanding and tolerant toward other cultures.
  - **Fun with Chinese:** This section introduces a common slang expression, an idiom, or a motto that either utilizes new vocabulary presented in the lesson or is closely related to the theme of the lesson. Drawings are included to help make this section more fun and eye-catching. Discussion questions are provided to offer another fun way to relate the common Chinese expressions to the theme of the lesson.
  - **Let's Go!:** This section gives students an opportunity to interact with Chinese in an authentic context. It assists the students to connect themselves to authentic Chinese societies and communities. This section promotes students' motivation and helps them develop survival skills for life in authentic Chinese societies.

Appendices: The appendices serve as a learning resource for both students and instructors. It can also be used for review exercises in class or for self-study. The Appendices include the following:

- Vocabulary List
- Simplified/Traditional Character Table
- Chinese Transcriptions of **Language in Use**
- English Transcriptions of **Language in Use**: These can be used for translation or interpretation practice, for self-study or in-class review.
- Index (Pinyin and English)
- Characters in The Character Book

Other Program Components

Workbook: Homework and Character Book

The **Homework** portion contains a homework assignment for each lesson in the main textbook. A typical assignment is 3–4 pages, including space for students to write their responses. Homework activities are divided among listening, character recognition and writing, grammar exercises, and communicative tasks.

The **Character** portion provides the Chinese characters for the core vocabulary in every lesson. It shows the following for each character:

1. Character with its stroke order indicated by numbers
2. Simplified form of the character
3. Traditional form of the character
4. Pinyin pronunciation, grammatical usage, and sample sentences or phrases
5. Stroke order illustrated by writing the character progressively
6. Radical of the character with its Pinyin pronunciation and meaning
7. Ghosted images for students to trace over
8. Dotted graph lines to aid students' practice

Blank boxes are also included for students to practice writing the character. As a handy reference, three types of indices are provided in the Character Book: (1) By number of strokes; (2) By Lesson number; (3) Alphabetic by Pinyin.

Instructor's Resource Manual

The **Instructor's Resource Manual** provides sample syllabi, daily schedules, the answer key for in-class and homework exercises, and sample test questions.

Audio Materials

The audio files for all the lesson texts, vocabulary, listening exercises, tongue twisters, and poems in the textbook, as well as the listening exercises in the **Homework Portion of the Workbook** are provided on audio CDs.

Companion Website, <www.prenhall.com/chineselink>

This open-access Web site will provide useful tools that will allow students to further their learning of the Chinese language and culture.

致谢 ACKNOWLEDGMENTS

While we have a sense of accomplishment for completing this project, we are also keenly aware and appreciative of the support and encouragement we have received from the many individuals who contributed. We would like to express our gratitude to everyone who offered us support, suggestions, and encouragement.

We would like to thank Mark Haney for his assistance with English proofreading of the manuscript during many different stages of its preparation. We also owe our thanks to Denny Chen for his delicate skills in tracing the stroke order of most of the Chinese characters in the character book manuscript. With Mark and Denny's devotion and patience, the **Chinese Link** project moved along smoothly and well.

We sincerely appreciate the illustrators for our manuscript and the custom copy, Chi-chen Wu, Chung-ning Lu, and Yi-ju Chen. Their wonderful line art with Chinese flavor helped the manuscript to be more vivid and pleasing. Their line art also provided good models for this project.

Thanks to our loving families in Taiwan and Mainland China and the sincere friends who served as our photographers and photo providers: Vincent Sha, Mark Shope, Wenze Hu, Su-ying Wu, Tsan-lung Wu, Su-yueh Wu, Yi-ching Liu, and Mark Haney. Their artistic and authentic photos bring our project to a professional level.

We would like to express our gratitude to the Elementary Chinese instructors and students at Carnegie Mellon University and St. Vincent College in 2003–2004 and 2004–2005 who took the time to assist us with comments and suggestions during the course of our revision of the manuscript. Thanks also go to our colleagues in the Department of Modern Languages at CMU for their consistent encouragement. Special thanks to our department head, Professor Richard Tucker, for his warm support, and to Dean Gary Quinlivan of St. Vincent College for his enthusiasm and promotion of Chinese Link.

We would like to give our sincerest thanks to the folks at Prentice Hall for bringing their talent and professional publishing experience to this project. Many thanks go to Rachel McCoy, Acquisitions Editor, for her enthusiasm, sincere dedication, and professional guidance. Many thanks also go to Nancy Stevenson, Senior Production Editor, and Mary Rottino, Assistant Director of Production, for their patient and detailed instructions and guidelines about production procedures. We would also like to thank Meriel Martínez Moctezuma, Supplements Editor, for carefully overseeing the production of the Instructor's Resource Manual, Workbook, and Audio program. Thanks to Claudia Fernandes, Publishing Coordinator, for handling the mail and details in a timely fashion. Thanks to Phil Miller for his faith and commitment to this project, and to Wanda España, Weedesign, whose creativity resulted in a wonderful design for this project.

Many thanks to Margaret Chan, Project Manager, and her Graphicraft team members. Their prompt communication and hard work helped this project to reach the production stage.

We would like to conclude by thanking our families, without whose love and support this project would not have been possible. Many thanks to our husbands, Mark, Denny, Dejun, and Jinghong, for enduring our long hours. Special thanks to our children, Carrie, Marion, Sara, and Ryan, for giving up a lot of time with their moms so that this project could be completed.

We extend our sincere thanks and appreciation to the colleagues who reviewed the manuscript and provided valuable input. Their detailed comments and insightful suggestions helped us to further refine our manuscript.

Gary Quinlivan, Saint Vincent College, PA
Xiaohong Wen, University of Houston, TX
Wenze Hu, Harvard University, MA
Weijia Huang, Brown University, RI
Mingjung Chen, De Anza College, CA
Dana Scott Bourgerie, Brigham Young University, UT
Zheng-sheng Zhang, San Diego State University, CA
Jun Yang, University of Chicago, IL
Jean Yu, The Hotchkiss School, CT

Sue-mei Wu
Yueming Yu
Yanhui Zhang
Weizhong Tian

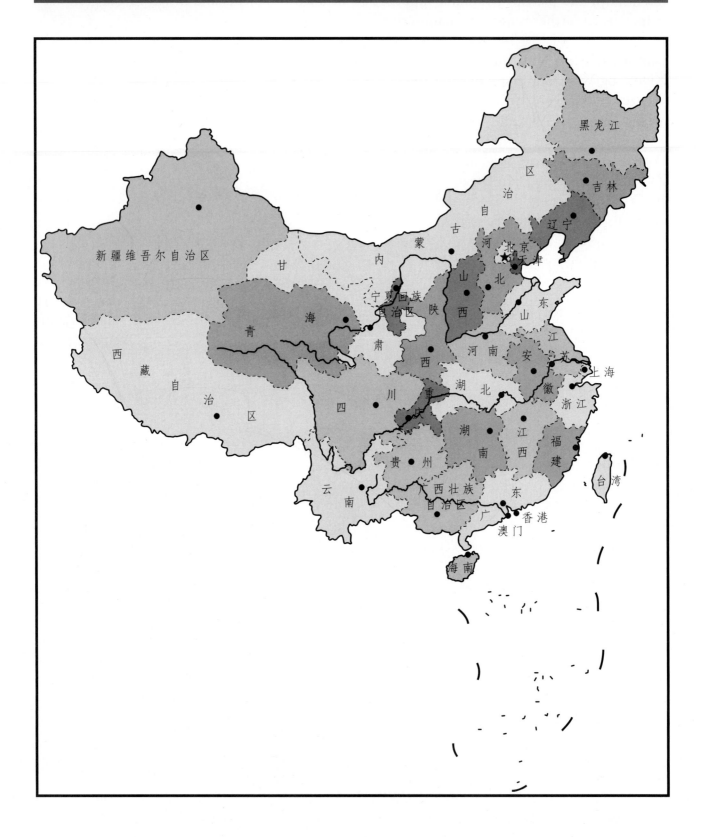

Chinese is a language spoken by about a quarter of the world's population. It is also one of the six working languages of the United Nations. It is called 汉语 [Hànyǔ] (Hanyu) in Chinese because it is spoken by the Han people, the largest ethnic group in China.

A member of the Sino-Tibetan language family, Chinese differs from other languages in many respects. Following are a few of its distinctive characteristics:

- It has no inflection of words to indicate person, gender, number, tense, or mood. The meaning of a sentence relies heavily on the context and word order.

- It is a tonal language. There are many Chinese words whose meanings are differentiated solely by which of the four tones is assigned to them.

- It comprises a large number of dialects, which share the same written form but can be mutually unintelligible when spoken. The Chinese dialects are generally categorized into eight groups: Mandarin (Northern), Northern Min (Northern Fujian), Southern Min (Southern Fujian, Taiwan), Xiang (Hunan), Gan (Jiangxi), Wu (Jiangsu and Zhejiang), Hakka (Guangdong, Guangxi), and Yue (Guangdong).

- The written form of the language consists of roughly square-shaped characters, each of which are formed by a number of strokes. The number of Chinese characters keeps growing. Scholars believe that 3,000 years ago there were around 4,500 characters in use. More recently the Kangxi Dictionary, compiled in 1710, lists about 48,000 characters. A dictionary published in 1994 lists around 86,000 characters! But don't let the sheer number of characters scare you away from studying Chinese. According to a list of commonly used Chinese characters published by China's Education Commission, only 3,500 characters are commonly used in daily life. It is generally acknowledged that a well-educated Chinese person has mastered 6,000 to 7,000 characters.

- Radicals often provide clues to the meaning of the character. The radical is also important for ordering and grouping characters. For example, dictionaries often have characters grouped by radical, and then by the number of strokes required to write the character. According to Chinese linguists, there are approximately 1,500 radicals in total, but most modern Chinese dictionaries only include 214.

About 400 years ago, a unified system of pronunciation for Chinese began to be established, which would be intelligible to everybody in the country. These efforts continued up until the beginning of the 20th century. As a result, *Guoyu* (the National Language) developed and became the language for all official communication. *Guoyu* takes Beijing Dialect as the standard for pronunciation and is based on dialects used in the northern part of the country. It also incorporates some language features of other dialects.

After the People's Republic of China was founded in 1949, some changes in the pronunciation of *Guoyu* were made and its name was changed to *Putonghua*, which means "Common Language." *Putonghua* has been the official language in Mainland China ever since, while *Guoyu* is still being used in Taiwan. In Singapore, Chinese is referred to locally as *Huawen*. In the West, "Mandarin Chinese" is the common term for Chinese.

Phonetic Transliteration Systems

In the last few centuries there have been efforts to develop a method of representing the Chinese language using the Latin alphabet. The most widely used system is called the *Pinyin* system. It was developed in Mainland China in the 1950s and officially adopted in 1979. *Pinyin*, which literally means "spell the sounds," is used to help people learn the pronunciation of characters or to look up words in dictionaries. The "Pinyin Foundation" section of this textbook gives you a more detailed introduction to this phonetic system.

Characters

Legend says that Chinese characters were created by Cang Jie, an official recorder of the Yellow Emperor, over 5,000 years ago. But the earliest use of a fully developed form of Chinese characters can be traced back to around 3,300 years ago in the Shang Dynasty. These writings, called the "Oracle Bone Scripts," consist of characters carved on ox bones or tortoise shells. Scholars believe that Chinese characters originally were pictographs that represented objects in the real world. Recent archeological discoveries also show that character-like pictographs existed as far back as 7,000 years ago. Xu Shen (58–147), a well-known linguist of the Eastern Han Dynasty (25–220 A.D.), analyzed the existing characters, examined their shapes, pronunciations and meanings, traced their roots, and finally compiled the first ever Chinese dictionary in history — *Shuo Wen Jie Zi* 《说文解字》— in which he collected over 9,000 characters categorized under 540 radicals. He concluded that Chinese characters were basically formed in six forms, called *Liu Shu* (the six writings):

- *Xiang xing* (Pictographs to represent real objects): e.g., 木、月、女,
- *Zhi shi* (Pictographs with an indicative sign; indirect symbols): e.g., 上、下、本,
- *Hui yi* (Meeting of ideas; compound characters): e.g., 明、休、好,
- *Xing sheng* (Picture and sound; semantic-phonetic combinations): e.g., 想、清、爸,
- *Zhuanzhu* (Transferable meaning; transformed characters): e.g., 考、老,
- *Jiajie* (Borrowed or loaned characters): e.g., 莫、其.

Shuo Wen Jie Zi is not only the first dictionary in Chinese history, it is also a scholarly masterpiece with great theoretical and practical value. Xu Shen's analysis of "Liu Shu" has been followed by scholars in China and other East Asian countries as well.

The section "The Chinese Writing System" provides a more detailed introduction on the rules for writing Chinese characters.

Simplification of Characters

Because of a belief that the complexity of Chinese characters constituted an obstacle to raising the nation's literacy level, and also to learning of the language by non-Chinese, efforts to simplify the characters began in the 19th century. In the 1950s, a simplified system of characters was promulgated in Mainland China. This system eliminated 1,053 variant characters and reduced the number of strokes for many other characters. The "Complete List of Simplified Characters" published in May 1964 listed 2,236 simplified characters. This system of simplified characters has become the major writing system used in Mainland China and Singapore. The traditional forms are still the standard way of writing in Taiwan and many overseas Chinese communities.

China has a history of several thousand years. In spite of periods of unity and disunity, China has remained intact as a country and is one of the only ancient civilizations that still exists today. It is believed that the Chinese writing system has played a crucial role by serving as an important binding factor in the cohesiveness of the country.

拼音基础 PINYIN FOUNDATION

I.

The Pinyin system is a tool used by native Chinese speakers in Mainland China to learn the sounds of Chinese, or to look up unknown characters in dictionaries. It uses the 26 letters of the Latin alphabet to represent the sounds of Chinese. Many of the letters are pronounced in a similar way to their English pronunciation, but not all of them. Some are, in fact, pronounced quite differently from what an English speaker might expect. In this section, for many of the Chinese sounds we have pointed out similar sounds in English for students to use as a reference point. However, it is very important to imitate your instructors and recordings of native speakers so that you learn standard Mandarin pronunciation.

II. Structure of Chinese Syllables

A Chinese syllable consists of three elements: initial, final, and tone.

TONE		
INITIAL	FINAL	
(Consonant)	(y/w)　　　　Vowel　　　(Ending)	
	(i u ü medial)　(a e o i u ü)　　(n ng)	

For example,

	Character	Meaning	Pinyin	Initial	Final			Type of final
1.	八	eight	bā	b	a (vowel)			simple final (a simple vowel)
2.	好	good	hǎo	h	a (vowel)	o (vowel)		compound final (a compound vowel)
3.	班	class	bān	b	a (vowel)	n (ending)		a nasal final
4.	忙	busy	máng	m	a (vowel)	ng (ending)		a nasal final
5.	也	also	yě	y	e (vowel)			final (with -y)
6.	我	I, me	wǒ	w	o (vowel)			final (with -w)
7.	亮	bright	liàng	l	i (medial)	a (vowel)	ng (ending)	a nasal final (with medial -i)
8.	国	country	guó	g	u (medial)	o (vowel)		double final (with medial -u)
9.	略	brief	lüè	l	ü (medial)	e (vowel)		double final (with medial -u (ü sound))

Notes:

1. There are four basic tones, which are indicated by marks placed over a vowel.
   For example, **bā bá bǎ bà**

2. In modern Chinese, there are 21 initials and 38 finals altogether. In a Chinese syllable, the vowel has to be present. Other components such as an initial or ending are optional.

3. The initial, if present, is always a consonant.

4. The final always contains a vowel. The final may be a simple final (a simple vowel, e.g., **bā**); a compound final (a compound vowel, e.g., **hǎo**; note that the tone mark is placed over the first vowel), or a nasal final, e.g., **bān** (vowel followed by a nasal consonant).

5. When -i-, -u-, and -ü- are not preceded by any initials, their Pinyin presentations are **y**, **w**, and **y**, respectively, e.g., **yě**, **wǒ**, and **yǔ**. If they are preceded by an initial, they are presented as **i**, **u**, and **ü** (as medial element, not the main vowel), e.g., **liàng**, **guó**, and **lüè**.

   There are three medials: **i**, **u**, and **ü**. They serve as transitional sounds, not as main vowels. For example, in liàng, guó, and lüè, **i**, **u**, and **ü** are the medial elements. **à**, **ó**, and **è** are the main vowels. Note that the tone marks are placed over the main vowels rather than over the medials.

III. Tones and Tone Marks

Chinese is a tonal language. This means different levels of pitch and the contour of its pronunciation are capable of differentiating meanings. There are four basic tones: the first tone, the second tone, the third tone, and the fourth tone.

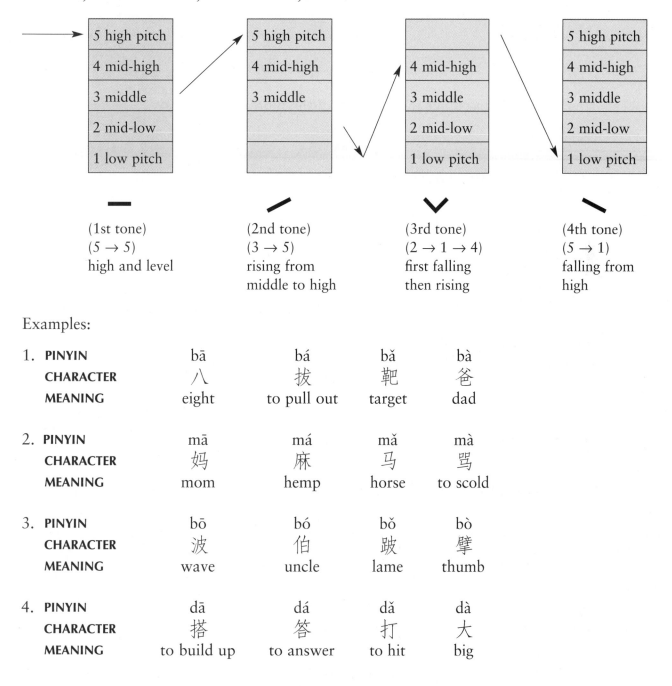

| | (1st tone)
(5 → 5)
high and level | (2nd tone)
(3 → 5)
rising from
middle to high | (3rd tone)
(2 → 1 → 4)
first falling
then rising | (4th tone)
(5 → 1)
falling from
high |

Examples:

1.	**PINYIN**	bā	bá	bǎ	bà
	CHARACTER	八	拔	靶	爸
	MEANING	eight	to pull out	target	dad

2.	**PINYIN**	mā	má	mǎ	mà
	CHARACTER	妈	麻	马	骂
	MEANING	mom	hemp	horse	to scold

3.	**PINYIN**	bō	bó	bǒ	bò
	CHARACTER	波	伯	跛	擘
	MEANING	wave	uncle	lame	thumb

4.	**PINYIN**	dā	dá	dǎ	dà
	CHARACTER	搭	答	打	大
	MEANING	to build up	to answer	to hit	big

IV. Vowels/Simple Finals

a   o   e   i   u   ü

- The letter **a** is pronounced like the "a" in English "father."

PRACTICE
(repeat after your teacher):   ba   ma   pa

- The letter **o** is pronounced like the "o" in English "more."

PRACTICE
(repeat after your teacher):   bo   po   mo

- The letter **e** sounds very similar to the "u" in English "bud."

PRACTICE
(repeat after your teacher):   de   ke   ne

- The letter **i** is pronounced like the "ee" in English "bee."
  (except after the initials: z c s, zh ch sh r, details later).

PRACTICE
(repeat after your teacher):   mi   pi   li

- The letter **u** is pronounced like the "ue" in "true" or "oe" in "shoe" in English.

PRACTICE
(repeat after your teacher):   gu   ku   lu

- The letter **ü** is pronounced like the [u] in French "tu." This sound is produced by first preparing to pronounce a long [i] sound, then holding that mouth position and rounding your lips as if to pronounce [u].

PRACTICE
(repeat after your teacher):   ju   qu   xu

V. Initials

There are 21 initials. They can be categorized into six groups (labials, velars, palatals, alveolars, dental sibilants, and retroflex) as illustrated below:

	Unaspirated	Aspirated[8]	Nasal	Fricative[9]	Voiced[10]
1. Labial[1]	b	p	m	f	
2. Alveolar[2]	d	t	n		l
3. Velar[3]	g	k		h	
4. Palatal[4]	j	q		x	
5. Dental[5] sibilant[6]	z	c		s	
6. Retroflex[7]	zh	ch		sh	r

Notes:

1. Labial: (speech sound) made using one or both lips.
2. Alveolar: (speech sound) made by putting the end of the tongue at the top of the mouth just behind the upper front teeth.
3. Velar: (speech sound) made with the back of the tongue against or near the soft part of the top of the mouth.
4. Palatal: (speech sound) made by putting the tongue against or near the hard palate. (Palate: the top inside part of the mouth)
5. Dental: (speech sound) made by putting the end of the tongue against the upper front teeth.
6. Sibilant: (speech sound) made by forcing air through a constricted passage.
7. Retroflex: (speech sound) made with the tip of the tongue curled upwards and backwards.
8. Aspirated: (speech sound) made with audible breath accompanying the articulation of the sound.
9. Fricative: (speech sound) made by impeding the flow of air through a narrow channel at the place of articulation.
10. Voiced: (speech sound) made when the vocal cords vibrate.

The following two groups are pronounced like their English counterparts.

1. Labials: b p m f

PRACTICE
ba bi bo bu   pa pi po pu   ma mi mo mu me   fa fo fu

2. Alveolars: d t n l

PRACTICE
da de du   ta ti te tu   na ni ne nu   la li le lu

Note: To practice what has been presented above, please see Pinyin Exercises, In-class Practice I.

3. Velars: g k h

The letter **g** sounds similar to the "g" in "go."
The letter **k** sounds similar to the "k" in "king."
The letter **h** sounds similar to the "h" in "happy."

Note that **g, k,** and **h** are never followed by the [i] sound.

PRACTICE
ge gu   ka ke ku   ha he hu

The sounds in groups 4, 5, and 6 below are some of the most challenging for learners of Chinese. Please note that the English counterpart sounds are listed here only as a rough approximation of the Chinese sounds. To pronounce these sounds correctly, it is very important to imitate your instructors and the recordings.

4. Palatals: j q x

The letter **j** sounds somewhat like the "g" in English "gesture" or the "j" in "jeep."
The letter **q** is formed like j above, but j is unaspirated, while q is aspirated. It sounds like "ch" in English "cheap."
The letter **x** sounds somewhat like "sh" in English "sheep."
Note that **j, q,** and **x** are never followed by the [u] sound.

PRACTICE
ji   qi   xi

5. Dental sibilants: z c s

The letter **z** sounds like "ds" in English "lad**s**."
The letter **c** is formed in the same way as "z" above but is aspirated while "z" is unaspirated. It sounds like "ts" in English "ca**ts**."
The letter **s** is very similar to "s" in English "son."

PRACTICE
za ze zu zi   ca ce cu ci   sa se su si

Note that with zi, ci, and si, the vowel [i] acquires a special sound quality. It is pronounced as [ɿ] (blade-alveolar vowel), a continuation of a [z] sound. The tongue is kept still. Be aware that it must not be pronounced like the simple final [i] (as in "bi," "pi," "mi," and "di").

6. Retroflexes: zh ch sh r

This group is pronounced by curling the tip of the tongue to touch the front of the hard palate, leaving a narrow opening between the tongue and roof of the mouth to allow some air to flow through.

zh sounds like "g" in English "**germ**."
ch sounds like "ch" in English "**church**."
sh sounds like "sh" in English "**shirt**."
r is pronounced like the "r" sound in English "plea**sure**," "trea**sure**," and "lei**sure**."

PRACTICE
zha zhe zhu zhi　　cha che chu chi
sha she shu shi　　re ru ri

Note that as with the [i] sound in "zi," "ci," and "si" above, in "zhi," "chi," "shi," and "ri" the vowel [i] also acquires a special sound quality. It is pronounced as [ʃ] (blade-palatal vowel), a continuation of a [zh] sound.

Summary: the pronunciation of -i sound

■ pronounced as [i] in **bi pi mi di ti**

■ pronounced as [ʔ] (blade-alveolar vowel) in **zi ci si**

■ pronounced as [ʃ] (blade-palatal vowel) in **zhi chi shi and ri**

Note: To practice what has been presented in points 3 to 6 (gkh; jqx; zcs; zh; ch; sh; r), please see Pinyin Exercises, In-class Practice II.

VI. Compound Finals

Compound finals comprise a main vowel and a secondary vowel. There are four types as illustrated below.

1. main vowel + secondary vowel　　**ai　ei　ao　ou**
2. medial i + main vowel　　**ia　iao　ie　iu (iou)#**
3. medial u + main vowel　　**ua　uo　uai　ui (uei)##**
4. medial ü + main vowel　　**üe/yue###**

Note: #Please see IX. Special Pinyin Rules for details (#rule 3; ##rule 2; ###rule 1: ü → y).

In group (1), the first vowel is the main vowel (and the tone mark is placed over it). It is stressed, and is the longer of the two vowel sounds. The following vowel is soft and brief. For example, "ai" is pronounced beginning with the [a] sound then gliding into the direction of the [i] sound. Groups (2), (3), and (4) are compound finals that begin with medials (transitional sounds) followed by main vowels.

PRACTICE
bai　pei　mao　dou　　jia　jiao　jie　jiu
zhua　zhuo　shuai　rui

Note: To practice VI Compound Finals, please see Pinyin Exercises, In-class Practice III.

VII. Nasal Finals

Finals ending with "**n**" are called front nasals, and finals ending with "**ng**" [ŋ] are called back nasals.

1. Front nasals (+ n):

vowel + n	**an**	**en**
medial i + main vowel + n	**ian**	**in**
medial u + main vowel + n	**uan**	**un** (uen)#
medial ü + main vowel + n	**üan**	**ün** (üen)##

Note: Please see IX. Special Pinyin Rules for details (#rule 4; ##rule 1).

To produce the front nasal final, first form the final vowel sound. Then, without stopping the air flow, form the ending "**n**." The [n] sound is pronounced similarly to "n" in the English "i**n**" and "noo**n**."

PRACTICE							
ban	pan	man	fan		gen	ken	hen
jian	qian	xian			jin	qin	xin
gun	kun	hun	wen (uen)#		huan	guan	kuan ([u] sound)
jun	qun	xun	([ü] sound)##		juan	quan	xuan ([ü] sound)

Notes: # Please see IX. Special Pinyin Rules for details (#rule 1).

Note that "j q x" can be followed by the [i] and [ü] sounds, but never by the [u] sound. So the umlaut (two dots) is omitted over the [ü] sound (##rule 5).

2. Back nasals (+ ng)

vowel + ng [ŋ]	**ang**	**eng**	**ong**
medial i + main vowel + ng	**iang**	**ing**	**iong**
	(yang)#	(ying)#	(yong)#
medial u + main vowel + ng	**uang**	**ueng**	
	(wang)##	(weng)##	

Note: #Please see IX. Special Pinyin Rules for details (#rule 1; ##rule 1).

To produce a back nasal final, form the final vowel sound. Then, without stopping the air flow, follow it with the nasal "ng."

PRACTICE									
bang	pang			deng	neng	feng		dong	long	kong
jiang	qiang	xiang	yang	jing	qing	xing	ying	jiong	qiong	xiong
wang	weng									

Note: To practice Nasal Finals, please see Pinyin Exercises, In-class Practice IV.

VIII.　Summary of Finals

Simple finals	a　o　e　i　u　ü
Compound finals	ai　ei　ao　ou ia　iao　ie　iu (iou) ua　uo　uai　ui (uei) üe/yue
Nasal finals	an　en　ang　eng　ong ian　in　iang　ing　iong uan　un (uen)　uang　ueng üan　ün (üen)

IX.　Special Pinyin Rules

1. i u ü without initial consonant.

   i → y　　　e.g.,　ya　ye　yao　yan　yong　you　yi　yin　ying
   u → w　　　e.g.,　wa　wo　wai　wang　wu　wei　wen
   ü → y　　　e.g.,　yu　yue　yuan　yun

2. When the final "uei" has an initial, it is written as "ui."

   uei → ui　　e.g.,　dui　tui　gui　kui　hui

3. When the final "iou" has an initial, it is written as "iu."

   iou → iu　　e.g.,　liu　niu　jiu　qiu　xiu

4. When the final "uen" has an initial, it is written as "un" e.g., sun.

   uen → un　　e.g.,　zun　cun　sun　zhun　chun　shun

5. The initials **j q x** are only followed by -i and -ü. They are never followed by -u. Therefore, when j q x are followed by the ü sound, the umlaut (two dots) above the u is omitted.

   　　　　　e.g.,　ju　qu　xu　　juan　quan　xuan　　jun　qun　xun

6. Initials **z c s** and **zh ch sh r** are only followed by -i and -u. They are never followed by the -ü sound.

7. When the initials are l and n, the two dots on the ü sound have to be present in order to differentiate it from the u sound.

   　　　　　e.g.,　lǜ　绿　"green"　　lù　路　"road"
   　　　　　　　　nǚ　女　"female"　　nǔ　努　"diligent"

8. Neutral tone: Some syllables are unstressed; this is known as the neutral tone. There is no need to place a tone mark over neutral tone syllables.

PRACTICE	
bàba 爸爸 (Dad)	māma 妈妈 (Mom)
gēge 哥哥 (older brother)	jiějie 姐姐 (older sister)

9. Retroflex final -er: In Mandarin Chinese, sometimes we can see a final [er] attached to another final to form a retroflex final. There are some special rules for the spelling as illustrated below. These rules are listed here only as a reference. Note that the final [er] sound occurs more frequently in northern China.

   ■   When -er attaches to another final:

      a.   In general, add only -r:

huār	花儿	(flower)	(huā + ér → huār)
hàomǎr	号码儿	(number)	(hàomǎ + ér → hàomǎr)
zhèr	这儿	(here)	(zhè + ér → zhèr)
yíxiàr	一下儿	(one time)	(yíxià + ér → yíxiàr)

      b.   with -ai -ei -an -en, drop the last letter and add -r:

nánhár	男孩儿	(boy)	(nánhái + ér → nánhár)
yíkuàr	一块儿	(together)	(yíkuài + ér → yíkuàr)
wár	玩儿	(play)	(wán + ér → wár)
yìdiǎr	一点儿	(a little)	(yìdiǎn + ér → yìdiǎr)
shùgēr	树根儿	(root)	(shùgēn + ér → shùgēr)

      c.   with zhi chi shi ri, drop -i and add -er.

shùzhēr	树枝儿	(branch)	(shùzhī + ér → shùzhēr)
shèr	事儿	(matter)	(shì + ér → shèr)

      d.   with -in, drop -n and add -er

xìer	信儿	(message)	(xìn + ér → xìer)

      e.   with -ng endings, drop -ng and add only -r.

dàshēr	大声儿	(louder)	(dàshēng + ér → dàshēr)
bǎndèr	板凳儿	(stool)	(bǎndèng + ér → bǎndèr)

10. When two syllables come together to form a word and the second syllable begins with a vowel, they are sometimes separated with an apostrophe " ' ":

xī ān	西安 (a city in China)	→ xī'ān
xiāng ài	相爱 (love each other)	→ xiāng'ài

   Without an apostrophe, [xī'ān] 西安 and [xiāng'ài] 相爱 may be misread as [xiān] 先 (first) and [xiān gài] 先盖 (to build first).

X. Special Tone Rules

1. Tone change for 3rd tone:

   - 3rd tone is pronounced as a full 3rd tone when it occurs alone.

     e.g.,　nǐ 你 (you)　　　hǎo 好 (good)　　hěn 很 (very)　　hǎo 好 (good)
     　　　yǔ 语 (language)　fǎ 法 (rule)　　biǎo 表 (surface)　yǎn 演 (perform)

   - When two 3rd tones co-occur, the first 3rd tone will be pronounced as the 2nd tone, but with its tone mark unchanged.

     $3 + 3 \rightarrow 2 + 3$

     e.g.,　nǐhǎo 你好 (hello)　　　　(pronounced as níhǎo)
     　　　hěnhǎo 很好 (very good)　　(pronounced as hénhǎo)
     　　　yǔfǎ 语法 (grammar)　　　 (pronounced as yúfǎ)
     　　　biǎoyǎn 表演 (perform)　　(pronounced as biáoyǎn)

   - Half 3rd tone[#]: 3rd tone + the 1st, 2nd, 4th tone or most neutral tones.

     nǐtīng 你听 (you listen)　　nǐshuō 你说 (you speak)　　nǐlái 你来 (you come)
     nǐkàn 你看 (you see)　　　hěnmáng 很忙 (very busy)　jiějie 姐姐 (older sister)

     Note: [#]Half 3rd tone: The rising part of the tone is curtailed. This results in a half-finished 3rd tone.

2. Conditional tone change for " 一 ":

   - When " 一 " stands alone, it is pronounced as 1st tone [**yī**].
   - When " 一 " + the 1st, 2nd, or 3rd tones, it is pronounced as the 4th tone [**yì**].

     yì + 1st tone　　yìtiān　　一天 (one day)
     yì + 2nd tone　　yìtóng　　一同 (together)
     yì + 3rd tone　　yìqǐ　　　一起 (together)

   - When " 一 " + the 4th tone, it is pronounced as the 2nd tone [**yí**].

     yímiàn 一面 (at the same time)　　yíjiàn 一件 (one piece of <e.g., clothing>)

3. Conditional tone change for " 不 ":

   - When " 不 " stands alone, or is followed by a 1st, 2nd, or 3rd tone, it is pronounced as the 4th tone [**bù**].

     bùmáng 不忙 (not busy)　　bùhǎo 不好 (not good)

   - When " 不 " + the 4th tone, it is pronounced as the 2nd tone [**bú**].

     búshì 不是 (is not)　　búduì 不对 (incorrect)　　búkàn 不看 (not see)

     Notes: 1. To practice IX. Special Pinyin Rules and X. Special Tonal Rules, please see Pinyin Exercises, In-class Practice V.
     　　　　2. To review the Pinyin Foundation, please see Pinyin Exercises, In-class Practice VI.

拼音表　PINYIN TABLE

Initials/Finals		—	b	p	m	f	d	t	n	l	g	k	h	j	q	x	zh	ch	sh	r	z	c	s
1	a	a	ba	pa	ma	fa	da	ta	na	la	ga	ka	ha				zha	cha	sha		za	ca	sa
2	o	o	bo	po	mo	fo																	
3	e	e			me		de	te	ne	le	ge	ke	he				zhe	che	she	re	ze	ce	se
4	ê																						
5	ai	ai	bai	pai	mai		dai	tai	nai	lai	gai	kai	hai				zhai	chai	shai		zai	cai	sai
6	ei	ei	bei	pei	mei	fei	dei		nei	lei	gei	kei	hei				zhei				zei		
7	ao	ao	bao	pao	mao		dao	tao	nao	lao	gao	kao	hao				zhao	chao	shao	rao	zao	cao	sao
8	ou	ou			mou	fou	dou	tou	nou	lou	gou	kou	hou				zhou	chou	shou	rou	zou	cou	sou
9	an	an	ban	pan	man	fan	dan	tan	nan	lan	gan	kan	han				zhan	chan	shan	ran	zan	can	san
10	en	en	ben	pen	men	fen			nen		gen	ken	hen				zhen	chen	shen	ren	zen	cen	sen
11	ang	ang	bang	pang	mang	fang	dang	tang	nang	lang	gang	kang	hang				zhang	chang	shang	rang	zang	cang	sang
12	eng	eng	beng	peng	meng	feng	deng	teng	neng	leng	geng	keng	heng				zheng	cheng	sheng	reng	zeng	ceng	seng
13	ong	ong					dong	tong	nong	long	gong	kong	hong				zhong	chong		rong	zong	cong	song
14	er	er																					
15	i	yi	bi	pi	mi		di	ti	ni	li				ji	qi	xi	zhi	chi	shi	ri	zi	ci	si
16	-i																						
17	ia	ya												jia	qia	xia							
18	iao	yao	biao	piao	miao		diao	tiao	niao	liao				jiao	qiao	xiao							
19	ie	ye	bie	pie	mie		die	tie	nie	lie				jie	qie	xie							
20	iu (iou)	you			miu		diu		niu	liu				jiu	qiu	xiu							
21	ian	yan	bian	pian	mian		dian	tian	nian	lian				jian	qian	xian							
22	in	yin	bin	pin	min				nin	lin				jin	qin	xin							
23	iang	yang							niang	liang				jiang	qiang	xiang							
24	ing	ying	bing	ping	ming		ding	ting	ning	ling				jing	qing	xing							
25	iong	yong												jiong	qiong	xiong							
26	u	wu	bu	pu	mu	fu	du	tu	nu	lu	gu	ku	hu	ju	qu	xu	zhu	chu	shu	ru	zu	cu	su
27	ua	wa									gua	kua	hua				zhua	chua	shua				
28	uo	wo					duo	tuo	nuo	luo	guo	kuo	huo				zhuo	chuo	shuo	ruo	zuo	cuo	suo
29	uai	wai									guai	kuai	huai				zhuai	chuai	shuai				
30	ui (uei)	wei					dui	tui			gui	kui	hui				zhui	chui	shui	rui	zui	cui	sui
31	uan	wan					duan	tuan	nuan	luan	guan	kuan	huan				zhuan	chuan	shuan	ruan	zuan	cuan	suan
32	un (uen)	wen					dun	tun		lun	gun	kun	hun				zhun	chun	shun	run	zun	cun	sun
33	uang	wang									guang	kuang	huang				zhuang	chuang	shuang				
34	ueng	weng																					
35	ü	yu							nü	lü				ju	qu	xu							
36	üe	yue							nüe	lüe				jue	que	xue							
37	üan	yuan												juan	quan	xuan							
38	ün (üen)	yun												jun	qun	xun							

In-class Practice I

Simple finals: a o e i u ü   *Labial initials: b p m f*   *Alveolar initials: d t n l*

> **USEFUL CLASSROOM EXPRESSIONS:**
>
> | 请你再说一遍。 | Qǐng nǐ zài shuō yí biàn. | Please say it again. |
> |---|---|---|
> | 对(了)。 | Duì(le). | Correct. |
> | 不对。 | Bú duì. | Incorrect. |
> | 第几声? | Dì jǐ shēng? | Which tone? |
> | 第一声 | dì yī shēng | the first tone |
> | 第二声 | dì èr shēng | the second tone |
> | 第三声 | dì sān shēng | the third tone |
> | 第四声 | dì sì shēng | the fourth tone |
> | 轻声 | qīng shēng | neutral tone |

F-1　Repeat after the instructor:

1. bā　bá　bǎ　bà
2. mī　mí　mǐ　mì
3. dē　dé　dě　dè
4. nū　nú　nǔ　nù

5. pō　pó　pǒ　pò
6. fā　fá　fǎ　fà
7. tī　tí　tǐ　tì
8. lǖ　lǘ　lǚ　lǜ

F-2　In each group, circle the syllable your instructor pronounces:

1. mū　mú　mǔ　mù
2. mō　mó　mǒ　mò
3. lī　lí　lǐ　lì
4. lǖ　lǘ　lǚ　lǜ

5. tū　tú　tǔ　tù
6. dū　dú　dǔ　dù
7. nā　ná　nǎ　nà
8. pō　pó　pǒ　pò

F-3　Read aloud the following syllables:

1. pá　bá
2. bó　pó
3. mǔ　nǔ

4. lù　nù
5. lú　lǘ
6. dī　tī

7. lǚ　nǚ
8. tā　tē
9. mō　mū

F-4   Read aloud the following words or phrases:

1.	lùdì	land	陆地	11.	bìmá	castor oil plant	蓖麻
2.	báhé	tug-of-war	拔河	12.	mǎlù	road, street	马路
3.	pífū	skin	皮肤	13.	dútè	unique	独特
4.	tèlì	special case	特例	14.	púfú	crawl	匍匐
5.	lǚbó	aluminum foil	铝箔	15.	fābù	issue, release	发布
6.	mùmǎ	wooden horse	木马	16.	mābù	rag	抹布
7.	bófù	uncle	伯父	17.	tūpò	break through	突破
8.	dìtú	map	地图	18.	dībà	dam	堤坝
9.	lǐfà	haircut	理发	19.	làbǐ	crayon	蜡笔
10.	tǐlì	physical strength	体力	20.	fùmǔ	parents	父母

F-5   In each pair, circle the one your instructor pronounces:

1. lǔ   nǚ   3. lù   nù   5. dū   dē
2. mā   mō   4. mò   mù   6. tā   tē

F-6   Fun with Pinyin

Read the following ràokǒulìng (tongue twister):

bóbo	伯伯	uncle
bàba	爸爸	dad
mǎ	马	horse
pá	爬	to climb
dǎ	打	to hit, play
tǔpō	土坡	muddy slope
lùbō	绿波	green water

Bóbo de mǎ,	伯伯的马，	Uncle's horse,
Bàba de é.	爸爸的鹅。	Father's goose.
Mǎ pá tǔpō,	马爬土坡，	The horse is climbing a muddy slope,
É dǎ lùbō.	鹅打绿波。	The goose is playing in the green water.

In-class Practice II

Velar initials: g k h　　　　　*Palatal initials: j q x*
Dental sibilant initials: z c s　*Retroflex initials: zh ch sh r*

USEFUL CLASSROOM EXPRESSIONS:		
请你再说一遍。	Qǐng nǐ zài shuō yí biàn.	Please say it again.
对(了)。	Duì(le).	Correct.
不对。	Bú duì.	Incorrect.
第几声?	Dì jǐ shēng?	Which tone?
第一声	dì yī shēng	the first tone
第二声	dì èr shēng	the second tone
第三声	dì sān shēng	the third tone
第四声	dì sì shēng	the fourth tone
轻声	qīng shēng	neutral tone

F-7　Repeat after the instructor:

1. shā shá shǎ shà
2. chū chú chǔ chù
3. sū sú sǔ sù
4. jī jí jǐ jì
5. xī xí xǐ xì

6. zū zú zǔ zù
7. zhē zhé zhě zhè
8. rū rú rǔ rù
9. qī qí qǐ qì
10. cū cú cǔ cù

F-8　Read the following words or phrases. Pay attention to the initials "j, q, x" and "z, c, s."

1. qìxī breath 气息
2. xīqǔ absorb 吸取
3. qìjù utensil 器具
4. jīxù savings 积蓄
5. qícì secondly 其次
6. jīqì machine 机器
7. qízǐ chess piece 棋子
8. zìjǐ oneself 自己
9. sījī driver 司机
10. xíjī raid 袭击
11. zájì acrobatics 杂技
12. zǐxì attentively 仔细
13. cíqì porcelain 瓷器
14. cíxù word order 词序
15. zìjù written pledge 字据
16. cūsú vulgar 粗俗
17. jìcè stratagem 计策
18. qǐsù sue 起诉
19. xìjù drama 戏剧
20. zìsī selfish 自私

F-9   Read the following words or phrases. Pay attention to the initials "j, q, x" and "zh, ch, sh, r."

1.	chúxī	New Year's Eve	除夕	11.	zhàqǔ	extort	榨取
2.	rèqì	heat	热气	12.	zhījǐ	intimate	知己
3.	xīshì	Western style	西式	13.	zhìxù	order	秩序
4.	xùshì	narrate	叙事	14.	zhúzì	word for word	逐字
5.	qìzhì	temperament	气质	15.	zhǔxí	chairman	主席
6.	qūshǐ	spur on	驱使	16.	chājù	gap	差距
7.	qízhì	flag	旗帜	17.	chíxù	continue	持续
8.	jīzhì	quick-witted	机智	18.	shíjī	opportunity	时机
9.	jīchǔ	foundation	基础	19.	shìqì	morality	士气
10.	jùchǐ	sawtooth	锯齿	20.	rúqī	on schedule	如期

F-10   Read the following words or phrases. Pay attention to the initials "z, c, s" and "zh, ch, sh, r."

1.	zǔzhī	organize	组织	11.	chúshī	chef	厨师
2.	sīshì	personal affairs	私事	12.	shìsú	secular	世俗
3.	zīzhù	subsidize	资助	13.	shùzì	figure	数字
4.	zhízé	duty	职责	14.	chūrù	discrepancy	出入
5.	qìchē	car	汽车	15.	rúcǐ	in this way	如此
6.	chìzì	deficit	赤字	16.	rǔzhī	milk	乳汁
7.	zhīchí	support	支持	17.	shízǐ	cobble	石子
8.	zhùcí	congratulatory speech	祝词	18.	shízì	learn to read	识字
9.	shísù	board and lodging	食宿	19.	chìrè	blazing	炽热
10.	shǐcè	annals	史册	20.	chūcì	the first time	初次

F-11 In each pair, circle the one your instructor pronounces:

1. rì shì	4. shī sī	7. zhà chà	10. cā zā
2. xī sī	5. qì xì	8. shú chú	11. zǔ sǔ
3. zhè zè	6. xì shì	9. jǐ xǐ	12. cè chè

F-12 Listen to the instructor pronounce each syllable, then fill in the initials:

Part I:

1. ____ē	4. ____í	7. ____à
2. ____ī	5. ____ù	8. ____ú
3. ____è	6. ____ì	9. ____ǐ

Part II:

10. ____è	13. ____ù	16. ____ā
11. ____ù	14. ____á	17. ____ì
12. ____é	15. ____ě	18. ____ǔ

F-13 Fun with Pinyin

Read the following ràokǒulìng (tongue twister):

shí shīzi	石狮子	stone lion
shī shīzi	湿狮子	wet lion
sǐ shīzi	死狮子	dead lion
sī shīzi	丝狮子	silk lion
chī shīzi	吃狮子	eat lion
cí shīzi	瓷狮子	porcelain lion

Sì zhī shí shīzi,	四只石狮子，	Four stone lions,
Shí zhī zhǐ shīzi.	十只纸狮子。	Ten paper lions.
Zhǐ shīzi bù kě chī,	纸狮子不可吃，	Paper lions cannot be eaten,
Shí shīzi bù kě sī.	石狮子不可撕。	Stone lions cannot be torn.

In-class Practice III

Compound finals: ai ei ao ou   ia iao ie iu   ua uo uai ui üe

USEFUL CLASSROOM EXPRESSIONS:		
请你再说一遍。	Qǐng nǐ zài shuō yí biàn.	Please say it again.
对(了)。	Duì(le).	Correct.
不对。	Bú duì.	Incorrect.
第几声?	Dì jǐ shēng?	Which tone?
第一声	dì yī shēng	the first tone
第二声	dì èr shēng	the second tone
第三声	dì sān shēng	the third tone
第四声	dì sì shēng	the fourth tone
轻声	qīng shēng	neutral tone

F-14 Repeat after the instructor:

1. juē   jué   juě   juè
2. jiā   jiá   jiǎ   jià
3. tuī   tuí   tuǐ   tuì
4. zhōu   zhóu   zhǒu   zhòu
5. fēi   féi   fěi   fèi
6. qiāo   qiáo   qiǎo   qiào
7. xiē   xié   xiě   xiè
8. niū   niú   niǔ   niù
9. zāo   záo   zǎo   zào
10. duō   duó   duǒ   duò

F-15 Listen to the instructor pronounce each syllable, then add the correct tone mark:

1. bie   4. hua   7. mao   10. zhua   13. shuo
2. shuai 5. biao   8. tou   11. nuo   14. lüe
3. zhou   6. liu   9. cui   12. ren   15. pei

F-16 Read aloud the following syllables:

1. huó   hóu   4. bǎo   biǎo   7. luó   lóu   10. shāo   xiāo
2. diū   duī   5. jué   xué   8. chāo qiāo   11. lín   liú
3. rào   ròu   6. lüè   nüè   9. chóu zhóu   12. xuē   xiū

F-17 Read aloud the following words or phrases:

1.	báicài	Chinese cabbage	白菜	11.	nǎilào	cheese	奶酪
2.	cáixué	scholarship	才学	12.	páiliè	put in order	排列
3.	còuqiǎo	luckily	凑巧	13.	quèqiè	exact	确切
4.	dàotuì	go backwards	倒退	14.	róudào	judo	柔道
5.	fēikuài	very fast	飞快	15.	sǎomiáo	scan	扫描
6.	gàobié	bid farewell to	告别	16.	shōuhuò	harvest	收获
7.	huàxué	chemistry	化学	17.	táoshuì	evade a tax	逃税
8.	jiézòu	rhythm	节奏	18.	tuóniǎo	ostrich	驼鸟
9.	liúxué	study abroad	留学	19.	wèilái	future	未来
10.	měimiào	wonderful	美妙	20.	zuòjiā	writer	作家

F-18 In each pair, circle the one your instructor pronounces:

1. jué xué   3. huó hóu   5. guò gòu   7. jiǔ xiǔ
2. lüè nüè   4. xuē xiū   6. shāo xiāo   8. rào ròu

F-19 Fun with Pinyin

Read the following ràokǒulìng (tongue twister):

huīmāo　灰猫　gray cat
huāniǎo　花鸟　spotted bird
táopǎo　逃跑　to run away

Huīmāo zhuī huāniǎo	**灰猫追花鸟**
Huīmāo tiào, huāniǎo jiào, Huīmāo tiào qǐ zhuā huāniǎo. Huāniǎo pà huīmāo, Bátuǐ jiù táopǎo.	灰猫跳，花鸟叫， 灰猫跳起抓花鸟。 花鸟怕灰猫， 拔腿就逃跑。
The Gray Cat Chases the Spotted Bird The gray cat leaps, the spotted bird cries, The gray cat leaps up to catch the spotted bird. The spotted bird is afraid of the gray cat, It flies away quickly.	

In-class Practice IV

Nasal finals: *an en*   *ian in*   *uan un*   *ang eng ong*   *iang ing iong*   *uang*

USEFUL CLASSROOM EXPRESSIONS:		
请你再说一遍。	Qǐng nǐ zài shuō yí biàn.	Please say it again.
对(了)。	Duì(le).	Correct.
不对。	Bú duì.	Incorrect.
第几声?	Dì jǐ shēng?	Which tone?
第一声	dì yī shēng	the first tone
第二声	dì èr shēng	the second tone
第三声	dì sān shēng	the third tone
第四声	dì sì shēng	the fourth tone
轻声	qīng shēng	neutral tone

F-20 Repeat after the instructor:

1. liān   lián   liǎn   liàn   5. tōng   tóng   tǒng   tòng
2. guān   guán   guǎn   guàn   6. qiāng   qiáng   qiǎng   qiàng
3. kūn   kún   kǔn   kùn   7. xīng   xíng   xǐng   xìng
4. mēng   méng   měng   mèng   8. jiōng   jióng   jiǒng   jiòng

F-21 Listen to the instructor pronounce each syllable, and then add the correct tone mark:

1. mian   3. zhun   5. zhuang   7. lun
2. ling   4. hen   6. qiang   8. rong

F-22 Read aloud the following syllables:

1. jūn   qūn   4. zhàn   zhèn   7. xūn   sūn   10. zhāng   jiāng
2. cóng   chóng   5. juān   jūn   8. xiàng   xuàn   11. rǎn   zhǎn
3. huán   huáng   6. tūn   tuān   9. qiáng   qióng   12. kěn   kǔn

F-23 Read aloud the following words or phrases:

1.	ānjìng	quiet	安静	11.	miànfěn	flour	面粉
2.	bàngwǎn	at dusk	傍晚	12.	niánqīng	young	年轻
3.	Chángchéng	the Great Wall	长城	13.	píngjūn	average	平均
4.	diànyǐng	movie	电影	14.	qiānzhèng	visa	签证
5.	fāngbiàn	convenient	方便	15.	ruǎnjiàn	software	软件
6.	guāngxiàn	ray	光线	16.	sēnlín	forest	森林
7.	hǎnjiàn	rare	罕见	17.	tiānrán	natural	天然
8.	jǐnzhāng	nervous	紧张	18.	xiāngcūn	village	乡村
9.	kěndìng	affirm	肯定	19.	zhèngcháng	normal	正常
10.	línggǎn	inspiration	灵感	20.	huánjìng	environment	环境

F-24 In each pair, circle the one your instructor pronounces:

1. zhèn	shè	5. xūn	sūn	9. jūn	qūn	13. háng	huáng
2. zhàn	zhèn	6. qiáng	qióng	10. kàn	kèn	14. rēng	zhēng
3. lín	líng	7. tūn	tuān	11. xiàng	xuàn	15. shāo	shōu
4. juān	jūn	8. huán	huáng	12. zhāng	jiāng	16. shùn	shèn

F-25 Listen to the instructor pronounce each syllable, then fill in the blank with the correct final:

1. k _____   5. x _____   9. r _____
2. h _____   6. zh _____   10. z _____
3. j _____   7. ch _____   11. c _____
4. q _____   8. sh _____   12. s _____

F-26 Fun with Pinyin:

Read the following ràokǒulìng (tongue twister):

dēngshān:	登山	to climb a mountain
Xiǎosān:	小三	Little San (name of a person)
sān lǐ sān:	三里三	three miles plus three feet
sān jiàn shān:	三件衫	three shirts

Dēngshān	登山	Climb the Mountain
Xiǎosān qù dēngshān,	小三去登山，	Little San went to climb a mountain,
Pǎo le sān lǐ sān.	跑了三里三。	He ran for three miles plus three feet.
Chū le yì shēn hàn,	出了一身汗，	He was sweaty all over,
Shī le sān jiàn shān.	湿了三件衫。	Three of his shirts were wet.

In-class Practice V

Special Pinyin and tonal rules

F-27 Listen to the instructor pronounce each syllable, then fill in the blank with the correct tone and final:

1. y ____	5. m ____	9. j ____	13. l ____
2. y ____	6. n ____	10. q ____	14. n ____
3. h ____	7. s ____	11. zh ____	15. b ____
4. zh ____	8. ch ____	12. ch ____	16. y ____

F-28 Tone change for the 3rd tone. Read aloud the following words or phrases:

Part I: 3rd + 3rd → 2nd + 3rd

1.	jǔzhǐ	manner	举止	6.	nǎohǎi	mind	脑海
2.	fǎmǎ	weight used on a balance	砝码	7.	měihǎo	fine	美好
3.	liǎojiě	understand	了解	8.	suǒyǒu	all	所有
4.	shǒubiǎo	watch	手表	9.	chǎnpǐn	product	产品
5.	shuǐguǒ	fruit	水果	10.	wǎnzhuǎn	tactful	婉转

Part II: Half 3rd tone

1.	hěn máng	very busy	很忙	7.	Fǎguó	France	法国
2.	wǒ de	my, mine	我的	8.	lǎoshī	teacher	老师
3.	wǒ shì	I am	我是	9.	kǎoshì	test	考试
4.	Qǐng wèn	May I ask . . . ?	请问	10.	Qǐng gēn wǒ shuō.	Please repeat after me.	请跟我说。
5.	Nǎ guó rén?	What nationality?	哪国人	11.	Dǒng le ma?	Do you understand?	懂了吗?
6.	Měiguó	US	美国	12.	Dì jǐ shēng?	Which tone?	第几声?

F-29 Repeat after the instructor. Mark the tones of "yi" (一) and "bu" (不) in accordance with the "yi-bu" tonal rules:

1.	yí	gè	one	一个	11.	bù	xíng	cannot	不行
2.	yì	bǎi	hundred	一百	12.	bù	néng	not be able	不能
3.	yì	qiān	thousand	一千	13.	bù	xiǎng	don't want	不想
4.	yí	wàn	ten thousand	一万	14.	bù	duō	not many	不多
5.	yí	zhào	trillion	一兆	15.	bù	shǎo	not few	不少
6.	yì	yuán	dollar	一元	16.	bú	dà	not big	不大
7.	yí	kuài	dollar	一块	17.	bù	xiǎo	not small	不小
8.	yì	jiǎo	ten cents	一角	18.	bú	pà	not afraid	不怕
9.	yì	máo	ten cents	一毛	19.	bú	liào	not expected	不料
10.	yì	fēn	cent	一分	20.	bù	zǎo	not early	不早

21.	yí	lùpíng'ān	have a safe trip	一路平安
22.	yì	gǔzuòqì	get something done in one vigorous effort	一鼓作气
23.	yì	hūbǎiyìng	be ready to go into action in their hundreds	一呼百应
24.	yì	míngjīngrén	amaze the world with a single brilliant feat	一鸣惊人
25.	yì	fānfēngshùn	have a good innings	一帆风顺
26.	bù	gōngzìpò	collapse of itself	不攻自破
27.	bú	jìnzétuì	not to advance is to go back	不进则退
28.	bù	tóngfánxiǎng	out of the common run	不同凡响
29.	bù	xiāngshàngxià	be equally matched	不相上下
30.	bú	dòngshēngsè	stay calm and collected	不动声色

F-30 Fun with Pinyin

Read the following ràokǒulìng (tongue twister):

gǔ: 鼓 drum
hǔ: 虎 tiger
bù: 布 cloth
bǔ: 补 patch

Gǔ hé hǔ	**鼓和虎**	**Drum and Tiger**
Yì zhī xiǎo huāgǔ,	一只小花鼓，	A little colored drum,
Gǔ lǐ huà zhī hǔ.	鼓里画只虎。	On the drum a tiger is drawn.
Hǔ pá gǔ pò bù lái bǔ,	虎爬鼓破布来补，	Tiger climbs, drum breaks, a cloth patch is applied,
Bùzhī shì bù bǔ gǔ?	不知是布补鼓？	Is the drum being patched?
Háishì bù bǔ hǔ?	还是布补虎？	Or the tiger being patched?

In-class Practice VI

Comprehensive Pinyin Review

F-31 Read aloud the following Pinyin:

1. yǔ	yǒu	5. jūn	zhēn	9. wō	ōu
2. xià	xiào	6. xiōng	jiōng	10. lián	liáng
3. niè	lèi	7. jié	zéi	11. lǔ	liǔ
4. zuō	cuō	8. dàng	dèng	12. lǔ	nǔ

F-32 Read and compare the following words or phrases:

1.	míngshēng	reputation	名声	4.	shǔsè	light of early dawn	曙色
	míngshèng	scenic spot	名胜		sùshè	dormitory	宿舍
2.	tiáojiě	mediate	调解	5.	chājù	disparity	差距
	tiáojié	adjust	调节		chájù	tea set	茶具
3.	shíqī	period	时期	6.	zhīshi	knowledge	知识
	shíqì	stoneware	石器		zhìshǐ	result in	致使

F-33 In each pair, circle the one your instructor pronounces:

1. lǔ	nǔ	4. lián	liáng	7. xià	xiào
2. bīn	bīng	5. xiōng	jiōng	8. jié	zéi
3. dàng	dèng	6. lǔ	liǔ	9. jūn	zhēn

F-34 Listen to the instructor pronounce the following classroom expressions, and then write them out in Pinyin:

1. 大家好。_____

2. 上课。_____

3. 中文怎么说? _____

4. 没有问题。_____

5. 第四声 _____

6. 请打开书。_____

F-35　Fun with Pinyin

Read the following ràokǒulìng (tongue twister):

xī:	锡	tin
qī:	漆	paint
xījiàng:	锡匠	tinsmith
qījiàng:	漆匠	lacquerer

Xījiàng hé qījiàng	**锡匠和漆匠**
Xījiàng mài xī, qījiàng mài qī, Xījiàng shuō qījiàng tōu le tāde xī, Qījiàng shuō xījiàng tōu le tāde qī, Bùzhī shì xījiàng tōu le qījiàng de qī, Háishì qījiàng tōu le xījiàng de xī.	锡匠卖锡，漆匠卖漆， 锡匠说漆匠偷了他的锡， 漆匠说锡匠偷了他的漆， 不知是锡匠偷了漆匠的漆， 还是漆匠偷了锡匠的锡。

Tinsmith and Lacquerer

Tinsmith sells tins; lacquerer sells paint,
The tinsmith charges the lacquerer with stealing his tins,
The lacquerer charges the tinsmith with stealing his paints,
Who knows whether the tinsmith has stolen the lacquerer's paints,
Or the lacquerer has stolen the tinsmith's tins.

Chinese characters can be thought of as square-shaped "signs" which fit into blocks that are independent of each other. Generally speaking, a character may consist of one, two, or three parts, each standing for an independent semantic unit. In general, the arrangement of these semantic units in Chinese characters falls into the following patterns:

1. One-semantic-unit characters:

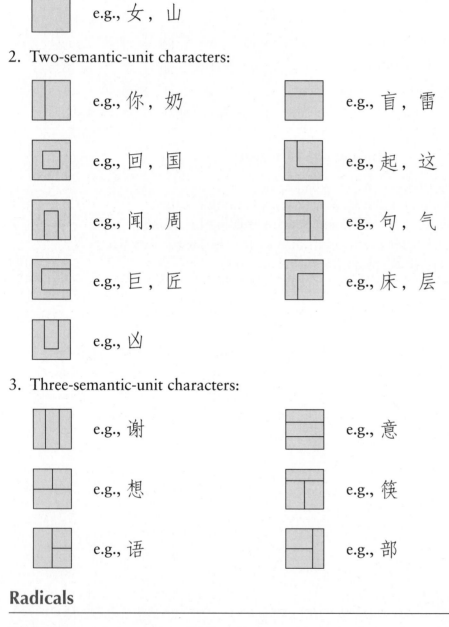

       e.g., 女 , 山

2. Two-semantic-unit characters:

       e.g., 你 , 奶   e.g., 盲 , 雷

       e.g., 回 , 国   e.g., 起 , 这

       e.g., 闻 , 周   e.g., 句 , 气

       e.g., 巨 , 匠   e.g., 床 , 层

       e.g., 凶

3. Three-semantic-unit characters:

       e.g., 谢   e.g., 意

       e.g., 想   e.g., 筷

       e.g., 语   e.g., 部

Radicals

Radicals are pictographs which represent objects in the real world. Some of them can stand alone as independent, one-semantic-unit characters. Examples include 人 (person), 口 (mouth), and 雨 (rain). Radicals may also be combined with other components to form a new character for which the radical serves as a clue to its meaning. Examples include 吹 (to blow) and 妹 (younger sister). Some radicals cannot be used as independent characters but only serve as a part of another character. Their function is to provide a semantic clue to the character, such as 宀 in 家 (home), 艹 in 菜 (vegetable), and 辶 in 逛 (to stroll). According to most dictionaries, there are 214 commonly used radicals in Chinese. Look at the following archaic examples of radicals:

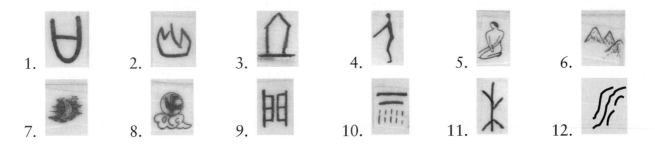

1.　　　2.　　　3.　　　4.　　　5.　　　6.

7.　　　8.　　　9.　　　10.　　　11.　　　12.

Below are their modern forms. Can you use the archaic forms as clues to figure out the meaning of the modern forms?

人 rén ( )	口 kǒu ( )	山 shān ( )	水 shuǐ ( )	日 rì ( )	月 yuè ( )
土 tǔ ( )	木 mù ( )	雨 yǔ ( )	火 huǒ ( )	女 nǚ ( )	门 mén ( )

Each of these characters, when combined with other components to form a new character, provides a clue to the meaning of that character. For example, 吃 [chī] (to eat) is formed by the radical 口 (mouth) and a phonetic clue 乞 [qǐ]. Characters with the radical 口 generally have meanings related to the mouth, such as 喝 [hē] (to drink), 唱 [chàng] (to sing) and 吸 [xī] (to suck). Here are some more examples:

心 xīn (heart)	耳 ěr (ear)	目 mù (eye)	手 shǒu (hand)	鱼 yú (fish)	马 mǎ (horse)
车 chē (vehicle)	门 mén (door)	刀 dāo (knife)	足 zú (foot)	金 jīn (metal)	玉 yù (jade)

练习一   **Practice (1)**

Circle the radicals in the following characters:

姐	鳄	晴	悲	驾	轮	劈	枝	聪	期
jiě	è	qíng	bēi	jià	lún	pī	zhī	cōng	qī
sister	crocodile	sunny	grief	to drive	wheel	cleave	branch	clever	period

Some of these characters also take a slightly different form when used as radicals. They often have a specific name commonly used by Chinese when referring to them as radicals. The following are those most frequently used:

人	rén – person	→	亻	*dān lìrén* – single standing person e.g., 你 (nǐ – you) 他 (tā – he)
手	shǒu – hand	→	扌	*tíshǒu* – lift hand e.g., 打 (dǎ – to strike) 拉 (lā – to pull)
水	shuǐ – water	→	氵	*sān diǎn shuǐ* – three dot water e.g., 江 (jiāng – river) 海 (hǎi – sea)
	bīng – ice	→	冫	*liǎng diǎn shuǐ* – two dot water e.g., 冷 (lěng – cold) 冰 (bīng – ice)
心	xīn – heart	→	忄	*shùxīn* – vertical heart e.g., 忙 (máng – busy) 情 (qíng – feelings)
火	huǒ – fire	→	灬	*sì diǎn huǒ* – four dot fire e.g., 煮 (zhǔ – to boil) 蒸 (zhēng – to steam)
刀	dāo – knife	→	刂	*lìdāo* – standing knife e.g., 到 (dào – to arrive) 利 (lì – sharp)
邑	yì – town	→	阝	*yòu ěr dāo* – right ear knife e.g., 都 (dōu – all) 那 (nà – that)
阜	fǔ – dam	→	阝	*zuǒ ěr dāo* – left ear knife e.g., 陡 (dǒu – steep) 陆 (lù – land)
犬	quǎn – dog	→	犭	*fǎn quǎn* – reversed dog e.g., 狗 (gǒu – dog) 狐 (chú – fox)

练习二　Practice (2)

F-36 Circle the radicals in the following characters:

冻	伯	怪	摔	信	踢	拔	煎	海	割
dòng	bó	guài	shuāi	xìn	tī	bá	jiān	hǎi	gē
freeze	uncle	strange	tumble	believe	kick	pull	fry	sea	cut

F-37 Match the following radicals with their original characters:

( )	( )	( )	( )	( )	( )
火	水	心	刀	手	人

a. 扌　　b. 刂　　c. 灬　　d. 亻　　e. 氵　　f. 忄

There are some radicals which are actually only part of the original characters, such as:

丝	sī – silk	→	糸(纟)	*jiǎosī (mì)* – tangled silk e.g., 纸 (zhǐ – paper)　　绸 (chóu – silk)
草	cǎo – grass	→	艹	*cǎo zì tóu* – top of grass character e.g., 花 (huā – flowers)　　菜 (cài – vegetable)

The following characters show very little change when used as radicals. For example,

金	jīn – gold	→	钅	e.g., 钟 (zhōng – clock)　　钱 (qián – money)
食	shí – food/eat	→	饣	e.g., 饭 (fàn – rice)　　饿 (è – hungry)
衣	yī – clothes	→	衤	e.g., 裙 (qún – skirt)　　裤 (kù – pants)
示	shì – display/reveal	→	礻	e.g., 礼 (lǐ – ritual)　　视 (shì – to view)
玉	yù – jade	→	王	e.g., 珍 (zhēn – treasure)　　珠 (zhū – pearl)
竹	zhú – bamboo	→	⺮	e.g., 篮 (lán – basket)　　笔 (bǐ – pen)
火	huǒ – fire	→	火	e.g., 炸 (zhà – to fry)　　爆 (bào – to explode)
足	zú – foot	→	𧾷	e.g., 跑 (pǎo – to run)　　跳 (tiào – to jump)

A few radicals do not have corresponding characters and can only be used as a component of a character to provide the semantic clue to the character:

宀	mián	*bǎo gài tóu*, precious cover head, which is used to imply "roof" e.g., 家 (jiā – home)　　室 (shì – room)
辶	chuò	*zǒuzhī*, walking zhi, used to imply walking or running e.g., 道 (dào – path/way)　　逃 (táo – to run/escape)

练习三　**Practice (3)**

Circle the radicals in the following characters:

缎	逛	珍	笛	钉	衫	饱	烧	神	寓
duàn	guàng	zhēn	dí	dīng	shān	bǎo	shāo	shén	yù
satin	stroll	treasure	flute	nail	jacket	full	burn	god	apartment

Strokes

The basic elements of Chinese characters are strokes. In order to know how to write Chinese characters, one must know how to write each stroke. Knowledge of strokes will not only lay the foundation for character writing, but is essential for looking up a word in a Chinese dictionary.

There are a total of 31 different kinds of strokes used in Chinese writing. Among these are eight basic strokes that are most commonly used. These eight strokes are illustrated as follows:

1. 横 héng (Horizontal stroke)	2. 竖 shù (Vertical stroke)	3. 撇 piě (Left-slanted stroke)	4. 捺 nà (Right-slanted stroke)
一　王	丨　中	丿　大	乀　文

5. 点 diǎn (Dot)	6. 提 tí (Up-lift stroke)	7. 钩 gōu (Hook)	8. 折 zhé (Bend stroke)
丶　游	㇀　泳	亅　小	乛　姐

In writing Chinese characters, the correct stroke order should be followed so that the characters look "right" to native Chinese. The following principles should be observed in the order of strokes:

Top first, then bottom:

　　e.g.,　交　⟶　亠　六　交

Left first, then right:

　　e.g.,　很　⟶　彳　很

Horizontal first, then vertical:

　　e.g.,　十　⟶　一　十

Left-slanted first, then right-slanted:

　　e.g.,　父　⟶　八　少　父

Center first, then both sides:

　　e.g.,　小　⟶　亅　小　小

Outside first, then inside:

　　e.g.,　同　⟶　冂　同

Enter first, and then close the door:

　　e.g.,　国　⟶　冂　国　国

练习四　Practice (4)

F-38 For each of the following characters, write out the first stroke:

　　交 _____　　月 _____　　水 _____　　去 _____　　中 _____
　　不 _____　　他 _____　　洪 _____　　吃 _____　　代 _____

F-39 Write the following characters progressively, following the correct stroke order:

　　再 _____

　　但 _____

　　因 _____

　　京 _____

　　看 _____

In writing Chinese characters, the following principles guide the directions of the strokes:

a. Start the horizontal strokes from the left and move to the right.
b. Start the vertical strokes from the top and move downwards.
c. Left-slanted strokes start from the upper right and go towards the lower left.
d. Right-slanted strokes move from top left to bottom right.

Here are some examples:

The shape of Chinese character strokes follows strict rules. A tiny change in the shape may change the meaning of the whole character. For example, 贝 [bèi] means "shell" and 见 [jiàn] means "to see." The top parts of the two characters are the same, but the bottom parts are different. Though the difference is not very conspicuous, it needs to be taken seriously. Otherwise, misunderstanding may result.

Writing Chinese characters may be difficult but it is also great fun. Character writing can be an art as well. If you put some effort into it, practice, and learn the cultural implications of characters, you may find writing Chinese an enjoyable and rewarding experience.

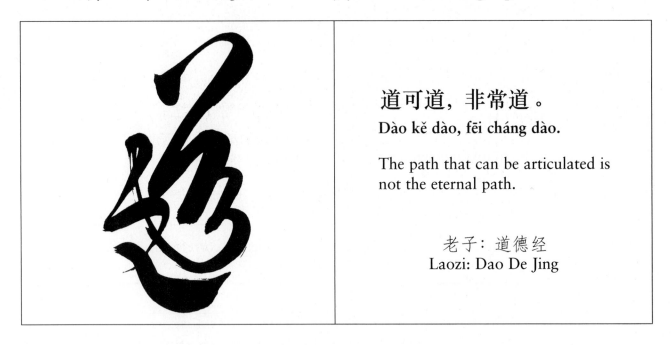

道可道，非常道。
Dào kě dào, fēi cháng dào.

The path that can be articulated is not the eternal path.

老子：道德经
Laozi: Dao De Jing

课 堂 用 语
Kè táng yòng yǔ

Chinese characters	Pinyin	Meaning
1. 同学们好。	Tóngxuémen hǎo.	Hello, students.
2. 你们好。	Nǐmen hǎo.	Hello, everyone.
3. 大家好。	Dàjiā hǎo.	Hello, everybody.
4. 老师好。	Lǎoshī hǎo.	Hello, teacher.
5. 你好。	Nǐ hǎo.	Hello.
6. 上课。	Shàng kè.	Class begins.
7. 下课。	Xià kè.	Class is dismissed.
8. 请跟我说。	Qǐng gēn wǒ shuō.	Please repeat after me.
9. 对(了)。	Duì (le).	Correct.
10. 不对。	Bú duì.	Incorrect.
11. 很好。	Hěn hǎo.	Very good.
12. 谢谢。	Xièxie.	Thank you.
13. 不客气。	Bú kèqi.	You are welcome.
14. 再见。	Zài jiàn.	Goodbye.
15. 请你再说一遍。	Qǐng nǐ zài shuō yíbiàn.	Please say it again.
16. 中文怎么说?	Zhōngwén zěnme shuō?	How do you say ____ in Chinese?
17. 英文怎么说?	Yīngwén zěnme shuō?	How do you say ____ in English?
18. 请打开书。	Qǐng dǎkāi shū.	Please open your book.
19. 请看第__页。	Qǐng kàn dì __ yè.	Please take a look at page __.
20. 请看第__题。	Qǐng kàn dì __ tí.	Please take a look at question __.
21. 请念课文。	Qǐng niàn kèwén.	Please read the text.
22. 请跟我念。	Qǐng gēn wǒ niàn.	Please read after me.
23. 请你念。	Qǐng nǐ niàn.	You read, please.
24. 请你写。	Qǐng nǐ xiě.	You write, please.
25. 懂了吗?	Dǒng le ma?	Do you understand?
26. 懂了。	Dǒng le.	Understand.
27. 不懂。	Bù dǒng.	Don't understand.
28. 有问题吗?	Yǒu wèntí ma?	Any questions?
29. 我有问题。	Wǒ yǒu wèntí.	I have questions.
30. 没有问题。	Méi yǒu wèntí.	No questions.

Chinese characters	**Pinyin**	**Meaning**
31. 练习练习	Liànxi liànxi.	Practice a bit.
32. 表演	biǎoyǎn	Perform
33. 作业	zuòyè	Homework
34. 生词	shēngcí	Vocabulary
35. 考试	kǎoshì	Test
36. 生词考试	shēngcí kǎoshì	Character quiz
37. 第一声	dì yī shēng	The first tone
38. 第二声	dì èr shēng	The second tone
39. 第三声	dì sān shēng	The third tone
40. 第四声	dì sì shēng	The fourth tone
41. 轻声	qīng shēng	Neutral tone
42. 第几声?	Dì jǐ shēng?	Which tone?

43.

一	二	三	四	五	六	七	八	九	十
yī	èr	sān	sì	wǔ	liù	qī	bā	jiǔ	shí
one	two	three	four	five	six	seven	eight	nine	ten

课堂用语练习 CLASSROOM EXPRESSIONS AND EXERCISES

Form groups of two to three students and practice the following situations:

Items 1–14

F-40 The teacher enters the classroom, greets the students, and starts the class. Try to use the following phrases: tóng xué men hǎo, nǐ hǎo, shàng kè, qǐng gēn wǒ shuō, duì (le), hěn hǎo, zài jiàn.

F-41 Students introduce themselves in turn to the class (greeting, their names, where they are from . . . etc.)

Example: Nǐmen hǎo. Wǒ shì ____. Wǒ cóng ____ lái. . . . Hǎo. Xièxie. Zàijiàn.
Hello, everyone, I am ___. I am from _____. . . . OK, thank you. Bye-bye.

Items 15–27

F-42 On campus you run into one of your Chinese classmates. Greet and introduce yourselves to each other in Chinese. (Include greeting, names, where you come from, very good, bye . . . etc.)

Items 28–42

F-43 In the library, you run into one of your Chinese classmates. Greet and introduce yourselves in Chinese, and then practice Pinyin and the four tones. (Remember to give your partners some feedback!)

F-44 Before class, you are waiting outside the classroom with your Chinese classmates. You would like to take the chance to get to know them better (and you might want to review yesterday's lessons).

F-45 On campus, you run into your Chinese teacher. Greet your teacher, and then ask some questions about Pinyin and tones, and how to say something in English or Chinese.

F-46 You have some Chinese friends and would like to ask them some questions. (For example, ask how to say the following words in Chinese or English: textbooks, Chinese, friends — some examples can be from Classroom Expressions items.)

F-47 You are the Chinese teacher teaching Pinyin practice, Lesson 1, Lesson 2, and Classroom Expressions.

词类简称 ABBREVIATIONS OF PARTS OF SPEECH

Adj. = adjective	形容词	[xíngróngcí]	e.g.,	好 [hǎo] (good) 美 [měi] (beautiful)
Adv. = adverb	副词	[fùcí]	e.g.,	很 [hěn] (very) 也 [yě] (also)
Aux. = auxiliary verb	助动词	[zhùdòngcí]		
Conj. = conjunction	连词	[liáncí]	e.g.,	可是 [kěshì] (but)
Int. = interjection	叹词	[tàncí]	e.g.,	啊 [a] (Ah?)
M.W. = measure word (or classifier)	量词	[liàngcí]	e.g.,	一本 [běn] 书 (a book)
N. = noun	名词	[míngcí]	e.g.,	老师 [lǎoshī] (teacher) 书 [shū] (book)
Num. = numeral	数词	[shùcí]	e.g.,	二 [èr] (two) 十 [shí] (ten)
Part. = particle	助词	[zhùcí]	e.g.,	吗 [ma] (turn a sentence into a question)
Prep. = preposition	介词	[jiècí]	e.g.,	在 [zài] (in; at) 从 [cóng] (from)
Pron. = pronoun	代词	[dàicí]	e.g.,	你 [nǐ] (you) 他 [tā] (he)
V. = verb	动词	[dòngcí]	e.g.,	学 [xué] (study) 说 [shuō] (speak) 跑 [pǎo] (run)
V.O. = verb + object	动宾	[dòng bīn]	e.g.,	说中文 [shuō Zhōngwén] (speak Chinese)
V.C. = verb + complement	动补	[dòng bǔ]	e.g.,	搬过来 [bān guò lái] (move over) 打破 [dǎ pò] (hit-broken)

第一课
LESSON

1

你好!
Hello!

教学目标 OBJECTIVES

- Conduct simple greetings in Chinese
- Ask simple yes/no questions
- Answer simple yes/no questions
- Discuss other people

Greetings are common in many different situations.

Shaking hands is a common gesture of greeting among Chinese people.

Chinese people use both hands when making a toast.

生词 VOCABULARY

核心词   Core Vocabulary

	SIMPLIFIED	TRADITIONAL	PINYIN		
1.	你	你	nǐ	Pron.	you
2.	好	好	hǎo	Adj.	good, well
3.	是	是	shì	V.	to be, (affirmative answer) yes
4.	学生 学	學生 學	xuésheng xué	N. V.	student to study, to learn
5.	吗	嗎	ma	Part.	(used at the end of a declarative sentence to transform it into a question)
6.	我	我	wǒ	Pron.	I, me
7.	呢	呢	ne	Part.	(used at the end of an interrogative sentence)
8.	也	也	yě	Adv.	also
9.	他	他	tā	Pron.	he, him
10.	不	不	bù	Adv.	(used to form a negative) not, no
11.	老师	老師	lǎoshī	N.	teacher

语文知识   LANGUAGE LINK

The Sentence Patterns provide models that will help you with the Language in Use section. In both sections, pay attention to the grammar points, vocabulary, and expressions.

句型   Sentence Patterns

A: 你好！
　　Nǐhǎo!

B: 你好！
　　Nǐhǎo!

A: 你是学生吗?
Nǐ shì xuésheng ma?

B: 我是学生。你呢?
Wǒ shì xuésheng. Nǐ ne?

A: 他也是学生吗?
Tā yě shì xuésheng ma?

B: 不,他不是学生。
Bù, tā bú shì xuésheng.

课文 Language in Use: 你好! Nǐhǎo!

MARY: 你好!
Nǐhǎo!

JOHN: 你好!
Nǐhǎo!

MARY: 你是学生吗?
Nǐ shì xuésheng ma?

JOHN: 我是学生。你呢?
Wǒ shì xuésheng. Nǐ ne?

MARY: 我也是学生。
Wǒ yě shì xuésheng.

JOHN: 他呢? 他是学生吗?
Tā ne? Tā shì xuésheng ma?

MARY: 他不是学生。他是老师。
Tā bú shì xuésheng. Tā shì lǎoshī.

注释 LANGUAGE NOTES

你好

你好 means "Hello!" It is a common greeting that may be used for "Good morning," "Good afternoon," or "Good evening."

Note: Tone change in 你好:
When two 3rd tones co-occur, the first 3rd tone is pronounced as a 2nd tone.

3rd tone + 3rd tone → 2nd tone + 3rd tone
你好   nǐhǎo   → pronounced as   [níhǎo]

Tone Change of 不 in 不是

Note: When 不 is followed by the 4th tone, it is pronounced as a 2nd tone as illustrated below:

不 + 4th tone → 不 is pronounced as a 2nd tone
不是   bù shì → pronounced as   [bú shì]

语法 GRAMMAR

Chinese Sentences

Chinese sentences usually consist of a subject and a predicate. For example,

Subject	Predicate
你	好

你好 ("Hello!" or "How are you?") is a common expression of greeting. 好 is an adjective. In Chinese, adjectives are stative verbs that can function independently as a predicate.

The Pronouns 我, 你 and 他

我, 你, and 他 are used as the 1st person, 2nd person, and 3rd person pronouns, respectively. Note that Chinese pronouns do not change case like English pronouns. For example, the pronoun 我 is used for both "I" and "me."

The Interrogative Particle 吗

The most common way to turn a sentence into a question is to place the particle 吗 at the end of the sentence.

你是老师 。
You are a teacher.

你是老师吗?
Are you a teacher?

他是学生 。
He is a student.

他是学生吗?
Is he a student?

The Modal Particle 呢

The particle 呢 is used after a noun, pronoun, or noun phrase to turn the sentence into a question that could be translated as "How about N?" 呢 is used when a topic or some piece of information is established or shared in the preceding statements. For example,

A: 你是学生吗?   Are you a student?
B: 我是学生 。你呢?   I am a student. How about you?
A: 我也是学生 。   I am also a student.

是 Sentences

是 is a linking verb. It functions almost as an equal sign between nouns, pronouns, or nouns and pronouns. For example,

我是学生 。他是老师 。   I am a student. He is a teacher.
(between a pronoun and a noun)

老师是中国人 [Zhōngguórén] 。   The teacher is Chinese.
(between two nouns)

To negate the 是 sentence, simply place the adverb 不 before 是. To turn the 是 sentence into a question, we may simply add the interrogative particle 吗 to the end of the sentence. The 是 sentences can be illustrated as follows:

Interrogative form: A是B吗?   e.g. 他是学生吗?   Is he a student?
Affirmative form: A是B   e.g. 他是学生 。   He is a student.
Negative form: A不是B   e.g. 他不是学生 。   He is not a student.

The Adverb 也

也 is an adverb placed before a verb. It is often translated as "also" or "too." Note that 也 cannot be placed at the beginning or end of a sentence as "also" or "too" can in English. For example, the English sentence, "I am a student and a teacher too" would be expressed as "我是学生，也是老师" in Chinese.

补充课文 ━◦◦◦━ **SUPPLEMENTARY PRACTICE**

This selection will help you test your comprehension of the grammar and vocabulary you have learned in this lesson. Be prepared to answer questions about the meaning of the passage.

你好! 我不是学生，我是老师。他也不是学生，他是教授。你呢? 你是学生吗? 你是教授吗?

Note: 教授 [jiàoshòu]: professor

练习   ACTIVITIES

I. Listening Exercises

1-1   In each pair, circle the one your instructor pronounces:

1. tā/dā	2. lǎo/nǎo	3. bō/pō	4. wǔ/nǔ	5. hé/lé
6. shì/xì	7. mà/nà	8. néng/léng	9. xué/jué	10. tǎo/dǎo

1-2   In each pair, circle the one your instructor pronounces:

1. bú/bó	2. láo/lái	3. nā/nē	4. mà/mù	5. shì/shè
6. xī/xū	7. yuè/yè	8. wǒ/wǔ	9. nǐ/ně	10. hà/hé

1-3   Listen to the instructor pronounce the following words, and then add the tone marks:

1. hao	2. laoshi	3. ni	4. ta	5. bu
6. ye	7. xuesheng	8. shi	9. wo	10. ne

1-4   Read the following poem, paying special attention to the tones and the rhythm:

Jìng Yè Sī (Lǐ Bó/Lǐ Bái)	静夜思 (李白)	Thoughts on a Tranquil Night (Li, Bo/Li, Bai)
Chuáng qián míng yuè guāng,	床前明月光，	In front of my bed, bright moonlight,
Yí shì dì shàng shuāng?	疑是地上霜 。	Can it be frost on the ground?
Jǔ tóu wàng míng yuè,	举头望明月，	Lifting my head, I gaze upon the bright moon,
Dī tóu sī gù xiāng.	低头思故乡 。	Lowering my head, I think of my hometown.

Note: 李白 Lǐ Bái is pronounced as Lǐ Bó in Classical Chinese.

II. Character Exercises

1-5　Read the following words and sentences:

学生	老师
他是学生。	我是老师。
他不是学生。	我不是老师。
他也不是学生。	我也不是老师。

Now try to use the following characters to make words, phrases, and then sentences:

1. 你　　2. 好　　3. 是　　4. 吗　　5. 我　　6. 呢

7. 也　　8. 他　　9. 不　　10. 生　　11. 学　　12. 师

1-6　Match the following characters with the English expressions:

老师	student
你好	and you
不	also
你呢	teacher
也	hello
学生	not

1-7　Create flashcards.

To help learn new characters, and also as an aid for future review, students are strongly encouraged to create flashcards for each lesson's vocabulary items. See the following example for a suggested format:

FRONT　　　　　　　　　　　　BACK

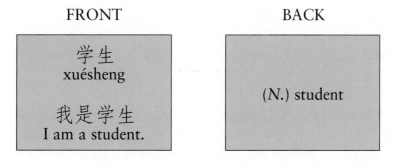

学生
xuésheng

我是学生
I am a student.

(*N.*) student

III. Grammar Exercises

1-8 Put the word given in the brackets in the appropriate place:

1. 你　学生　　。　　　　　　　(是)
2. 不　是　老师　　。　　　　　(我)
3. 他　不　是　学生　　。　　　(也)
4. 你　不　是　老师　？　　　　(吗)

1-9 Fill in the blanks with either 也, 不, or 是 to complete the dialogue:

A: 请问 [qǐng wèn] (may I ask)，你 ＿＿ 学生吗?
B: 我 ＿＿ 学生。你 ＿＿ ＿＿ 学生吗?
A: 不，我 ＿＿ ＿＿ 学生，我 ＿＿ 老师。他 ＿＿ ＿＿ 老师。
B: 老师好!
A: 你好!

1-10 Fill in the blanks with "吗" or "呢":

A: 你好! 你是学生 ＿＿ ?
B: 是，你 ＿＿ ? 你也是学生 ＿＿ ?
A: 不，我不是学生。我是老师。
B: 他也是老师 ＿＿ ?
A: 不，他是学生。

IV. Communicative Activities

1-11 Picture talk: With the help of the clues provided, give an introduction for each of the following pictures (say as much as you can).

I
Lǐ Xiǎowén
(student)

You
Wú Hànzhōng
(teacher)

He
Wáng Xuéwén
(student)

She
Dīng Wényīng
(professor)

1-12 Find a partner, choose a role from the pictures above, and create a dialogue.

1-13 Suppose you are at a welcoming party for new students. Try to introduce yourself to a new student and start a conversation. Remember, your professor is also at the party.

文化点滴　CULTURE NOTES

问候语 [Wèn hòu yǔ]
Basic Chinese Greetings

Chinese greetings can be classified into two types: (1) exchanged greetings and (2) question-and-answer greetings.

(1) Exchanged greetings:

Both parties say the same words or phrases almost at the same time. The most common ones are "你好！""早！" and "嗨！"

Exchanged greetings	Features
你好 [Nǐ hǎo!] (Hello!)	• Usually used for the first meeting. • Often used by receptionists when taking an incoming phone call or greeting visitors.
早 [Zǎo!] (Morning!)	• Used in the early and late morning.
嗨 [Hāi!] (Hi!)	• Taken from English "Hi!"

(2) Question-and-answer greetings:

Like the English "How are you?" and its answer, "Fine," these simple questions and answers are often fixed expressions. They should not be taken literally as questions and answers. The common greetings are "你好吗?""怎么样?" and "你吃了吗?"

Question	Common answer		Feature
你好吗？ [Nǐ hǎo ma?] 好吗？ [Hǎo ma?] *How are you?*	很好 [Hěn hǎo] 还好 [Hái hǎo] 不错 [Bú cuò]	*Fine.* *All right.* *Not bad.*	• Frequently used when you haven't seen someone for a while.
怎么样？ [Zěn me yàng?] *What's up?* *What's new?*	很好 [Hěn hǎo] 还好 [Hái hǎo] 不错 [Bú cuò]	*Fine.* *All right.* *Not bad.*	• Can also be taken as an invitation to start a conversation.
(你)吃了吗？ [(Nǐ) chī le ma?] *Have you eaten yet?*	吃了 [Chī le] 还没 [Hái méi]	*I have.* *I haven't yet.*	• Used close to meal times. • Not really asking whether you have eaten or not.

Another interesting aspect of Chinese greetings is that they often consist of stating the obvious, as in the following examples:

When running into an acquaintance while grocery shopping, a Chinese person might say:

A：买菜啊？   [Mǎi cài a?]   (So you're) grocery shopping, eh?
B：嗯，买菜。   [En, mǎi cài.]   Yes, (I'm) grocery shopping.

Other examples might include:

看电视啊？   [Kàn diàn shì a?]   (So you're) watching TV, eh?
做功课啊？   [Zuò gōng kè a?]   (So you're) doing homework, eh?

Shaking hands is a common Chinese gesture of greeting or introduction.

During an election, candidates show up everywhere to greet, campaign, and ask for votes. Several candidates visited this wedding banquet (in Taiwan).

Questions:

1. When you come to Chinese class, which greeting do you use to your classmates? How about to your teacher? How about when you run into your Chinese friends in a Chinese restaurant?

2. Can you provide any similar greetings in English or other languages?

趣味中文 FUN WITH CHINESE

> 学而时习之。
>
> to learn/study and review it from time to time

xué	ér	shí	xí	zhī
学	而	时	习	之
learn/study	and	often	review	it

This famous saying of Confucius encourages his disciples to study.

Question:

Are there any similar sayings in English or other languages to encourage students to study?

行动吧! LET'S GO!

服务台 **Service Stand**

This is 吴大中's first time traveling in China, Taiwan, and Hong Kong. He has had several chances to greet people with 你好. He has also sought out the sign below several times, beginning with when he needed to ask for information at the airport.

Useful words and expressions:

服务(服務) [fúwù]: service
服务台(服務台) [fúwùtái]: information counter
台 [tái]: stand, counter

第二课
LESSON

2

您贵姓?
What's Your Surname?

- Exchange names
- Get to know each other
- Find out who someone else is

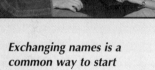

Exchanging names is a common way to start getting to know one another.

Upon first meeting someone in a business setting, it is common to exchange business cards, which usually include one's full name and title.

生词 VOCABULARY

核心词   Core Vocabulary

	SIMPLIFIED	TRADITIONAL	PINYIN		
1.	您	您	nín	Pron.	(polite) you
2.	贵	貴	guì	Adj.	noble, honored, expensive
3.	姓	姓	xìng	N. V.	surname, family name to be surnamed
4.	请问 请 问	請問 請 問	qǐng wèn qǐng wèn	 V.	may I ask (polite) please to ask
5.	的	的	de	Part.	(a structural particle)
6.	英文	英文	Yīngwén	N.	English (language)
7.	名字	名字	míngzi	N.	name
8.	中文	中文	Zhōngwén	N.	Chinese (language)
9.	叫	叫	jiào	V.	to call
10.	什么	什麼	shénme	Pron.	what
11.	她	她	tā	Pron.	she, her
12.	谁	誰	shéi/shuí (shéi also pronounced as shuí in some regions)	Pron.	who, whom
13.	同学	同學	tóngxué	N.	classmate

专名   Proper Nouns

	SIMPLIFIED	TRADITIONAL	PINYIN		
1.	李文中	李文中	Lǐ Wénzhōng	N.	(name) Wenzhong Li
2.	吴小美	吳小美	Wú Xiǎoměi	N.	(name) Xiaomei Wu
3.	于英	于英	Yú Yīng	N.	(name) Ying Yu

补充词　Supplementary Vocabulary

	SIMPLIFIED	TRADITIONAL	PINYIN		
1.	汉语	漢語	Hànyǔ	N.	Chinese (language)
2.	英语	英語	Yīngyǔ	N.	English (language)

语文知识　LANGUAGE LINK

The Sentence Patterns provide models that will help you with the Language in Use section. In both sections, pay attention to the grammar points, vocabulary, and expressions.

句型　Sentence Patterns

A: 请问您贵姓?
Qǐng wèn nín guì xìng?

B: 我姓李。
Wǒ xìng Lǐ.

A: 你叫什么名字?
Nǐ jiào shénme míngzi?

B: 我叫吴小美。
Wǒ jiào Wú Xiǎoměi.

A: 她是谁?
Tā shì shéi?

B: 她是于英。
Tā shì Yú Yīng.

课文   Language in Use: 您贵姓？ Nín guì xìng?

MARY: 你好！请问您贵姓？
Nǐhǎo! Qǐng wèn nín guì xìng?

JOHN: 我姓李，我的英文名字是John Lee，中文名字是
Wǒ xìng Lǐ, wǒ de Yīngwén míngzi shì John Lee, Zhōngwén míngzi shì

李文中。你呢？请问你叫什么名字？
Lǐ Wénzhōng. Nǐ ne? Qǐng wèn nǐ jiào shénme míngzi?

MARY: 我叫Mary。我的英文名字是Mary Wood，
Wǒ jiào Mary. Wǒ de Yīngwén míngzi shì Mary Wood,

中文名字是吴小美。
Zhōngwén míngzi shì Wú Xiǎoměi.

JOHN: 她呢？她是谁？
Tā ne? Tā shì shéi?

MARY: 她是我的同学于英。
Tā shì wǒ de tóngxué Yú Yīng.

注释 LANGUAGE NOTES

The Verb 叫; 请问

The verb 叫 ("to call" or "to be called") is used to ask one's full name or given name. "请问" means "May I ask . . ." "请 . . ." is an expression of polite request.

Remember to add "请问" (May I ask . . .) to be polite when asking someone's name in Chinese.

For example,

请问，你叫什么名字?   May I have your name, please?

Chinese Names 姓名

A person's name in Chinese has two parts: the surname 姓 and the given name 名. The word order of a Chinese name is different from that of an English name. In a Chinese name, the surname comes before the given name. For example, in the Chinese names 吴小美, 李文中, and 于英, 吴, 李, and 于 are the surnames. 小美, 文中, and 英 are the given names. Chinese given names are commonly one or two syllables. In all but a few cases, Chinese surnames are one syllable.

Surname	Given name
吴	小美
李	文中
于	英

语法 GRAMMAR

您

您 is the polite form of the pronoun for the second person singular 你. It is normally used to address one's elders or those with a higher social status. For example,

<u>Situation:</u> A student and a teacher
Student: 李老师，您好!   How are you, Teacher Li?
Teacher: 你好。   How are you?

For the sake of politeness or courtesy it is also used to address someone of similar age or social status, but only at the first meeting.

<u>Situation:</u> A and B are about the same age, and this is their first meeting
A: 您好!   Hi! *or* How are you?
B: 您好!   Hi! *or* How are you?

您贵姓

您贵姓 is a polite way of asking someone's surname. The person who is asked the question "您贵姓?" commonly replies with his/her surname or his/her full name. Note that one should never use 贵姓 in the reply when somebody asks your surname.

For example,

A: 请问，您贵姓？   May I ask your surname?
B: 我姓李。   My surname is Li.

A: 请问，您贵姓？   May I ask your surname?
B: 我姓李。我叫李文中。   My surname is Li, and my full name is Wenzhong Li.

The Interrogative Pronouns   什么，谁

As an interrogative pronoun, 什么 can be used alone to ask "what?" Its most common usage, however, is to be placed before a general noun when requesting more specific information. For example, the Chinese sentence "你叫什么名字？" can be thought of as "You are called *what* name?" and translated as "What's your name?" The word order in Chinese "who, what, where, which, when, how" questions is usually different from that in English. Chinese does not place the question word at the beginning of the sentence. In Chinese, the question word occurs where the expected answer would be. That is, the question and the answer have a similar word order as illustrated below.

你叫<u>什么名字</u>?   What's your name?
我叫<u>小美</u>。   I am called 小美.

谁 (who, whom) is an interrogative pronoun. As mentioned above, the Chinese word order of a question formed with an interrogative word is the same word order as would be used in the answer. Thus we see question-and-answer combinations like the following:

Question: 他们是<u>谁</u>?   Who are those people?
Answer: 他们是<u>我的同学</u>。   They are my classmates.

The position of 谁 in the question is the same as the position of 我的同学 in the answer.

Again, remember that this contrasts with the English word order. Another thing to remember is that there is no need to put 吗 at the end of the sentence to mark it as a question, since the interrogative word already fulfills this function.

The Particle   的

In Chinese word order, a modifier typically precedes the word or phrase it modifies. The possessive construction is formed by placing the particle 的 after a noun to form the possessor. It is similar to the "'s" of English indicating the genitive association.

For example,

我的 modifier	名字 modified	my name
教师的 modifier	名字 modified	teacher's name
老师的 modifier	学生 modified	teacher's students

补充课文 ⊶ SUPPLEMENTARY PRACTICE

This selection will help you test your comprehension of the grammar and vocabulary you have learned in this lesson. Be prepared to answer questions about the meaning of the passage.

大家好！我来自我介绍一下。我姓吴，我叫吴小美，我的英文名字是Mary Wood。你呢？请问您贵姓？你叫什么名字？她呢？她是谁？你不知道，对不对？没关系，我来告诉你吧。她是我的同学，她叫于英。

Notes: 大家 [dàjiā]: everybody
来 [lái]: come (placed in front of a verb, indicates the intention of doing something)
自我介绍 [zìwǒjièshào]: self-introduction
一下 [yíxià]: a little bit
知道 [zhīdào]: to know
告诉 [gàosu]: to tell

练习 ACTIVITIES

I. Listening Exercises

2-1 In each pair, circle the one your instructor pronounces:

1. nín/lín   2. wén/mén   3. xǐng/qǐng   4. zì/zhì   5. níng/míng
6. qiào/jiào   7. tǒng/dǒng   8. miǎo/xiǎo   9. yìng/xìng   10. shénme/zénme

2-2 In each pair, circle the one your instructor pronounces:

1. guǐ/gěi   2. yīng/yīn   3. shén/shéi   4. wài/wèi   5. mén/mín
6. jiào/jiù   7. zì/cì   8. xǐng/xiǎo   9. tóng/tíng   10. mèi/miàn

2-3   Listen to the instructor pronounce the following words, then add the tone marks:

1. mingzi   2. tongxue   3. qing   4. Yingwen   5. shenme
6. nin shi   7. shei   8. guixing   9. Zhongwen   10. jiao

2-4   Form groups of three to four members. Take turns reading the following tongue twister out loud, as quickly as you can. Each group will select one member to represent the group in a class competition.

sìshí: 四十   forty

shísì: 十四   fourteen

shì: 是   is, are

Sìshí shì sìshí.	四十是四十。	Forty is forty.
Shísì shì shísì.	十四是十四。	Fourteen is fourteen.
Sìshí búshì shísì.	四十不是十四。	Forty is not fourteen.
Shísì yě búshì sìshí.	十四也不是四十。	Fourteen is not forty, either.

II. Character Exercises

2-5   Read the following words, phrases, and sentences:

名字	姓
什么名字	贵姓
你叫什么名字?	您贵姓?
你的老师叫什么名字?	请问您贵姓?
你的中文老师叫什么名字?	请问您的老师贵姓?

Now try to use the following characters to make words, phrases, and then sentences:

1. 您   2. 姓   3. 请   4. 问   5. 的   6. 英
7. 文   8. 中   9. 叫   10. 她   11. 谁   12. 同

2-6   Write the Chinese characters for the following words:

1. name _____ _____   2. please _____   3. who _____

4. ask _____   5. surname _____   6. English _____ _____

7. to call _____   8. what _____ _____

2-7 Create flashcards.

To help learn new characters, and also as an aid for future review, students are strongly encouraged to create flashcards for each lesson's vocabulary items. See the following example for a suggested format:

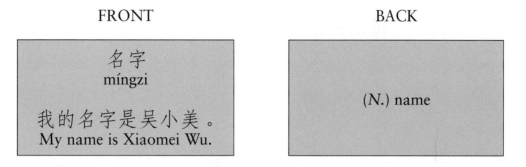

FRONT

名字
míngzi

我的名字是吴小美。
My name is Xiaomei Wu.

BACK

(N.) name

III. Grammar Exercises

2-8 Substitution exercises: Create sentences following the examples given:

1. 她是谁？
   她是小美。

你	李文中
小美	我的同学
于英	我的老师

2. 你叫什么名字？
   我叫李文中。

他	吴小同
你的同学	于学文

3. 请问，你的名字是什么？
   我的名字是李文中。

她的	于文英
你的老师的	李师美
他的同学的	吴同文
你的中文老师的	文汉中

2-9 Form pairs. Following the example given, ask and answer as many questions as you can on each of the following sentences:

For example,　　　我的同学叫小美。

你的同学叫小美吗?

谁叫小美?

谁的同学叫小美?

你的同学叫什么名字?

你的同学的名字是什么?

Hint: 谁,什么,什么名字,谁的,贵姓。

1. 她是李小英。
2. 我姓吴。
3. 我的老师的名字是于文中。
4. 我的同学姓文,他的中文名字是文同生。

IV. Communicative Activities

2-10 Form groups of three. Each group should have a piece of paper. Go around the classroom and get acquainted with as many people as you can. First introduce yourself, then find out what other students' names are. Write them down in Pinyin on the paper. Based on the information you have collected, design a roster of your classmates for later use.

For example,

	xìng 姓 surname	míngzi 名字 name
1.	Wáng	Xiǎoměi
2.	. . .	. . .
3.	. . .	. . .
4.	Wú	Wénzhōng

2-11 Introductions:

Write your name on the blackboard. Add the Pinyin and the English translation for each character in your name. Then introduce yourself to the class.

Useful expressions:

大家 [dàjiā] (everyone) 好　　　　　　　　　　　你们 [nǐmen] ([pl.] you) 好

我姓......　　　　　　　　　　　　　　　我叫......

我的英文名字是......,中文名字是......

我是学生,不是老师。

他/她是我的同学。他/她的英文名字是......,中文名字是......

文化点滴 CULTURE NOTES

中文姓名 [Zhōngwén xìngmíng]
Chinese Names

Chinese names have two parts: a 姓 [xìng] (surname) and a 名 [míng] (given name). In a Chinese name, the surname precedes the given name.

In general, the surname is inherited from the father. Chinese surnames are usually referred to as the 百家姓 [bǎi jiā xìng] (hundreds of family surnames), which is the name of a famous listing of Chinese surnames. Most Chinese surnames are monosyllabic, such as 赵 [Zhào], 钱 [Qián], 孙 [Sūn], 李 [Lǐ], which happen to be the first four surnames on the 百家姓 list. A few surnames are disyllabic (having two syllables), the most common being 欧阳 [Ōuyáng] and 司马 [Sīmǎ].

A child's given name is significant and meaningful. It is generally chosen by the parents and usually has one or two characters.

Naming a child generally involves two important considerations. First, the given names that the parents choose usually reflect the parents' hopes for their child. Parents always hope to have a virtuous child who becomes successful and achieves great things. For boys, honor, success, strength, bravery, and brilliance are common themes in names. Girls' names are usually related to beauty, purity, and elegance.

Siblings sometimes have similar or identical elements in their given names. The shared elements can be either the first or the second character of a two-character given name, as illustrated below:

美 [měi] beautiful, fine the first character is shared	杰 [jié] heroic, outstanding the second character is shared
美玲 [Měilíng] beautiful, cute, and bright	志杰 [Zhìjié] ambitious and outstanding
美玉 [Měiyù] beautiful, fine, and delicate	俊杰 [Jùnjié] handsome and outstanding
美秀 [Měixiù] beautiful and brilliant	豪杰 [Háojié] talented and outstanding

In order to help the child have a prosperous and lucky future, parents, especially those in Taiwan, usually also consult with a fortuneteller. The fortuneteller will match the name with the child's birthday and provide advice.

Common one-syllable Chinese surnames:

Zhào	Qián	Sūn	Lǐ		Féng	Chén	Chǔ	Wèi		Zhū	Qín	Yóu	Xǔ
赵	钱	孙	李		冯	陈	褚	卫		朱	秦	尤	许
Kǒng	Cáo	Yán	Huà		Qī	Xiè	Zōu	Yù		Shào	Sū	Pān	Gě
孔	曹	严	华		戚	谢	邹	喻		邵	苏	潘	葛
Zhōu	Wú	Zhèng	Wáng		Jiǎng	Shěn	Hán	Yáng		Xuē	Lǚ	Shī	Zhāng
周	吴	郑	王		蒋	沈	韩	杨		薛	吕	施	张
Jīn	Wèi	Táo	Jiāng		Léi	Hè	Dòu	Zhāng		Rén	Fàn	Péng	Láng
金	魏	陶	姜		雷	贺	窦	章		任	范	彭	郎
Yú	Tián	Yáo	Lín		Dīng	Yú	Fāng	Huáng		Hé	Gāo	Xià	Kē
于	田	姚	林		丁	余	方	黄		何	高	夏	柯
Bāo	Xú	Liáng	Zhōng		Hú	Hóng	Cuī	Liú		Qiáo	Liǔ	Gān	Dèng
包	徐	梁	钟		胡	洪	崔	刘		乔	柳	甘	邓
Máo	Jiāng	Zhān	Zhuāng		Gǒng	Niú	Zēng	Yóu		Bì	Wū	Guō	Móu
毛	江	詹	庄		巩	牛	曾	游		毕	巫	郭	牟
Xiè	Dài	Dǒng	Láo		Qiū	Mò	Jiǎ	Miáo		Shǐ	Tāng	Mèng	Táng
谢	戴	董	劳		邱	莫	贾	苗		史	汤	孟	唐

Common two-syllable Chinese surnames:

Sīmǎ	Ōuyáng	Xiàhóu	Zhūgě	Huángfǔ
司马	欧阳	夏侯	诸葛	皇甫
Dōngfāng	Lìnghú	Duānmù	Shàngguān	Gōngsūn
东方	令狐	端木	上官	公孙

**Jade, wood, and stone are common materials used for carving chops.
Various calligraphic styles can be chosen to add artistic effects.**

A frequently heard sentence in everyday Chinese life is, "Please sign your name and put your chop on it." Chops are also known as seals; they are specially carved stamps that the Chinese use almost as a signature. A chop is still required to legalize a contract, pick up registered mail, withdraw money from the bank, acknowledge receipt of official documents, etc.

Questions:

1. What are the similarities and differences between naming in Chinese and English (or other languages)? (e.g., How is a child's name given? Are there any special considerations?)

2. Do you have any stories to share (e.g., the story of your name; Chinese people you know who share some elements in their names)?

趣味中文　FUN WITH CHINESE

> 同名同姓
> having the same given name and surname

tóng	míng	tóng	xìng
同	名	同	姓
same	name	same	surname

China has one of the largest populations in the world. There are around
1.3 billion people in Mainland China. As a result, it is very common
to have the same given name and surname as someone else.

Question:

Have you ever encountered a "同名同姓" situation? What would
you do if you did?

行动吧! LET'S GO!
....

身份证   ID Card

美英 is helping her Chinese friend translate his identity card for a lawyer.
Can you help?

Useful words and expressions:

身份证(身份證) [shēnfèn zhèng]: identity card
性别 [xìngbié]: sex
男 [nán]: male
女 [nǔ]: female
民族 [mínzú]: ethnicity
汉(漢) [hàn]: Han (ethnic group)
出生 [chūshēng]: to be born
年 [nián]: year
月 [yuè]: month
日 [rì]: date
住址 [zhùzhǐ]: address
北京市 [Běijīng shì]: Beijing (Beijing City)
中山路 [Zhōngshān lù]: Zhongshan Road
公安局 [gōng'ān jú]: police bureau
号(號) [hào]: number
编号(編號) [biānhào]: ID number
签发(簽發) [qiānfā]: to be issued
有效期限 [yǒuxiào qīxiàn]: valid date

姓名：王大中
性别：男　　　民族：汉
出生：1970年8月19日
住址：北京市中山路10号

北京市公安局　2002年6月26日　签发　有效期限10年
编号：111111197008191111

Your translation: _____

_____

_____

Questions:
1. 他叫什么名字？　_____
2. 他是从哪儿来的？_____

复习   Review

Read Aloud

Read the following sentences aloud. Pay attention to pronunciation and tones.

1. **A:** 他是学生。
   B: 他不是学生。

2. **A:** 他也是学生。
   B: 他也是学生吗?

3. **A:** 他是学生吗?
   B: 他不是学生吗?

4. **A:** 我是他的同学，你呢?
   B: 我不是他的同学，你呢?

Conversation

Find a partner and practice the following dialogues:

1. **A:** 你好! 请问，您贵姓?
   B: 我姓____。你呢?

2. **A:** 请问，你叫什么名字?
   B: 我的英文名字是_____，中文名字是_____。

3. **A:** 请问，你的中文老师是谁?
   B: 我的中文老师是____ 老师。

Write Chinese

Write your Chinese name in both Pinyin and Chinese characters.

For example,   Wú   Xiǎoměi
                 吴   小 美

我 的 名 字 是: _____

Simplified and Traditional Characters

Read each character aloud. Write its simplified form. Then create a phrase and a sentence using the character.

For example,   學 → 学 → 学生 → 我是学生。

嗎 ( )   師 ( )   貴 ( )   請 ( )   問 ( )   麼 ( )   誰 ( )

你是哪国人?
Which Country Are You From?

- Find out someone's nationality
- Ask which language they speak
- Talk about each others' nationalities and languages

China has visitors from all over the world.

Chinese like to make friends with people of all nationalities.

Shanghai attracts many foreign students interested in studying Chinese language and culture.

生词 VOCABULARY

核心词 Core Vocabulary

	SIMPLIFIED	TRADITIONAL	PINYIN		
1.	哪	哪	nǎ/něi (nǎ also pronounced as něi in some regions)	Pron.	which
2.	国	國	guó	N.	country
3.	人	人	rén	N.	person
4.	很	很	hěn	Adv.	very, quite
5.	对了	對了	duìle		by the way (a phrase used to start a new topic)
6.	法国	法國	Fǎguó Fàguó (pronunciation in Taiwan)	N.	France
7.	美国	美國	Měiguó	N.	United States
8.	英国	英國	Yīngguó	N.	Britain
9.	中国	中國	Zhōngguó	N.	China
10.	说	說	shuō	V.	to speak
11.	会	會	huì	Aux.	can, be able to
12.	一点儿儿	一點兒兒	yìdiǎr ér		a little (retroflex ending)
13.	法文	法文	Fǎwén	N.	French (language)
14.	和	和	hé hàn (pronunciation in Taiwan)	Conj.	and

补充词 Supplementary Vocabulary

SIMPLIFIED	TRADITIONAL	PINYIN		
1. 德国 德国人 德语(德文)	德國 德國人 德語(德文)	Déguó Déguórén Déyǔ (Déwén)	N. N. N.	Germany German (person) German (language)
2. 韩国 韩国人 韩语(韩文)	韓國 韓國人 韓語(韓文)	Hánguó Hánguórén Hányǔ (Hánwén)	N. N. N.	Korea Korean (person) Korean (language)
3. 加拿大 加拿大人	加拿大 加拿大人	Jiānádà Jiānádàrén	N. N.	Canada Canadian (person)
4. 泰国 泰国人 泰语(泰文)	泰國 泰國人 泰語(泰文)	Tàiguó Tàiguórén Tàiyǔ (Tàiwén)	N. N. N.	Thailand Thai (person) Thai (language)
5. 日本 日本人 日语(日文)	日本 日本人 日語(日文)	Rìběn Rìběnrén Rìyǔ (Rìwén)	N. N. N.	Japan Japanese (person) Japanese (language)
6. 西班牙 西班牙人 西班牙语 (西班牙文)	西班牙 西班牙人 西班牙語 (西班牙文)	Xībānyá Xībānyárén Xībānyáyǔ (Xībānyáwén)	N. N. N.	Spain Spanish (person) Spanish (language)

语文知识 LANGUAGE LINK

The Sentence Patterns provide models that will help you with the Language in Use section. In both sections, pay attention to the grammar points, vocabulary, and expressions.

句型 Sentence Patterns

A: 你是哪国人？
Nǐ shì nǎ guó rén?

B: 我是法国人。
Wǒ shì Fǎguórén.

A: 你会说中文吗？
Nǐ huì shuō Zhōngwén ma?

B: 我会说中文。
Wǒ huì shuō Zhōngwén.

课文   Language in Use: 你是哪国人？Nǐ shì nǎ guó rén?

李文中：   小美，你好吗？
Xiǎoměi, nǐhǎo ma?

吴小美：   我很好。对了，文中，你是哪国人？
Wǒ hěnhǎo. Duìle, Wénzhōng, nǐ shì nǎ guó rén?

李文中：   我是法国人。你呢？你是美国人吗？
Wǒ shì Fǎguórén. Nǐ ne? Nǐ shì Měiguórén ma?

吴小美：   不是，我不是美国人，我是英国人。
Bú shì, wǒ bú shì Měiguórén, wǒ shì Yīngguórén.

李文中：   老师呢？
Lǎoshī ne?

吴小美：   他是中国人。他说中文。
Tā shì Zhōngguórén. Tā shuō Zhōngwén.

李文中：   你会说中文吗？
Nǐ huì shuō Zhōngwén ma?

吴小美：   我会说一点儿中文，我也会说法文和英文。
Wǒ huì shuō yìdiǎr Zhōngwén, wǒ yě huì shuō Fǎwén hé Yīngwén.

注释 LANGUAGE NOTES

你好吗? How Are You?

"你好吗?" is a common greeting. The common reply is "我很好".

For example,

A: 你好吗?
B: 我很好, 你呢?

Adverb 很(他很好)

很 is an adverb meaning "very" that occurs before verbs or adjectives. (For more details on the adverb 很, please refer to Lesson 4.)

Note: 是 is not used to link a subject and an adjective in a descriptive sentence, such as the English sentence "He is good." That sentence would be expressed in Chinese as "他很好。"

对了

对了 is often used in informal conversation to start a new topic so that the transition won't sound too abrupt. It is similar to "by the way" in English.

For example,

A: 小美, 你好吗?   How are you, Xiaomei?
B: 我很好。对了, 文中, 你是哪国人?   I am fine. By the way, Wenzhong, what's your nationality?

语法 GRAMMAR

哪(哪国人) Which Nationality?

哪 is a question word that means "which." "哪国人" is an interrogative phrase used to ask someone's nationality. For example,

他是哪国人?   What's his nationality?

国名和国人 Country Names and People

In Chinese, the character 国 means "country, nation." 国 is placed after a one-syllable character to form a country name. If there are two or more syllables, 国 is not used. See the following examples:

One syllable (with 国)

Country	Pinyin	Meaning
美国	Měiguó	United States
德国	Déguó	Germany
英国	Yīngguó	Britain
泰国	Tàiguó	Thailand
中国	Zhōngguó	China
韩国	Hánguó	Korea
法国	Fǎguó	France

More than two syllables (without 国)

Country	Pinyin	Meaning
日本	Rìběn	Japan
越南	Yuènán	Vietnam
印尼	Yìnní	Indonesia
印度	Yìndù	India
伊朗	Yīlǎng	Iran
伊拉克	Yīlākè	Iraq
西班牙	Xībānyá	Spain
墨西哥	Mòxīgē	Mexico
加拿大	Jiānádà	Canada
新加坡	Xīnjiāpō	Singapore
意大利	Yìdàlì	Italy
俄罗斯	Éluósī	Russia
马来西亚	Mǎláixīyà	Malaysia

To indicate a person from a certain country, simply add 人 after the country name.

People	Pinyin	Meaning
美国人	Měiguórén	American
德国人	Déguórén	German
英国人	Yīngguórén	British
泰国人	Tàiguórén	Thai
中国人	Zhōngguórén	Chinese
日本人	Rìběnrén	Japanese
法国人	Fǎguórén	French
越南人	Yuènánrén	Vietnamese
印尼人	Yìnnírén	Indonesian
印度人	Yìndùrén	Indian
伊朗人	Yīlǎngrén	Iranian
伊拉克人	Yīlākèrén	Iraqi
西班牙人	Xībānyárén	Spanish
墨西哥人	Mòxīgērén	Mexican
加拿大人	Jiānádàrén	Canadian
意大利人	Yìdàlìrén	Italian
韩国人	Hánguórén	Korean
新加坡人	Xīnjiāpōrén	Singaporean
马来西亚人	Mǎláixīyàrén	Malaysian

Chinese people commonly add 人 after a place or city to indicate where they are from. For example,

我是北京人。	Wǒ shì Běijīngrén.	I am from Beijing.
他是台北人。	Tā shì Táiběirén.	He is from Taipei.
老师是上海人。	Lǎoshī shì Shànghǎirén.	The teacher is from Shanghai.
你是香港人。	Nǐ shì Xiānggǎngrén.	You are from Hong Kong.

说 and 语言

The character 说 means "to speak." "我会说中文" means "I can speak Chinese." In Taiwan and some other regions of China, 讲 [jiǎng] is used in place of 说 (我会讲中文). In most cases the word for a language is formed by adding 文 or 语 after the country name (without 国). For example,

英文 English	法文 French	德文 German	日文 Japanese
英语 English	法语 French	德语 German	日语 Japanese

Note: Chinese is expressed as either 中文 or 汉语.

The subtle difference between 文 and 语 is that 文 tends to refer to written language and literature, while 语 tends to refer to spoken language.

一点儿

一点儿 is a phrase used before a noun to indicate "a little."

Note: When 一 is followed by 1st, 2nd, and 3rd tone, it is pronounced as [yì]. Therefore "一点儿" should be pronounced as [yì diǎr].

一点儿 (a little) [yì diǎr] + Noun	
我会说一点儿中文。	I can speak a little Chinese.
我也会说一点儿法文。	I can also speak a little French.

Conjunction 和

和 is a common conjunction for nouns and pronouns. Note that it may be translated as English "and." However, it is not equivalent to the all-purpose English conjunction "and." (In English, the conjunction "and" can be used for nouns and pronouns, for verbs, and between sentences or clauses.) Following are some examples of the use of 和:

老师和学生都[dōu](all)很忙[máng](busy)。	Teacher and student are both busy.
我和我的室友都是中国人。	My roommates and I are all Chinese.
他们是丁明和方小文。	They are Ming Ding and Xiaowen Fang.

补充课文 ━◦◦◦━ SUPPLEMENTARY PRACTICE

This selection will help you test your comprehension of the grammar and vocabulary you have learned in this lesson. Be prepared to answer questions about the meaning of the passage.

我是美国人，我会说英文和法文，我也会说一点儿中文。他是我的中文老师，我的老师很好。他是中国人，他说中文，他也说一点儿英文。对了，你呢？请问，你是哪国人？你会说什么语言？你会说中文吗？

Note: 语言 [yǔyán]: language

练习 ACTIVITIES

I. Listening Exercises

3-1   In each pair, circle the one your instructor pronounces:

1. nǎguó	Fǎguó	2. liàn Zhōngwén	niàn Zhōngwén
3. suō	shuō	4. Tàiyǔ	Dǎiyǔ
5. Rìběn	Lǐběn	6. Déwēn	Éwén

3-2   In each pair, circle the one your instructor pronounces:

1. Měiguó	Měiguō	2. yìrén	yīrén
3. nàběn	nǎběn	4. Fāguó	Fǎguó
5. shuòshì	shuōshì	6. Hànyǔ	Hányǔ

3-3   Form groups of three to four. Read the following poem in your group, paying special attention to the rhythm.

Yóuzǐ Yín (Mèng Jiāo)	游子吟 (孟郊)	Song of the Parting Son (Meng, Jiao)
Cí mǔ shǒuzhōng xiàn,	慈母手中线，	A loving mother with thread in her hands,
Yóuzǐ shēnshàng yī.	游子身上衣。	For the parting son weaves the gown.
Línxíng mìmì féng,	临行密密缝，	Before he leaves she stitches carefully,
Yì kǒng chíchí guī.	意恐迟迟归。	Fearing his return will be long delayed.
Shéi yán cùn cǎo xīn,	谁言寸草心，	Who believes that the heart of young grass,
Bào dé sān chūn huī?	报得三春晖？	Can repay three springs of sunshine?

II. Character Exercises

3-4 Read the following words, phrases, and sentences:

人	说
国人	说中文
美国人	我会说中文。
我是美国人。	我不会说中文。
我不是美国人。	我会说中文，不会说日文。
我不是英国人，也不是美国人。	老师也会说中文，他也不会说日文。

Now try to use the following characters to make words, phrases, and then sentences:

1. 哪   2. 国   3. 很   4. 对   5. 法   6. 美
7. 会   8. 点   9. 儿   10. 和   11. 人   12. 说

3-5 Draw lines to match the simplified and traditional forms of the following characters:

点	说	谁	贵	学	师	国	吗
說	國	嗎	師	點	誰	學	貴

3-6 Stroke and radical exercises:

1. Write several characters you have learned which start with a horizontal stroke "—":

一 : _____

2. Write several characters you have learned which start with a vertical stroke "丨":

丨 : _____

3. Write several characters you have learned which start with a left-slanted stroke "丿":

丿 : _____

3-7 Create flashcards.

To help learn new characters, and also as an aid for future review, students are strongly encouraged to create flashcards for each lesson's vocabulary items. See the following example for a suggested format:

FRONT   BACK

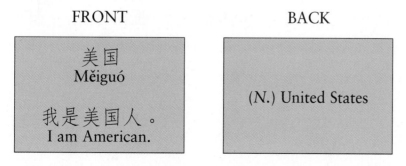

美国
Měiguó

我是美国人。
I am American.

(N.) United States

III. Grammar Exercises

3-8   The following are the names of countries. Please tell the class how to refer to the nationality and the language for each of them:

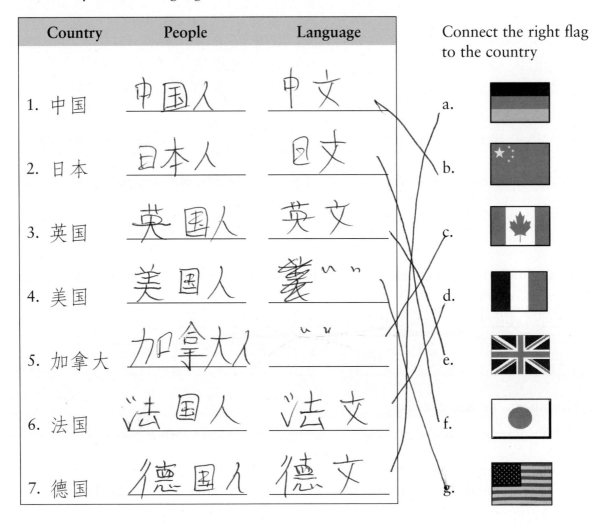

Country	People	Language		Connect the right flag to the country
1. 中国	中国人	中文	a.	
2. 日本	日本人	日文	b.	
3. 英国	英国人	英文	c.	
4. 美国	美国人	美〞	d.	
5. 加拿大	加拿大人	〞	e.	
6. 法国	法国人	法文	f.	
7. 德国	德国人	德文	g.	

3-9   Substitution exercises:

1. **A:** 你是哪国人?
   B: 我是中国人。
   A: 你会说英文吗?
   B: 我不会说英文,我会说中文。

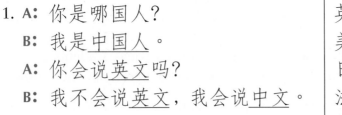

英国人	法文	英文
美国人	日文	英文
日本人	中文	日文
法国人	德文	法文
德国人	西班牙文	德文
韩国人	法文	韩文

2. A: 你会说<u>中文</u>吗？

   B: 我会说<u>中文</u>，我也会说一点儿<u>英文</u>。

英文	法文
法文	德文
德文	日文
日文	西班牙文
西班牙文	韩文
韩文	中文

3-10 Fill in the blanks with appropriate words to complete the following sentences:

(Words: 叫, 会, 说, 是, 不, 也)

1. 我 <u>是</u> 中国人。
2. 她 <u>会</u> <u>说</u> 英文，也 <u>会</u> <u>说</u> 一点儿法文。
3. 他 <u>叫</u> 李中，他 <u>是</u> 美国人。
4. 我 ＿＿ 吴英。我 ＿＿ 法国人。我 ＿＿ 法语。
5. 小文 ＿＿ 英国人。他 ＿＿ ＿＿ 说日文，他 ＿＿ ＿＿ 英文。
   他 ＿＿ ＿＿ ＿＿ 一点儿中文。

IV. Communicative Activities

3-11 In the exercises for Lesson 2, you gathered information about your classmates and created a list of all the students in the class. Now you need to update the list with new information. First check the accuracy of the information you gathered last time by asking the following questions (among others — use whatever you find necessary). Then, update your list of information to add the country each is from and the language each speaks.

1. 我是……。
2. 请问，你是……吗？
3. 请问，你叫……？
4. 你的中文名字……？

文化知识 ⟨⟐⟐⟐⟩ Culture Link

文化点滴　CULTURE NOTES

中国人的家乡观念
[Zhōngguórén de jiāxiāng guānniàn]
Chinese Concept of "Native Town"

One of the items you are usually required to fill out on forms in China is your 家乡 [jiāxiāng] (native town/hometown). This term refers to the place from which your family originally came. While the English term "hometown" typically refers to where a person was born or grew up, this is not necessarily the case with the Chinese term. Given the increased mobility of modern society it is not unreasonable or even uncommon for Chinese to list as their hometown a place they have never seen in their lives.

Whether they grew up there or not, Chinese people often feel a sense of attachment to their family's hometown as well as a sense of affinity with others who share the same hometown. In fact, among overseas Chinese there are various townsman societies whose major goal is to help their fellow townsmen in difficulty. You will find 广东同乡会 [Guǎngdōng tóngxiānghuì] (the Guangdong Fellow Townsman Society), 宁波同乡会 [Níngbō tóngxiānghuì] (the Ningbo Fellow Townsman Society), 福建同乡会 [Fújiàn tóngxiānghuì] (the Fujian Fellow Townsman Society), and recently 温州同乡会 [Wēnzhōu tóngxiānghuì] (the Wenzhou Fellow Townsman Society).

"叶落归根 [yè luò guī gēn]," which means "fallen leaves settle on their roots," is a phrase very much appreciated by Chinese. No matter where they are or how many generations separate them from it, many Chinese would like to visit their hometown at least once in their lifetime. This is evident when you consider that, after 40 years of separation between Mainland China and Taiwan, countless Taiwanese people still visit the Mainland.

In modern society, the feeling of attachment among Chinese to their hometown has become much weaker. People no longer have to rely on their townsmen for support and help. However, meeting someone from your hometown is still a pleasure, and traveling to one's hometown still remains a dream of many Chinese.

Traditionally, families have a small altar for remembering deities and ancestors, and for seeking their blessings and protection.

Questions:

1. Is there a similar saying in English (or other languages) that communicates the concept of "叶落归根"? Do you have any related stories to share?

2. In what situations in your country do you need to indicate your "家乡"?

趣味中文　FUN WITH CHINESE

说来话长。
It's a long story.

shuō	lái	huà	cháng
说	来	话	长
speak	come	words	long

说来话长 is commonly used Chinese slang. It is usually used to refer to something that is very complicated.

Question:

Do you have any stories that are examples of "说来话长"? Would you like to share one with the class?

行动吧！ LET'S GO!

···

网上语言家教中心
On-line Language Tutoring Center

Mary is filling in her data at an online language tutoring center. Below is what she filled out.

Useful words and expressions:

个人(個人) [gèrén]: personal
资料(資料) [zīliào]: data, information
性别 [xìngbié]: sex
女 [nǚ]: female
男 [nán]: male
国籍(國籍) [guójí]: nationality
电话(電話) [diànhuà]: telephone
电子邮件(電子郵件) [diànzǐ yóujiàn]: e-mail address
能 [néng]: be able to
教 [jiāo]: to teach

Mary Lee 李文英 的 个人资料：

英文姓名：Mary Lee
中文姓名：李文英
性别：女
国籍：英国
电话：311-1122
电子邮件：marywenying@zhongwen.edu
能教的语言：英文，西班牙文，法文，德文

Questions:

1. Mary 的中文名字叫什么？ _____

2. 她是哪国人？ _____

3. 她能教什么语言？ _____

第四课
LESSON

4

你学什么?
What Do You Study?

- Ask what something is
- Explain what something is
- Ask about majors in school
- Talk about courses

A senior high school in Taiwan.

In a Taiwan school, you will see many girls wearing uniforms with long skirts.

Fudan University in Shanghai.

生词 VOCABULARY

核心词 Core Vocabulary

	SIMPLIFIED	TRADITIONAL	PINYIN		
1.	那	那	nà/nèi (nà also pronounced as nèi in some regions)	Pron.	that
2.	书	書	shū	N.	book
3.	这	這	zhè/zhèi (zhè also pronounced as zhèi in some regions)	Pron.	this
4.	本	本	běn	M.W.	(measure word for book)
5.	文学	文學	wénxué	N.	literature
6.	工程	工程	gōngchéng	N.	engineering
7.	难	難	nán	Adj.	difficult
8.	太	太	tài	Adv.	too
9.	可是	可是	kěshì	Conj.	but, yet, however
10.	功课	功課	gōngkè	N.	homework, assignment
11.	多	多	duō	Adj.	many, much
12.	我们	我們	wǒmen men	Pron.	we, us (used after a personal pronoun or a noun to show plural number)
13.	少	少	shǎo	Adj.	few, little

补充词 Supplementary Vocabulary

	SIMPLIFIED	TRADITIONAL	PINYIN		
1.	系	系	xì	N.	department
2.	数学	數學	shùxué	N.	mathematics
3.	计算机 (电脑)#	計算機 (電腦)	jìsuànjī (diànnǎo)	N.	computer
4.	专业 (主修)##	專業 (主修)	zhuānyè (zhǔxiū)	N.	major
5.	辅修	輔修	fǔxiū	N.	minor
6.	容易	容易	róngyì	Adj.	easy
7.	忙	忙	máng	Adj.	busy
8.	累	累	lèi	Adj.	tired
9.	作业	作業	zuòyè	N.	homework, assignment
10.	考试	考試	kǎoshì	N.	exam
11.	有点儿	有點兒	yǒudiǎr	Adv.	a little
12.	还好	還好	hái hǎo		not bad, okay

Notes: # In Mainland China, a computer is called "计算机"; now it is also commonly called "电脑".
In Taiwan, it is called "电脑".
主修 is mainly used in Taiwan, while 专业 is used in Mainland China.

语文知识 LANGUAGE LINK

The Sentence Patterns provide models that will help you with the Language in Use section. In both sections, pay attention to the grammar points, vocabulary, and expressions.

句型   **Sentence Patterns**

A: 那是一本什么书?
Nà shì yìběn shénme shū?

B: 那是一本英文书。
Nà shì yìběn Yīngwén shū.

A: 你学什么?
Nǐ xué shénme?

B: 我学英国文学,你呢?
Wǒ xué Yīngguó wénxué, nǐ ne?

A: 工程难吗?
Gōngchéng nán ma?

B: 不太难。
Bú tài nán.

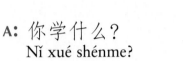

课文   **Language in Use: 你学什么? Nǐ xué shénme?**

吴小美:　文中,那是你的书吗?
　　　　　Wénzhōng, nà shì nǐ de shū ma?

李文中:　那是我的书。
　　　　　Nà shì wǒ de shū.

吴小美:　那是一本什么书?
　　　　　Nà shì yìběn shénme shū?

李文中:　那是一本英文书。
　　　　　Nà shì yìběn Yīngwén shū.

吴小美:　这本呢?这是一本什么书?
　　　　　Zhè běn ne? Zhè shì yìběn shénme shū?

李文中：　这是一本中文书。
　　　　　Zhè shì yìběn Zhōngwén shū.

吴小美：　对了，你学什么？
　　　　　Duì le, nǐ xué shénme?

李文中：　我学英国文学，你呢？
　　　　　Wǒ xué Yīngguó wénxué, nǐ ne?

吴小美：　我学工程。
　　　　　Wǒ xué gōngchéng.

李文中：　工程难吗？
　　　　　Gōngchéng nán ma?

吴小美：　不太难。可是功课很多。
　　　　　Bú tài nán. Kěshì gōngkè hěnduō.

李文中：　我们的功课也不少。
　　　　　Wǒmen de gōngkè yě bùshǎo.

注释　LANGUAGE NOTES

英国文学

英国文学 means "English literature." When referring to the literature of a certain country, in Chinese the country name is followed by the word for literature, 文学. For example,

中国文学	Chinese literature
美国文学	American literature
法国文学	French literature
德国文学	German literature
日本文学	Japanese literature

语法 GRAMMAR

Demonstrative Pronouns　这，那

这 ("this") and 那 ("that") are the most commonly used demonstrative pronouns in Chinese. They can be used with 是 to form 这是 ("this is"), 那是 ("that is").

那是什么？　　　　　What is that?
这是我的中文书。　　This is my Chinese book.

量词 　(Measure Word/Classifier) (1)：本

本 is a measure word (also called a classifier). One of the special characteristics of Chinese is that it makes extensive use of measure words. That is, when denoting the number of entities, the number alone cannot function as an attributive but must be combined with a measure word inserted between the number and the noun it modifies. For example,

Numeral	Measure word	Noun
一	本	书

English also makes limited use of measure words, such as "pieces" in "three pieces of cake." However, in Chinese, their use is much more pervasive. In Chinese, measure words must also be placed between demonstrative pronouns (这 and 那) and nouns.

• The measure word 本 is for bound items such as books and magazines.	两本中文书 Two Chinese books. 这本书是中文书。 This book is a Chinese book. 那本书是英文书。 That book is an English book.
	那本 That one. (when referring to a book)

Adverb 　很

很 is an adverb that occurs before the adjective it modifies. Note that 很 has two senses depending on whether it is stressed or not. When it is stressed, it means "very." For example,

我很忙。　I am very busy.　　　　　　工程很难。　Engineering is very difficult.

However, in most cases, 很 is not stressed. Its unstressed usage has to do with the reality that in Chinese the adjectives are inherently comparative. For example,

爸爸忙，妈妈不忙。　　　　Father is busy. Mother is not busy.
他好，我不好。　　　　　　He is doing fine. I am not doing well.

These two sentences imply comparison between father and mother, and he and I. But how can we simply say "Father is busy" or "He is doing fine"? The way we do this is to use 很 without stressing it: "爸爸很忙", "他很好". Therefore the sentence, "我很忙" could mean either "I am very busy" or simply "I am busy," depending on whether the 很 is stressed.

Suffix   们(我们，你们，他们)

们 is a plural suffix that is commonly placed after the singular pronouns, such as 我，你，他 to form their plural pronouns 我们，你们，他们. For example,

Singular	Plural
我 (I, me)	我们 (we, us)
你 (you, you)	你们 (you, you)
他 (he, him)	他们 (they, them)
她 (she, her)	她们 (they, them)

This suffix may also be placed after animate nouns to give an intimate feeling to the people named. Note that it is never added to inanimate nouns. For example,

老师们
朋友们

Grammar Summary   语法小结

Chinese words:

So far we have learned the following words:

personal pronouns	我 你 他 她 您
demonstrative pronouns	这 那
interrogative pronouns	什么 谁 哪
nouns	老师 学生 名字 中文 英文 书
verbs	是 姓 说 学 叫
adverbs	也 很 太
adjectives	好 忙 累 多 少 难
particles	吗 呢 的
negation	不
conjunctions	和 可是
optative verbs	会
measure word (classifier)	本

Chinese sentences:

Chinese sentences usually consist of a subject and a predicate. Chinese is a non-inflectional language. That means it does not change word endings to reflect person, gender, tense, number, or case. In place of word endings, word order (the arrangement of words) plays an important role in indicating these different grammatical relationships. In general, Chinese word order is:

> Subject   +   Adverbial   +   Verb   +   Object
> (Adverbial: e.g., prepositional phrase, auxiliary verb, adverb)

For example,

我说中文。　　　　I speak Chinese.
我学工程。　　　　I study engineering.

So far we have learned about the following types of sentences:

1. Sentences with an adjectival predicate. (The main element of the predicate is an adjective.)

Subject	Predicate (adjective)	
我	很好。	I am fine.
老师	很忙。	Teacher is busy.
工程	不难。	Engineering is not difficult.
他们	都很累。	They are all very tired.
中文书	不太多。	Chinese books are quite few.

2. 是 sentences. (The main element of the predicate is 是.)

Subject	Predicate	
我	是学生。	I am a student.
你	也是学生。	You are also a student.
他	不是老师。	He is not a teacher.

3. Sentences with a verbal predicate. (The main element of the predicate is a verb.)

Subject	Predicate	
我	会说中文。	I can speak Chinese.
我	学文学。	I study literature.
他	不叫李文中。	He is not named Wenzhong Li.

4. Interrogative sentences.

   a. 吗 and 呢 sentences

   你是老师。　　　　You are a teacher.
   你是老师吗?　　　Are you a teacher?

   A: 你是学生吗?　　Are you a student?
   B: 是，我是学生，你呢?　Yes, I am a student. How about you?
   A: 我也是学生。　　I am also a student.

   b. Sentences with an interrogative pronoun. (Remember that the question word occurs where the expected answer would be.)

   这是什么书?　　　　这是中文书。
   他是谁?　　　　　　他是李文中。
   你是哪国人?　　　　我是美国人。

补充课文 ━oœ━ SUPPLEMENTARY PRACTICE

This selection will help you test your comprehension of the grammar and vocabulary you have learned in this lesson. Be prepared to answer questions about the meaning of the passage.

你们好！我叫美英，是大学生。我是二年级的学生，我学中国文学。这是我的书，这是一本中国文学书。中国文学不太难，可是功课不少。你们呢？你们学什么？是工程吗？那是你们的工程书吗？工程难吗？功课多吗？

Notes: 大学生 [dàxuéshēng]: college student
二年级 [èrniánjí]: sophomore, second year

练习 ACTIVITIES

I. Listening Exercises

4-1 Listen to the instructor and fill in each blank with the correct Pinyin:

1. zhuān _____
2. kǎo _____
3. _____ yè
4. _____ kè
5. kuài _____
6. wén _____
7. gōng _____
8. _____ yì
9. bù _____

4-2 Listen to the instructor and mark the following words with the correct tones:

1. kecheng
2. shuxue
3. yinyue
4. duoshao
5. tai nan
6. keneng
7. wenxue shu
8. zhexie

4-3   Form groups of three to four. Take turns reading the following tongue twister out loud, as quickly as you can. Each group will select one member to represent the group in a class competition.

mā: 妈   mom

má: 麻   hemp

mǎ: 马   horse

mà: 骂   to scold

Māma Mà Mǎ	妈妈骂马	**Mom Scolded the Horse**
Māma zhòng má,	妈妈种麻，	Mom planted some hemp,
Wǒ qù fàng mǎ.	我去放马。	I let the horse out.
Mǎ chīle má,	马吃了麻，	The horse ate the hemp,
Māma mà mǎ.	妈妈骂马。	Mom scolded the horse.

4-4   Listen to the instructor and write down the sentences in Pinyin:

1. _____

2. _____

3. _____

4. _____

II. Character Exercises

4-5   Read the following words, phrases, and sentences:

书	学
什么书	文学
工程书	中国文学
谁的工程书	学中国文学
同学的工程书	谁学中国文学
我的同学的工程书	美国人学中国文学

Now try to use the following characters to make words, phrases, and then sentences:

1. 那   2. 这   3. 本   4. 工   5. 程   6. 难

7. 太   8. 可   9. 功   10. 课   11. 多   12. 们

4-6 Match the following English sentences with the Chinese equivalents:

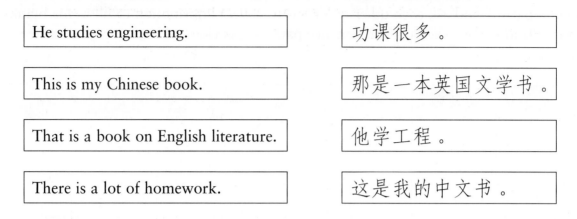

He studies engineering.	功课很多。
This is my Chinese book.	那是一本英国文学书。
That is a book on English literature.	他学工程。
There is a lot of homework.	这是我的中文书。

III. Grammar Exercises

4-7 Substitution exercises:

1. 这是什么？
   这是……。

   | 一本书 |
   | 小美的英文名字 |
   | 他的功课 |

2. 那是什么？
   那是……。

   | 一本法文书 |
   | 他的中文名字 |
   | 我的美国文学功课 |

4-8 Select an expression from each group and create a valid Chinese sentence. Create as many sentences as you can.

法国	学生	很难
工程	书	很好
中文	老师	很贵
美国	功课	很多

Note: 贵 [guì]: expensive

IV. Communicative Activities

4-9 Find a partner and ask each other questions to collect information to fill in the blanks in the form below. Then use the sentence patterns provided to introduce your partner to the class.

英文名字	中文姓	中文名字	哪国人	学生/老师	说……文	学……

Sentence patterns and expressions to be used in the introduction:

这是…… (那是……)   姓   叫   他/她是……   说   学

文化点滴　CULTURE NOTES

中国的教育制度 [Zhōngguó de jiàoyù zhìdù]
The Chinese Educational System

In 1978, Mainland China implemented a 九年义务教育制
[jiǔnián yìwù jiàoyù zhì] (nine-year compulsory schooling system).
In Taiwan, also, children are required to have nine years of compulsory
schooling. After nine years of study, they either go on to further study
at a senior high school, attend a vocational school, or enter the work force.
This is, however, not a free choice because students must pass a national
entrance exam to get into a senior high school. Students who receive
lower scores will either have to go to a vocational school or enter the work
force. Upon graduation from senior high school, students must take the
national entrance exam, called 高考 [gāo kǎo] in Mainland China and
大学联考 [dàxué liánkǎo] in Taiwan to determine which colleges or
universities they can get into, and even what majors they may pursue.
The exam used to take place only in early July each year in both Mainland
China and Taiwan, but it has been moved to early June in the Mainland.
In addition, it is now offered once in the winter in both places. It is one
of the biggest events in the entire country, and students usually begin
concentrated preparation for the exam a year or more beforehand.

Before the mid-1990s, most schools in Mainland China were government-run
and basically tuition was free. Today, free tuition is a thing of the past. Since
the late 1980s, more and more private schools funded by big businesses
or wealthy individuals have appeared. There are also "aristocratic schools"
— usually private boarding schools run by big businesses that charge very
high tuition and claim to provide the highest quality of education. Only a
small number of people can afford to send their children to these schools.

University students in Mainland China used to be assigned a job by the
university upon graduation, but they did not have too many choices. This
situation has also changed. As in many other countries, students need to
find a job on their own. More and more students are pursuing graduate
studies to become more competitive in the job market.

With the rapid changes in China's society, it can be anticipated that more
extensive and substantial changes will take place in the field of education in
China in the next decade.

Students play outside during physical education class in junior high school in Taiwan. Students generally wear uniforms, even for physical education class.

Students hope for good luck in the national college entrance exam.

Students study math, English, physics, chemistry, biology and more for the upcoming college entrance exam.

In order to help them improve their academic performance, Chinese parents often send their children to after-school learning centers.

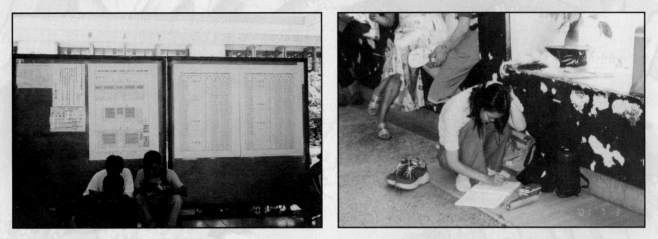

In Taiwan, July is a very important month for high school students. Everybody hopes to perform his/her best on the 大学联考 [dàxué liánkǎo] (national college entrance exam). Every minute counts! These students are cramming between sessions of the exam.

The national college entrance exams involve the whole family. Here family members wait outside to provide food, support, and encouragement between exam sessions.

In case students or parents cannot take the pressure (or the summer heat!) and don't feel well, they are welcome to visit the medical service group.

Questions:

1. What are the similarities and differences between the school systems of China and the U.S. (e.g., subjects, school hours)? How about other countries?

2. To gain admission to college, would you prefer to take entrance exams or go through an application process? Why?

趣味中文   FUN WITH CHINESE

> 书中自有黄金屋，书中自有颜如玉。
> Inside the books themselves, there are gold houses and beauties.

shū	zhōng	zì	yǒu	huángjīn	wū
书	中	自	有	黄金	屋
book	inside	itself	have	gold	house

shū	zhōng	zì	yǒu	yán	rú	yù
书	中	自	有	颜	如	玉
book	inside	itself	have	face	as if	jade

颜如玉 refers to beauties. This expression indicates that whoever studies hard will achieve good results, such as a gold house (getting rich) and a beautiful wife. In old China, there was a civil service examination system called 科举制度 [kē jǔ zhì dù]. Local and district competitions had to be passed in order to get to the final examination, the imperial examination 殿试 [diàn shì]. As a result, it was considered normal to spend several years preparing to pass the various local exams and become a candidate for the final imperial examination. The candidate who scored highest was called 状元 [zhuàngyuán], and was usually granted an audience with the emperor and awarded a high official status. This person usually achieved both fame and wealth, and married a princess or daughter of a high official.

Question:

Form groups of two to three, then tell a story that is an example of "书中自有黄金屋，书中自有颜如玉。"

行动吧! LET'S GO!

补习班   After-school Learning Center

于小英 is a college student majoring in English. She teaches English at two after-school learning centers to earn some extra money. Look at the signs for the two centers (below) and then answer the questions.

Useful words and expressions:

补习班(補習班) [bǔxíbān]:
  after-school learning center
中心 [zhōngxīn]: center
理化 [lǐhuà]: physics and chemistry
安亲班(安親班) [ān qīn bān]:
  after-school childcare center
钢琴(鋼琴) [gāngqín]: piano

家教 [jiājiào]: private tutor
数学(數學) [shùxué]:
  mathematics
幼儿(幼兒) [yòu'ér]: child
音乐(音樂) [yīnyuè]:
  music
招牌 [zhāopái]: shop sign

Center A

Center B

1. What subjects does Center A provide?

2. What subjects does Center B provide?

3. 大文 is a junior high school student. To help him perform better on the college entrance exam, he would like to attend after-school learning centers to improve his mathematics and English. Which shop signs below would 大文 be interested in?

   a. 大天英数补习班   b. 大天电脑中心
   c. 大天理化家教   d. 大天幼儿安亲班

4. 美美 was a music major at college. She runs a piano tutoring center. Let's help her create a shop sign.

复习　Review

LESSON 3 AND LESSON 4

Conversation

Find a partner and practice the following dialogues:

1. 请问，你是哪国人？
   我是＿＿＿＿＿ (e.g. 美国人)。我不是中国人，也不是英国人。

2. 你会说中文吗？
   我会说中文。我也会说＿＿＿＿＿ (e.g. 法文) 和英文。
   我不会说＿＿＿＿＿ (e.g. 日文)。

3. 请问，你是法国人吗？
   我不是＿＿＿＿＿，我是＿＿＿＿＿。
   你的中文老师是中国人吗？

4. 这是一本什么书？
   这是一本 ＿＿＿＿＿ (e.g. 工程书，中国文学书)。

5. 那是谁的书？
   那是 ＿＿＿＿＿ (e.g. 我的同学的书)，是 ＿＿＿＿＿ (e.g. 我的同学的中国文学书)。

6. 我是美国人，我学中文。你的同学学什么？
   他学 ＿＿＿＿＿ (e.g. 工程)。
   他的功课 ＿＿＿＿＿ (e.g. 很多，很难)。

   Note: 难 [nán]: difficult

Fill in the Blanks

You are at the consulate applying for a visa to visit China. You are asked to write down your Chinese name and your citizenship in Chinese characters.

姓名 [xìngmíng] Name: ＿＿＿＿＿＿＿＿＿＿＿＿＿＿＿＿＿＿

国籍 [guójí] Nationality: ＿＿＿＿＿＿＿＿＿＿＿＿＿＿＿＿

Write Chinese

Read the sentences, then practice writing the underlined characters. Pay attention to stroke order.

Lesson 3: 请问，你是<u>哪国</u>人？我是法国人，我<u>会说一点儿</u>中文<u>和</u>英文。

_____

_____

Lesson 4: <u>那本书</u>是工程书。<u>这</u>本书很<u>难</u>，可是，<u>我们</u>的<u>功课</u>不太多。

_____

_____

Simplified and Traditional Characters

Read each character aloud. Write its simplified form. Then make a phrase and a sentence using the character.

For example, 學 → 学 → 学生 → 我是学生。

國 (　)　　說 (　)　　點 (　)　　兒 (　)　　書 (　)　　這 (　)　　難 (　)

課 (　)　　們 (　)

这是我朋友
This Is My Friend

- Introduce people
- Make small talk
- Find out what someone owns

Friends play important roles in our lives. Chinese enjoy hanging out, going out to eat, hiking, and traveling with their friends.

Friends get together to chat, order take-out, and have some tea and wine. Dig in and have fun!

生词 VOCABULARY

核心词 Core Vocabulary

	SIMPLIFIED	TRADITIONAL	PINYIN		
1.	朋友	朋友	péngyou	N.	friend
2.	来	來	lái	V.	to come; (used before a verb to indicate that one is about to do something)
3.	介绍	介紹	jièshào	V. N.	to introduce introduction
4.	一下	一下	yíxià		(used after a verb to indicate a brief action)
5.	室友	室友	shìyǒu	N.	roommate
6.	有	有	yǒu	V.	to have
7.	几	幾	jǐ		how many
8.	两	兩	liǎng	Num.	two , a couple of ...
9.	个	個	gè	M.W.	(the most commonly used measure word for people, buildings, characters, etc.) General things not for books
10.	他们	他們	tāmen	Pron.	they, them
11.	都	都	dōu	Adv.	all, both
12.	常	常	cháng	Adv.	often, frequently
13.	跟	跟	gēn	Prep.	with

专名 Proper Nouns

	SIMPLIFIED	TRADITIONAL	PINYIN		
1.	王红	王紅	Wáng Hóng	N.	(name) Hong Wang
2.	丁明	丁明	Dīng Míng	N.	(name) Ming Ding
3.	方小文	方小文	Fāng Xiǎowén	N.	(name) Xiaowen Fang

补充词　Supplementary Vocabulary

	SIMPLIFIED	TRADITIONAL	PINYIN		
1.	没有	沒有	méiyǒu	V.	to not have, to be without
2.	女朋友	女朋友	nǚpéngyou	N.	girlfriend
3.	男朋友	男朋友	nánpéngyou	N.	boyfriend
4.	认识	認識	rènshi ,	V.	to know , *recognize*

语文知识　LANGUAGE LINK

The Sentence Patterns provide models that will help you with the Language in Use section. In both sections, pay attention to the grammar points, vocabulary, and expressions.

[handwritten margin notes: 朋 从 yuǎn fāng 来 不 yì lè hū; confucian analects]

句型　Sentence Patterns

A: 这是我室友，王红。
Zhèshì wǒ shìyǒu, Wáng Hóng.

这是我朋友，文中。
Zhèshì wǒ péngyou, Wénzhōng.

B: 你好！
Nǐhǎo!

C: 你好！
Nǐhǎo!

A: 你有室友吗？
Nǐ yǒu shìyǒu ma?

B: 有，我有室友。我有
Yǒu, wǒ yǒu shìyǒu. Wǒ yǒu

两个室友。
liǎngge shìyǒu.

[handwritten notes at bottom:]
Wèi (polite measure word for How many people?)

qían (money)

duō shào qían? (How much $)

课文   Language in Use: 这是我朋友 Zhè shì wǒ péngyou

吴小美: 文中，来！我来介绍一下。这是我室友，王红。
Wénzhōng, lái! Wǒ lái jièshào yíxià. Zhèshì wǒ shìyǒu, Wáng Hóng.

这是我朋友，文中。
Zhèshì wǒ péngyou, Wénzhōng.

李文中: 你好！
Nǐhǎo!

王红: 你好！你有室友吗？
Nǐhǎo! Nǐ yǒu shìyǒu ma?

李文中: 有，我有室友。
Yǒu, wǒ yǒu shìyǒu.

王红: 你有几个室友？
Nǐ yǒu jǐge shìyǒu?

李文中: 我有两个室友。
Wǒ yǒu liǎngge shìyǒu.

王红: 他们都是谁？
Tāmen dōu shì shéi?

李文中: 他们是丁明和方小文。他们都是中国人。
Tāmen shì Dīng Míng hé Fāng Xiǎowén. Tāmen dōu shì Zhōngguórén.

我常跟他们说中文。
Wǒ cháng gēn tāmen shuō Zhōngwén.

注释　LANGUAGE NOTES

我来介绍一下

我来介绍一下 is a common expression used for introducing people. It means "Let me introduce you." 介绍 is a verb meaning "to introduce," 一下 is used after a verb to indicate a brief action. It is adopted here to make the tone softer and more informal to ease the task of introducing people to each other.

For example,

文中，来，我来介绍一下，这是我室友王红。
Wenzhong, come! Let me introduce you. This is my roommate, Hong Wang.

室友

室友 means "roommate." In Mainland China, 同屋 [tóngwū] is also used.

跟

跟 "with" is a preposition that precedes an object to form a prepositional phrase, and it is often placed before the verb as an adverbial adjunct.

我常跟他说中文。　　I often speak Chinese with him.

The Measure Word (Classifier)　个

个 is a measure word used for people.

Numeral	+	Measure word	+	Noun	
一		个		人	one person
两		个		室友	two roommates

语法　GRAMMAR

有　Sentences　(没有)

有 means "have" or "there is (are)" in Chinese. Its negative form is 没有 [méiyǒu]. Its interrogative is formed by putting 吗 at the end of the sentence.

Interrogative form:	你有室友吗?	Do you have roommates?
Affirmative form:	我有一个室友。	I have one roommate.
Negative form:	我没有室友。	I don't have any roommates.

Question Word   几

几 is a question word used for asking "How many?" When asking about amounts under ten, 几 is used. It is placed before the measure word. For example,

Question word	Measure word	Noun	English
几	个	人	How many persons?
几	本	书	How many books?

Adverb   都

都 is an adverb meaning "all." It occurs before a predicate. It refers to persons or things already mentioned in the sentence. For example,

他们都是中国人。	They are all Chinese.
我们都学工程。	They all study engineering.
老师和学生都说中文。	The teacher and students all speak Chinese.

都   With   不

都不 means "none"; 不都 means "not all (some do, some don't)."

我们都不是日本人。	None of us is Japanese.
我们不都是日本人。	Not all of us are Japanese.

都   With   也

也 always precedes 都 as 也都.

他们也都是中国人。	They are all also Chinese.
我们也都学工程。	They all also study engineering.

Location of Adverbs   也都常很   (Summary of   也都常很)

So far we have learned the adverbs 也, 都, 常, 很: "also," "all," "often," and "very." They all occur before verbs or adjectives to modify them. When more than one of these words occur together, there are certain word order rules to follow, as illustrated below:

1. 我们　　　　　常　　说中文。　　　We often speak Chinese.
   我们　　　都　常　　说中文。　　　We all often speak Chinese.
   我们　也　都　常　　说中文。　　　We all also often speak Chinese.

2. 我们　　　都　很　忙。　　　　　　We are all very busy.
   我们　也　　　很　忙。　　　　　　We are also very busy.
   我们　也　都　很　忙。　　　　　　We are all also very busy.

补充课文 ⟶ SUPPLEMENTARY PRACTICE

This selection will help you test your comprehension of the grammar and vocabulary you have learned in this lesson. Be prepared to answer questions about the meaning of the passage.

你们好！我来介绍一下我的室友。我有两个室友，一个叫美美，一个叫文英，她们都是我的好朋友。美美是英国人，文英是法国人，我是美国人。

我们都学英国文学，也学中文，我们都会说英文和一点儿中文。

我们有很多中国朋友，他们都是留学生，我们常跟他们说中文，他们都很好，常常帮助我们练习中文。

你们呢？你们有室友吗？有几个？

Notes: 留学生 [liúxuéshēng]: international students
帮助 [bāngzhù]: to help
练习 [liànxí]: to practice

练习　ACTIVITIES

I. Listening Exercises

5-1 In each pair, circle the one the instructor pronounces:

1. shíyóu　shìyǒu
2. liǎnggè　liànggé
3. jiéshào　jièshào
4. zhèshí　zhèshì
5. dǒushì　dōushì
6. pēngyou　péngyou

5-2 Listen to the instructor and fill in the initials for each of the following:

1. ___ǒu ___ì
2. ___iè ___ào
3. ___éng ___ou
4. ___áng ___ái
5. ___ué ___èn
6. ___è ___iē
7. ___ǔ ___ǎ
8. ___iú ___ēn
9. ___iǎng ___ié

5-3 Read the following poem, paying special attention to the tones and rhythm:

Chūn Xiǎo (**Mèng Hàorán**)	**春晓** （**孟浩然**）	**Spring Morning** (Meng, Haoran)
Chūn mián bù jué xiǎo,	春眠不觉晓，	Morning comes unannounced to my spring slumber,
Chù chù wén tí niǎo.	处处闻啼鸟。	I hear birds calling all around.
Yè lái fēng yǔ shēng,	夜来风雨声，	In the night came sounds of wind and showers,
Huā luò zhī duō shǎo.	花落知多少。	Many of the flowers must have fallen.

II. Character Exercises

5-4 Read the following words, phrases, and sentences:

这	有
这是	我有
这是王红	我有室友
这是我朋友王红	我有美国室友
这是我的中国朋友王红	我有两个美国室友
这是我们的中国朋友王红	我有两个很好的美国室友

Now try to use the following characters to make words, phrases, and then sentences:

1. 友   2. 来   3. 介   4. 绍   5. 下   6. 室
7. 几   8. 两   9. 个   10. 都   11. 常   12. 跟

5-5 Write out the Pinyin and the simplified form of each of the following characters and then create a phrase with the character:

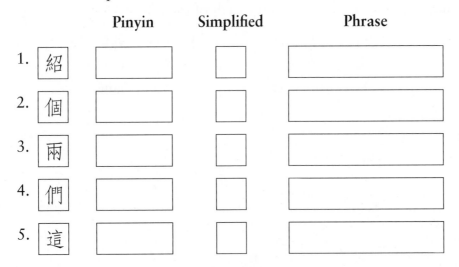

		Pinyin	Simplified	Phrase
1.	紹			
2.	個			
3.	兩			
4.	們			
5.	這			

III. Grammar Exercises

5-6　Substitution exercises:

1. 他们是谁?
   我来介绍一下。这是<u>吴小美</u>，
   那是<u>李文中</u>。

丁明	方文
我的同学	我的室友
我的文学老师	工程老师

2. 你有<u>课</u>吗?
   我有<u>中文课</u>，没有<u>法文课</u>。

书	中文书	英文书
室友	中国室友	日本室友
中文名字	英文名字	中文名字

3. 你有几<u>个室友</u>?
   我有<u>两个室友</u>。

本	工程书	三
个	中国朋友	很多

4. <u>小美</u>和<u>小文</u>都不<u>是学生</u>。

文明	李中	是老师
于英	吴学程	学文学
英文	法文	难

5-7　Based on the following pairs of sentences, write a new sentence using the clues provided in parentheses:

For example,　　他会说英文。他会说中文。(也)
　　　　　　→ 他会说英文，也会说中文。

1. 丁文是小美的室友。方中也是小美的室友。(有)

   _____

2. 红美会说中文。小文也会说中文。(们，都)

   _____

3. 这是我的室友大红，她也学英文。(介绍)

   _____

4. 大中是我朋友。小美是我朋友。(和，都)

   _____

IV. Communicative Activities

5-8 Picture talk: Use your imagination to say as much as you can based on the pictures below. You must use (but not limit yourself to) the following words, expressions, and sentence patterns.

这是……。
那是……。
介绍一下
他们
有(没有)
都
两

_____

_____

_____

_____

_____

_____

_____

_____

_____

_____

_____

_____

_____

_____

文化知识 ⟨⟨⟩⟩ Culture Link

文化点滴　CULTURE NOTES

中国的称谓文化
[Zhōngguó de chēngwèi wénhuà]
Chinese Forms of Address
The Art beneath Complexity

Addressing people in China is indeed complex. Even native Chinese occasionally become bewildered, especially when traveling to a new place or simply coming into contact with a new social circle.

In general, "先生 [xiānsheng]" (Mister) and "小姐 [xiǎojie]" (Miss) are regarded as the proper forms of address for initiating talk with an adult stranger in large cities. But "xiǎojie" (Miss) is suitable for young women only. "大姐/大嫂 [dàjiě/dàsǎo]" (Older Sister) and "伯母 [bómǔ]" (Aunt) should be used for addressing middle-aged or older women, respectively.

Professional titles are always preferred in business communications or governmental affairs. For example, if Mr. Zhang is a manager, it is polite to call him "张经理 [Zhāng jīnglǐ] (Manager Zhang)" rather than "张先生 [Zhāng xiānsheng] (Mr. Zhang)". But, if he is a vice-manager, instead of calling him "张副经理 [Zhāng fù jīnglǐ] (Vice-Manager Zhang)", which would make him feel his prestige is diminished, you should call him "张经理 [Zhāng jīnglǐ] (Manager Zhang)". The word "副 [fù] (vice)" should be dropped.

In social circles, individuals are addressed according to their age compared to the addresser. You should not address people much older than you by their full names. If you know the senior person well, the surname followed by "伯父/叔叔 [bófù/shūshu] (Uncle)" or "伯母/阿姨 [bómǔ/āyí] (Aunt)" is well accepted. If you are not familiar with the senior person, a simple address of "伯伯 [bóbo] (Uncle)" or "阿姨 [āyí] (Aunt)" is safe. People close to your age may be addressed by their full name, especially when it has only two Chinese characters. If you feel very familiar with the person, and the name has three Chinese characters, you may address them with only the given name. "小 [xiǎo] (little)" plus the surname is another

Eating, karaoke singing, and playing Majiang (打麻将 [dǎ májiàng]) are very common activities among Chinese acquaintances. These activities help them get to know each other better and expand their social circles. How to address people in an appropriate way is really a learned art!

popular way to address people when they are your age or younger. For example, if someone is named "张红 [Zhāng Hóng]", you can call him "小张 [Xiǎo Zhāng]". When talking to children, they can simply be called "小朋友 [xiǎo péngyou] (little friend)" or their given names.

People are almost never offended when addressed with the pronoun "您 [nín] (the esteemed you)". This especially applies when you are seeking help from an adult stranger. But when a friend is addressed with "您 [nín]," there is usually a hint of distance, irony, or sneering.

Questions:

1. What are the similarities and differences between the means of addressing people in Chinese and English (or other languages)?

2. Form groups of two to three enact situation involving addressing people (e.g., visit your Chinese friend's parents; meet people at a Chinese company; meet your girl/boyfriend's relatives for the first time . . .).

趣味中文   FUN WITH CHINESE

> 有朋自远方来，不亦乐乎?
> Isn't it a delight to have friends coming from afar?

yǒu	péng	zì	yuǎnfāng	lái
有	朋	自	远方	来
have	friend	from	a distant place	come

bú	yì	yuè	hū
不	亦	乐	乎
not	particle	happy	question particle

有朋自远方来，不亦乐乎?

This is another famous saying of Confucius. "不亦……乎?" is a rhetorical question meaning "isn't it . . . ?" in Classical Chinese. It carries a tone of courtesy. "乐" is pronounced as [yuè] in Classical Chinese, while it is pronounced as [lè] in modern Chinese. The whole sentence means you are very happy when your friends come to visit you, especially when they come from afar.

Question:

Form groups of two to three, then act out a "有朋自远方来，不亦乐乎?" situation.

行动吧！ LET'S GO!

婚友联谊中心
Marriage and Friendship Social Center

Read the following newspaper advertisement and translate it into English.

Useful words and expressions:

联谊(聯誼) [liányì] (pronounced as [liányí] in Taiwan):
   social contact
中心 [zhōngxīn]: center
未婚 [wèihūn]: unmarried
先 [xiān]: first
认识(認識) [rènshi]: to know
再 [zài]: then, again
交往 [jiāowǎng]: to have friendly relations
手机(手機) [shǒujī]: cell phone

婚友联谊中心

未婚男女介绍，先认识，再交往。
手机：0800-555-5555

Translation: _____

_____

_____

我的家
My Family

- Introduce yourself
- Talk about your family

Three generations living together is still a common pattern in Chinese societies.

In Taiwan, where there is no one-child policy like Mainland China, a nuclear family commonly includes two or three children.

生词 VOCABULARY

核心词 Core Vocabulary

	SIMPLIFIED	TRADITIONAL	PINYIN		
1.	家	家	jiā	N.	home, family
2.	大家	大家	dàjiā	P.	all, everybody
3.	从	從	cóng	Prep.	from
4.	在	在	zài	V. Prep.	to be at; be in at, in
5.	一	一	yī	Num.	one
6.	四	四	sì	Num.	four
7.	爸爸	爸爸	bàba *fùqin*	N.	father
8.	妈妈	媽媽	māma *mǔqin*	N.	mother
9.	姐姐	姐姐	jiějie	N.	elder sister
10.	工作	工作	gōngzuò	N. V.	job to work
11.	工程师	工程師	gōngchéngshī	N.	engineer
12.	男 男朋友	男 男朋友	nán nánpéngyou	N. N.	male boyfriend
13.	没有	沒有	méiyǒu	V.	to not have, to be without
14.	辆	輛	liàng	M.W.	(measure word for vehicles)
15.	车	車	chē	N.	car
16.	只	隻	zhī	M.W.	(measure word for certain animals, boats, or containers, or for one of a pair)
17.	狗	狗	gǒu	N.	dog
18.	爱	愛	ài	V.	to love

专名   Proper Nouns

SIMPLIFIED	TRADITIONAL	PINYIN		
1. 纽约	紐約	Niǔyuē	N.	New York

补充词   Supplementary Vocabulary

SIMPLIFIED	TRADITIONAL	PINYIN		
1. 自我介绍	自我介紹	zìwǒjièshào	N. V.	self-introduction, to introduce oneself
2. 自己	自己	zìjǐ	N.	oneself
3. 兄弟姐妹	兄弟姐妹	xiōngdìjiěmèi	N.	siblings *(Brotherhood)*
4. 哥哥	哥哥	gēge	N.	elder brother
5. 妹妹	妹妹	mèimei	N.	younger sister
6. 弟弟	弟弟	dìdi	N.	younger brother
7. 女 女朋友	女 女朋友	nǚ nǚpéngyou	N. N.	female girlfriend
8. 孩子	孩子	háizi	N.	child
9. 宠物	寵物	chǒngwù	N.	pet
10. 猫	貓	māo	N.	cat

by pen

gěi →to give

亲属称谓 [Qīnshǔ chēngwèi]   Addressing One's Relatives

	Relatives on the father's side		Relatives on the mother's side	
grandparents	爷爷 [yéye] 祖父 [zǔfù] grandfather	奶奶 [nǎinai] 祖母 [zǔmǔ] grandmother	外公 [wàigōng] 外祖父 [wàizǔfù] 姥爷 [lǎoye] maternal grandfather	外婆 [wàipó] 外祖母 [wàizǔmǔ] 姥姥 [lǎolao] maternal grandmother
uncles	伯伯 [bóbo] father's elder brother 叔叔 [shūshu] father's younger brother	伯母 [bómǔ] wife of father's elder brother 婶婶 [shěnshen] wife of father's younger brother	舅舅 [jiùjiu] mother's brother	舅妈 [jiùmā] wife of mother's brother
aunts	姑姑 [gūgu] 姑妈 [gūmā] father's sister	姑父 [gūfù] 姑丈 [gūzhàng] husband of father's sister	阿姨 [āyí] 姨妈 [yímā] mother's sister	姨父 [yífù] 姨丈 [yízhàng] husband of mother's sister
cousins#	堂哥 [tánggē] 堂姐 [tángjiě] 堂弟 [tángdì] 堂妹 [tángmèi]	堂嫂 [tángsǎo] 堂姐夫 [tángjiěfu] 堂弟妹 [tángdìmèi] 堂妹夫 [tángmèifu]	表哥 [biǎogē] 表姐 [biǎojiě] 表弟 [biǎodì] 表妹 [biǎomèi]	表嫂 [biǎosǎo] 表姐夫 [biǎojiěfu] 表弟妹 [biǎodìmèi] 表妹夫 [biǎomèifu]
nephews	侄子 [zhízi] brother's son		外甥 [wàisheng] sister's son	
nieces	侄女 [zhínǚ] brother's daughter		外甥女 [wàishengnǚ] sister's daughter	

Note: #Children of your father's brothers are 堂 [táng] cousins
New word: 嫂 [sǎo] sister-in-law.

职业 [Zhíyè] Occupations

	SIMPLIFIED	TRADITIONAL	PINYIN		
1.	会计师	會計師	kuàijìshī	N.	accountant
2.	经纪人	經紀人	jīngjìrén	N.	agent
3.	建筑师	建築師	jiànzhùshī	N.	architect
4.	老板	老闆	lǎobǎn	N.	boss
5.	商人	商人	shāngrén	N.	businessman
6.	大学生	大學生	dàxuéshēng	N.	college student
7.	顾问	顧問	gùwèn	N.	consultant
8.	医生	醫生	yīshēng	N.	doctor
9.	经济师	經濟師	jīngjìshī	N.	economist
10.	教育工作者	教育工作者	jiàoyù gōngzuòzhě	N.	educator
11.	工程师	工程師	gōngchéngshī	N.	engineer
12.	官员	官員	guānyuán	N.	government official
13.	家庭主妇	家庭主婦	jiātíng zhǔfù	N.	housewife
14.	留学生	留學生	liúxuéshēng	N.	international students
15.	律师	律師	lǜshī	N.	lawyer
16.	邮递员 (邮差)	郵遞員 (郵差)	yóudìyuán (yóuchāi)	N.	mailman
17.	经理	經理	jīnglǐ	N.	manager
18.	护士	護士	hùshi	N.	nurse
19.	飞行员	飛行員	fēixíngyuán	N.	pilot
20.	程序员 (程序设计师)	程序員 (程序設計師)	chéngxùyuán (chéngshì shèjìshī)	N.	computer programmer
21.	教授	教授	jiàoshòu	N.	professor

(handwritten note next to "doctor": in the country chinese medicals dr. daifu)

SIMPLIFIED	TRADITIONAL	PINYIN		
22. 房地产顾问	房地產顧問	fángdìchǎn gùwèn	N.	real estate agent
23. 秘书	秘書	mìshū	N.	secretary
24. 推销员	推銷員	tuīxiāoyuán	N.	salesman
25. 职员	職員	zhíyuán	N.	staff
26. 老师	老師	lǎoshī	N.	teacher
27. 导游	導遊	dǎoyóu	N.	tourist guide

语文知识   LANGUAGE LINK

The Sentence Patterns provide models that will help you with the Language in Use section. In both sections, pay attention to the grammar points, vocabulary, and expressions.

句型   Sentence Patterns

A: 你家在哪儿?
Nǐ jiā zài nǎr?

B: 我家在纽约。
Wǒ jiā zài Niǔyuē.

Note: 哪儿 [nǎr]: where

A: 你是从纽约来的吗?
Nǐ shì cóng Niǔyuē lái de ma?

B: 是，我是从纽约来的。
Shì, wǒ shì cóng Niǔyuē lái de.

A: 你家有几个人?
Nǐ jiā yǒu jǐge rén?

B: 我家有四个人:爸爸、
Wǒ jiā yǒu sìge rén: bàba,

妈妈、姐姐和我。
māma, jiějie hé wǒ.

A: 你爸爸是<u>做</u>什么的?
Nǐ bàba shì zuò shénme de?

B: 我爸爸是工程师。
Wǒ bàba shì gōngchéngshī.

Note: 做 [zuò]: to do

课文   Language in Use: 我的家 **Wǒ de jiā**

大家好! 我叫吴小美,我是从纽约来的,我学工程。
Dàjiā hǎo! Wǒ jiào Wú Xiǎoměi. Wǒ shì cóng Niǔyuē lái de. Wǒ xué gōngchéng.

我来介绍一下我的家。我家在纽约,有四个人:爸爸、妈妈、姐姐
Wǒ lái jièshào yíxià wǒ de jiā. Wǒ jiā zài Niǔyuē, yǒu sìge rén: bàba, māma, jiějie

和我。爸爸是英国人,妈妈是美国人。他们都在纽约工作。
hé wǒ. Bàba shì Yīngguó rén, māma shì Měiguó rén. Tāmen dōu zài Niǔyuē gōngzuò.

爸爸是工程师,妈妈是老师,我和姐姐都是学生。姐姐有
Bàba shì gōngchéngshī, māma shì lǎoshī, wǒ hé jiějie dōu shì xuésheng. Jiějie yǒu

男朋友,我没有。我们有两辆车,
nánpéngyou, wǒ méiyǒu. Wǒmen yǒu liǎngliàng chē,

一只狗。我的家很好。我很爱我的家。
yìzhī gǒu. Wǒ de jiā hěnhǎo. Wǒ hěn ài wǒ de jiā.

注释　LANGUAGE NOTES

大家好

"大家好!" is a common greeting meaning "Hello, everyone!"

四个人和四口人

"四个人" means four people. 个 is the measure word (classifier). When talking about family members, it is very common to use 口 [kǒu] (mouth) as the measure word, indicating how many mouths (people) need to be fed in the family.

男朋友

"Boyfriend" in Chinese is 男朋友, while 男的朋友 means "male friend." This is parallel to 女朋友 and 女的朋友 which mean "girlfriend" and "female friend" respectively.

语法　GRAMMAR

是 . . . 的　Construction

When an event has already taken place and we want to emphasize when, where, or how the event occurred, the "是…的" construction is used.

他是　在大学的时候[shíhou] 学中文的。 　　　(when he was in college)	It was when he was in college that he studied Chinese.	(focus on when)
他是　在北京 学中文的。 　　　(in Beijing)	It was in Beijing where he studied Chinese.	(focus on where)
他是　跟李老师 学中文的。 　　　(with Teacher Li)	It was with Teacher Li that he studied Chinese.	(focus on how)

The 是…的 construction may also be used without a time, place, or manner expression. In such cases, 是…的 does not imply a past event, but is used to emphasize the predicate that appears between 是 and 的. For example,

我是学英国文学的。　It is English literature that I study.
Note that "I study English literature" can be expressed as "我学英国文学" or "我是学英国文学的", but the latter is more emphatic.

在

在 can be a verb or a preposition meaning "be at, be in" and "at, in," respectively. It is placed before a noun to indicate location.

For example,

- 在 used as a verb meaning "be at, be in"
  他在家。　　　　　　He is at home.
  李老师在中国。　　　Teacher Li is in China.

- 在 used as a preposition meaning "at, in." 在 occurs before a place word (forming a prepositional phrase) to express where an action is carried out.

Subject	在	Place word	Verb	
我爸爸	在	纽约	工作。	My Dad works in New York.

When 在 is used as a preposition, the 在 phrase is placed before the verb phrase. Note that this word order is different from that of English.

几 = jǐ

量词(2) 个，辆，只，本.　Questions: 几个，几辆，几只，几本

As we mentioned in previous lessons, Chinese is a language that makes extensive use of measure words.

The following are some guidelines for the use of Chinese measure words:

Measure word	Features	Examples	
个	• The most commonly used measure word • Used to denote the number of people, buildings, characters etc.	一个人 一个室友 两个老师 四个汉字 [hànzì]	(one person) (one roommate) (two teachers) (four characters)
辆	• Used for vehicles	两辆车	(two cars)
只	• Used for animals	一只狗	(one dog)
本	• Used for bound items such as books or magazines	两本中文书	(two Chinese books)

几个，几辆，几只，几本
When asking about amounts under ten, the question word 几 is used.

For example,

你家有几个人?	How many people are there in your family?
你有几辆车?	How many cars do you have?
你妈妈有几只狗?	How many dogs does your mom have?
你姐姐有几本书?	How many books does your older sister have?

补充课文 ─○○○ SUPPLEMENTARY PRACTICE

This selection will help you test your comprehension of the grammar and vocabulary you have learned in this lesson. Be prepared to answer questions about the meaning of the passage.

书友：学文，来，我来介绍一下，这是我爸爸、妈妈和妹妹。爸爸、妈妈、妹妹，这是我室友学文。

学文：你们好！

爸爸，妈妈，妹妹：你好！

爸爸：来，请坐。请问，你是从哪儿来的？你家在哪儿？

学文：我是从中国来的，我家在北京。

妈妈：你家都有哪些人？

学文：我家有爸爸，妈妈和我。

妹妹：我们有宠物，我们养了一只狗，你呢？你家有狗吗？

学文：我们家没有狗，可是我们有猫。

书友：你们养了几只猫？

学文：我妈妈很爱猫，我们家养了三只猫。

爸爸：你爸爸，妈妈工作吗？他们都做什么？

学文：我爸爸工作，妈妈不工作。我爸爸是老师，妈妈是家庭主妇。

妹妹：对了，你有女朋友吗？

学文：没有，我没有女朋友。你呢，你有男朋友吗？

妹妹：有，我有男朋友。

书友：我妹妹的男朋友叫明明。他很爱车，他有四辆车。

学文：你男朋友好像很有钱！

Notes: 请坐 [qǐngzuò]: Please be seated
哪些 [nǎxiē]: What . . .
养 [yǎng]: to raise
了 [le]: an aspect particle indicating completion
家庭主妇 [jiātíng zhǔfù]: housewife
好像 [hǎoxiàng]: seems like
有钱 [yǒuqián]: rich
你 [nǐ]: you. In simplified characters, 你 is used for both the male and female "you." In traditional characters, 妳 is sometimes used for the female "you."

练习　ACTIVITIES

I. Pinyin Exercises

6-1 Read the following Pinyin words and pay special attention to any tone changes:

A. 3rd tonal change

1. wǒ jiā	2. Niǔyuē	3. lǎoshī	4. hěnduō
5. nǐ lái	6. Fǎguó	7. Měiguó	8. nǎ guó
9. hěnhǎo	10. Xiǎoměi	11. yě yǒu	12. hěnshǎo
13. qǐngwèn	14. jǐge	15. liǎngliàng	16. kǎoshì

B. "一" [yī] and "不" [bù] tonal change

17. yídìng	18. yìdiǎr	19. yíxiàr	20. yī èr sān sì
21. bù shuō	22. bú duì	23. bùhǎo	24. búcuò

6-2 Listen to the instructor read the paragraph and fill in the blanks with the correct Pinyin:

1. Wǒ shì _____ de.

2. Wǒ jiā _____.

3. Wǒ bàba _____ māma _____ shì _____.

4. Wǒ _____ yǒu nán péngyou, wǒ _____.

5. Wǒ _____ wǒde _____.

6-3 Form groups of three to four. Take turns reading the following tongue twister out loud, as quickly as you can. Each group will select one member to represent the group in a class competition.

rènmìng	任命	appointment
rénmíng	人名	name
cuò	错	wrong

Rènmìng, Rénmíng	**任命，人名**	**Appointments and Names**
Rènmìng shì rènmìng,	任命是任命，	Appointments are appointments,
Rénmíng shì rénmíng.	人名是人名。	Names are names.
Rènmìng, rénmíng bùnéng cuò,	任命，人名不能错，	Appointments and names should not be messed up,
Cuò le rénmíng rènmìng cuò.	错了人名任命错。	If they are, appointments will be names, and vice versa.

II. Character Exercises

6-4   Read the following words, phrases, and sentences:

家	车
我的家	我的车
这是我的家。	这是我的车。
我很爱我的家。	这是我哥哥的车。
姐姐也很爱我们的家。	这是我哥哥和我的车。
我们大家都很爱我们的家。	这也是我哥哥和我的车。

Now try to use the following characters to make words, phrases, and then sentences:

1. 大   2. 从   3. 在   4. 四   5. 爸   6. 妈

7. 作   8. 男   9. 没   10. 辆   11. 只   12. 爱

6-5   Write out the characters for the following Pinyin words:

1. bàba   ☐☐   2. māma   ☐☐

3. jiějie   ☐☐   4. dàjiā   ☐☐

5. gōngzuò   ☐☐   6. yíliàng chē   ☐☐☐

7. yìzhī gǒu   ☐☐   8. gōngchéngshī   ☐☐☐

6-6   Match the simplified forms of the following words with their traditional forms:

国	绍	两	爱	只	个	辆	师

(1)   (2)   (3)   (4)   (5)   (6)   (7)   (8)

愛   兩   國   輛   師   個   紹   隻

III. Grammar Exercises

6-7 Substitution exercises:

1. 你是从哪儿来的?
   我是从<u>纽约</u>来的。

北京	[Běijīng]	Beijing
上海	[Shànghǎi]	Shanghai
香港	[Xiānggǎng]	Hong Kong
台北	[Táiběi]	Taipei
波士顿	[Bōshìdùn]	Boston

2. 你是在哪儿学中文的?
   我是在<u>纽约</u>学中文的。

中国		
北京大学		
加州	[Jiāzhōu]	California
华盛顿特区	[Huáshèngdùntèqū]	
	Washington, D.C.	

3. 你是学什么的?
   我是学<u>中国文学</u>的。

工程		
数学	[shùxué]	mathematics
英国文学		

4. 你爸爸是做什么的?
   我爸爸是<u>工程师</u>。

英文老师		
医生	[yīshēng]	doctor
律师	[lǜshī]	lawyer
商人	[shāngrén]	businessman

5. 你在哪儿?
   我在<u>家</u>。

学校		
大学		
姐姐家		
宿舍	[sùshè]	dorm

6. 小美有几<u>个老师</u>?
   小美有<u>两个老师</u>。

四	本	中文书
一	只	狗
两	辆	车
一	个	姐姐
三	只	猫

IV. Communicative Activities

6-8   Go around the classroom and talk to as many people as you can. Ask questions on the following topics, among others:

1. 他/她的名字

2. 他/她学什么?

3. 他/她家在哪儿?

4. 他/她的家人

Note: 家人 [jiārén]: family members

6-9   Three or four students should give short introductions about themselves and their families. The rest should listen and prepare to ask questions about their introductions.

文化点滴　CULTURE NOTES

中国家庭 [Zhōngguó jiātíng]
Chinese Families

Traditional Chinese families were established on the theory of Confucianism, and large families have been valued in China for thousands of years. It was common for several generations to live together under one roof. Four generations living together was considered a sign of family prosperity and happiness. The man of the senior generation was the leader of the family and had the greatest authority in making decisions regarding all important issues, including the education, marriage, and careers of younger members of the family. It was assumed that younger generations would obey their elders, even if they did not see eye to eye, and would take care of them in their old age. Indeed, filial piety, the respect and care of elders in the family, was traditionally considered the most important of all qualities.

Today the situation has changed drastically because of the enforcement of the government's one-child-per-family policy and influences from other cultures. Chinese households now usually consist of the nuclear family, although it is still common for the elderly to live with their children. The only child often takes the role of family head and exercises great influence on family decisions. Filial piety is no longer emphasized, especially among the younger generation.

Families in China had been stable for thousands of years until very recently. This, to a large extent, was due to the traditional Chinese emphasis on family and the relationship between husband and wife. Marriages were based on responsibility more than love, and divorce was forbidden. Women could marry only once in their lifetime. Men were supposed to shoulder the responsibility of taking care of the family. A man who could not keep his family stable would face pressure from all directions. In modern China, until very recently, families remained stable because young men and women still attached great importance to marriage and would spend a long time getting to know each other before they finally got married. Frequently both husband and wife worked, which contributed to the equality between them.

An elder's birthday is an occasion for family members to gather together and celebrate.

The situation began to change in the 1990s. As more western ideas of freedom are introduced to China and the gap between the rich and the poor widens, people are paying more attention to freedom than to responsibility. As a result, the divorce rate has been increasing. To protect the interests of women and children, a new marriage law was enacted in 2001. It is hoped that good, old traditions will be maintained while people are allowed to enjoy more freedom.

Questions:

1. How are families organized in your country? Are there any similarities with or differences from Chinese families?

2. On what occasions does your family usually get together? What do you usually do?

趣味中文　FUN WITH CHINESE

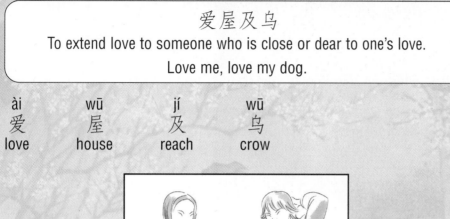

爱屋及乌
To extend love to someone who is close or dear to one's love.
Love me, love my dog.

ài	wū	jí	wū
爱	屋	及	乌
love	house	reach	crow

爱屋及乌 literally means that if one loves the house,
one tends to love even the birds perching on it.

Question:

Think of examples of "爱屋及乌". Then, form groups of two to three
to act out a "爱屋及乌" situation.

行动吧!　LET'S GO!

宣传标语　Propaganda Posters

李美美 is from Beijing. She has observed that while Beijing is changing
and becoming more modernized, residents are still encouraged to love and
cherish the city. Take a look at the propaganda slogans on the posters from
Beijing on the next page.

Useful words and expressions:

宣传(宣傳) [xuānchuán]: propaganda
标语(標語) [biāoyǔ]: slogan
碧水 [bìshuǐ]: green water
蓝天(藍天) [lántiān]: blue sky
绿色(綠色) [lǜsè]: green
家园(家園) [jiāyuán]: home
做 [zuò]: to be
文明 [wénmíng]: civilized
市民 [shìmín]: city citizen
树(樹) [shù]: to establish
社会(社會) [shèhuì]: society
新风(新風) [xīnfēng]: new atmosphere

Questions:

1. How would you translate these two slogans?

2. Did you notice the parallel pattern of the two slogans?

第七课
LESSON
7

你住哪儿？
Where Do You Live?

教学目标　OBJECTIVES

- Ask someone's address
- Tell them your address
- Describe a place
- Ask/give phone numbers

These mailboxes for an apartment complex are each clearly marked with an address.

Balconies are used for hanging laundry to dry. Note that many buildings have steel bars over windows to prevent thieves from entering.

生词 VOCABULARY

核心词 Core Vocabulary

	SIMPLIFIED	TRADITIONAL	PINYIN		
1.	住	住	zhù	V.	to live
2.	哪儿	哪兒	nǎr	Pron.	where
3.	宿舍	宿舍	sùshè	N.	dorm
4.	多少	多少	duōshǎo	Pron.	how many, how much
5.	号	號	hào	N.	number
6.	房间	房間	fángjiān	N.	room
7.	大	大	dà	Adj.	big
8.	电话	電話	diànhuà	N.	phone
9.	小	小	xiǎo	Adj.	small
10.	号码	號碼	hàomǎ	N.	number
11.	二	二	èr	Num.	two
12.	三	三	sān	Num.	three
13.	五	五	wǔ	Num.	five
14.	六	六	liù	Num.	six
15.	七	七	qī	Num.	seven
16.	八	八	bā	Num.	eight
17.	九	九	jiǔ	Num.	nine
18.	手机	手機	shǒujī	N.	cell phone
19.	校外	校外	xiàowài	N.	off campus

专名　Proper Nouns

SIMPLIFIED	TRADITIONAL	PINYIN		
1. 陈爱文	陳愛文	Chén Àiwén	N.	(name) Aiwen Chen
2. 张友朋	張友朋	Zhāng Yǒupéng	N.	(name) Youpeng Zhang

补充词　Supplementary Vocabulary

SIMPLIFIED	TRADITIONAL	PINYIN		
1. 校内	校內	xiàonèi	N.	on campus
2. 公寓	公寓	gōngyù	N.	apartment
3. 房子	房子	fángzi	N.	house, room
4. 十	十	shí	Num.	ten
5. ○	○	líng	Num.	zero

Formal Way to Write Zero to Ten in Chinese

líng	yī	èr	sān	sì	wǔ	liù	qī	bā	jiǔ	shí
○	一	二	三	四	五	六	七	八	九	十
零	壹	贰	叁	肆	伍	陆	柒	捌	玖	拾

Note: In some situations, "one" is also pronounced as [yāo] in Mainland China (e.g., phone numbers and room numbers).

语文知识　LANGUAGE LINK

The Sentence Patterns provide models that will help you with the Language in Use section. In both sections, pay attention to the grammar points, vocabulary, and expressions.

没 mei
有 you

Ku cry
lihaide alot.

black kindof 人
Hei zhong ren
bai zhong ren
白 kindof 人

句型   **Sentence Patterns**

A: 你住在哪儿?
Nǐ zhù zài nǎr?

B: 我住宿舍。
Wǒ zhù sùshè.

A: 多少号?
Duōshǎo hào?

B: 三一四号。
Sān yī sì hào.

A: 你的房间大吗?
Nǐde fángjiān dà ma?

B: 房间很小。
Fángjiān hěn xiǎo.

A: 你的电话号码是多少?
Nǐde diànhuà hàomǎ shì duōshǎo?

B: (一四二)二六八九三七五。
(Yī sì èr) èr liù bā jiǔ sān qī wǔ.

课文 Language in Use: 你住哪儿？Nǐ zhù nǎr?

陈爱文： 友朋，你住在哪儿？
Yǒupéng, nǐ zhù zài nǎr?

张友朋： 我住宿舍。
Wǒ zhù sùshè.

陈爱文： 多少号？
Duōshǎo hào?

张友朋： 三一四号。
Sān yī sì hào.

陈爱文： 你的房间大吗？有没有电话？
Nǐde fángjiān dà ma? Yǒuméiyǒu diànhuà?

张友朋： 房间很小。有电话。
Fángjiān hěn xiǎo. Yǒu diànhuà.

陈爱文： 你的电话号码是多少？
Nǐde diànhuà hàomǎ shì duōshǎo?

张友朋： (一四二)二六八九三七五。
(Yī sì èr) èr liù bā jiǔ sān qī wǔ.

陈爱文： 你有手机吗？
Nǐ yǒu shǒujī ma?

张友朋： 有。号码是 (一四二)五一二六八三七。
Yǒu. Hàomǎ shì (yī sì èr) wǔ yī èr liù bā sān qī.

你也住宿舍吗？
Nǐ yě zhù sùshè ma?

陈爱文： 不，我不住宿舍，我住校外。
Bù, wǒ bú zhù sùshè, wǒ zhù xiàowài.

注释 LANGUAGE NOTES

哪儿 and 哪里

哪儿 means "where." It is common to use "里 [lǐ]" to replace 儿 as in 哪里 [nǎlǐ] (where). It also applies to "here" as in 这儿 [zhèr] and 这里 [zhèlǐ] and "there" as in 那儿 [nàr] and 那里 [nàlǐ].

多少号

多少 is the question word for asking about a number. "多少号?" means "Which number?"

有没有

有 means "have," 没有 means "don't have." 有没有 is a question meaning "have or not have." It is equivalent to "有...吗?"

手机

手机 literally means "hand machine." It is used to refer to a "cellular phone." Chinese also refer to cell phones as 大哥大 [dàgēdà], and 行动电话 [xíngdòng diànhuà] (mobile phone) in Taiwan, and 移动电话 [yídòng diànhuà] in Mainland China.

语法 GRAMMAR

住

住 means "to live." Because the verb 住 typically is used to indicate a location, the locative preposition 在 ("at, in") sometimes is omitted. For example,

Where do you live?	你住在哪儿?	or	你住哪儿?
I live in room 314.	我住在三一四号。	or	我住三一四号。
I do not live in the dorm.	我不住在宿舍。	or	我不住宿舍。

住址的写法 **Word Order for Addresses**

Chinese word order for addresses is from larger scope to smaller scope. It is opposite to that of English. See the contrast below,

#245 Baker Street   美国宾州匹兹堡市   or   美国宾州匹兹堡市
Pittsburgh, PA 15143   15143贝克街245号   贝克街245号
USA   邮政编码：15143

Notes: 宾州 [Bīnzhōu]: Pennsylvania State
州 [zhōu]: state
匹兹堡 [Pǐzībǎo]: Pittsburgh
市 [shì]: city
邮政编码 [yóu zhèng biān mǎ]: zip code
邮递区号 [yóu dì qū hào]: zip code, used in Taiwan
街 [jiē]: street

#2 Zhongshan Road   中国北京市100083中山路2号
Beijing, 100083
China

Notes: 北京市 [Běijīng shì]: Beijing City
市 [shì]: city
路 [lù]: road

Topic-Comment Sentences

The topic-comment sentence pattern is one in which a noun or phrase serves as a topic, and is followed by a clause commenting on the topic. Other examples we have learned so far are as follows:

Topic	Comment	English
你的房间	大吗？	Is your room big?
我的房间	很大。	My room is big.
工程	难吗？	Is engineering difficult?
工程	不太难。	Engineering is not too difficult.
功课	多吗？	Is there a lot of homework?
功课	也不少。	There is also a lot of homework.

多少 and 几

多少 and 几 "how many, how much" are both used in asking about numbers. The differences between 多少 and 几 are detailed below:

几	多少
For fewer than 10 objects	For more than 10 objects
Must occur with a measure word	May occur with or without a measure word
For countable nouns only	For both countable and noncountable nouns

补充课文 ⟳ SUPPLEMENTARY PRACTICE

This selection will help you test your comprehension of the grammar and vocabulary you have learned in this lesson. Be prepared to answer questions about the meaning of the passage.

大家好! 这是我的宿舍。我的宿舍是四一三号, 房间很小, 有一个电话, 我的电话号码是(一四二)九三二六五八七。我有三个室友, 他们都有手机。我们都很喜欢我们的宿舍。你呢? 你也住在宿舍吗? 宿舍大吗? 你有没有手机? 号码是多少? 他呢? 他是我们的新同学吗? 他住宿舍还是校外?

Notes: 喜欢 [xǐhuān]: to like
  新 [xīn]: new
  还是 [háishì]: or

练习 ACTIVITIES

I. Pinyin Exercises

7-1   In each pair, circle the one your instructor pronounces:

1. xùshè   sùshè
2. duōshǎo   dōushǎo
3. diànhuà   diànhuā
4. hǎomā   hàomǎ
5. shǒujī   shǎojī
6. qiàowāi   xiàowài

7-2   Listen to the instructor read the sentences and fill in the blanks with the correct Pinyin:

1. Nǐ _____ nǎr?
2. Nǐde _____ dà ma?
3. Wǒ _____ diànhuà.
4. Nǐde diànhuà _____ shì _____ ?

7-3　Read the lyrics to the following Chinese folk song, paying special attention to the tones and rhythm:

Yí qù èr sān lǐ	**一去二三里**	**A Walk of Two or Three Miles**
Yí qù èr sān lǐ,	一去二三里，	I strolled for two or three miles,
Yān cūn sì wǔ jiā.	烟村四五家 。	Saw four or five villages in the fog.
Tíng tái liù qī zuò,	亭台六七座，	Viewed six or seven pavilions,
Bā jiǔ shí zhī huā.	八九十枝花 。	And enjoyed many flowers.

II. Character Exercises

7-4　Read the following words and phrases:

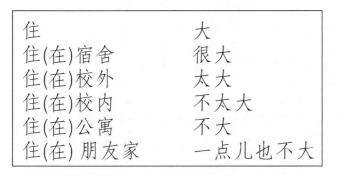

住	大
住(在)宿舍	很大
住(在)校外	太大
住(在)校内	不太大
住(在)公寓	不大
住(在) 朋友家	一点儿也不大

Now try to use the following characters to make words, phrases, and then sentences:

1. 宿　　2. 号　　3. 房　　4. 电　　5. 话　　6. 小
7. 码　　8. 手　　9. 机　　10. 校　　11. 外　　12. 间

7-5　Match the English translations with the correct characters, and then read them aloud:

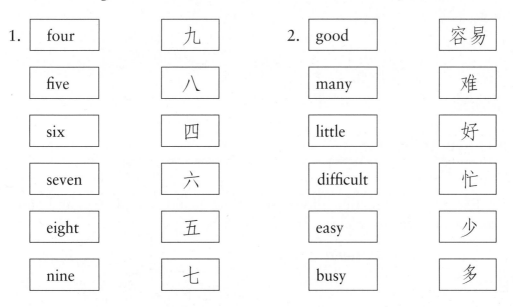

1.			2.		
four	九		good	容易	
five	八		many	难	
six	四		little	好	
seven	六		difficult	忙	
eight	五		easy	少	
nine	七		busy	多	

III. Grammar Exercises

7-6   Substitution exercises:

1. 你住哪儿？
   我住在<u>宿舍</u>，<u>二一六</u>号。

校内
校外
公寓   五二三

2. 你的电话号码是多少？
   是<u>(124)268-9375</u>。

(192)886-7532
(148)623-5790
我没有电话

3. 你的<u>房间</u><u>大</u>吗？
   我的<u>房间</u>很<u>小</u>。

功课	难
学习	忙
中文书	多
学习 [xuéxí] study	

7-7   Read the following sentences, then ask questions on the underlined words:

1. 我住在<u>宿舍</u>。
2. 我住在<u>三五六</u>号。
3. 我的房间<u>不大</u>。
4. 你的功课<u>很多</u>。
5. 我哥哥<u>有手机</u>。
6. 我哥哥的手机号码是<u>(一五五)二六七三九四八</u>。
7. 他有<u>四</u>个兄弟姐妹。
8. 他有<u>两</u>个妹妹。
9. 她和她的室友都<u>很忙</u>。
10. 老师也是<u>中国人</u>。

IV. Communicative Activities

7-8   Classroom activities:

Form pairs. Exchange information about each other, including addresses and phone numbers, then act out for the class.

Hints: Words or phrases that can be used:

住在哪儿？   有没有电话？   电话号码是多少？

有室友吗？   有几辆车？   功课多吗？

Useful words and expressions:

脆弱 [cuìruò]: fragile
邮件(郵件) [yóujiàn]: mail item
小心 [xiǎoxīn]: careful
轻放(輕放) [qīngfàng]: to handle gently
注意 [zhùyì]: watch out
事项(事項) [shìxiàng]: item
顾客(顧客) [gùkè]: customer
依 [yī]: according to
内装物(內裝物) [nèizhuāngwù]: contents
妥为封装(妥為封裝) [tuǒwéi fēngzhuāng]: to pack carefully
邮政(郵政) [yóuzhèng]: postal service
寄 [jì]: to send
东西(東西) [dōngxi]: things, stuff
贴(貼) [tiē]: to paste

Questions:

1. Translate the sticker on the right.
2. 你寄什么东西要贴这个?

复习   Review

Conversation

Ask your partner the following questions. Then report the information you collect to the class.

1. 请问，你住在哪儿? 你住宿舍吗? (什么宿舍? 多少号? 你住校外吗?)
2. 你有室友吗? 他们是谁? 他们都是哪国人?
3. 你们的宿舍(房子)有电话吗? 号码是多少?
4. 你的房间大吗?
5. 你有手机吗? 号码是多少? 你室友也有手机吗?
6. 你有中国朋友吗? 有几个? 他们都是从哪儿来的?
7. 你呢? 你是从哪儿来的?
8. 你家有几个人? 他们是谁? 他们都好吗? 他们忙吗?
9. 你们家有宠物 [chǒngwù] (pets) 吗? (狗/猫)
10. 你家有几个房间? 房间大吗?
11. 你有车吗? 什么车? 你的功课多吗? 难吗? 你是在哪儿学中文的?
12. 你有车吗? (什么车?) 你爸爸呢? 你家有几辆车?

Character Writing

<u>Situation:</u> You win a lottery while you are traveling in China! You need to confirm your birthday and address in order to claim it. Pay attention to stroke order.

Useful words:

年 [nián]: year   月 [yuè]: month   日 [rì]: day   生日 [shēngrì]: birthday

州 [zhōu]: state   街 [jiē]: street   路 [lù]: road   楼 [lóu]: floor

邮编 [yóubiān]: zip code

号 [hào]: number: 一 (1), 二 (2), 三 (3), 四 (4), 五 (5), 六 (6), 七 (7), 八 (8), 九 (9),
十 (10), 十一 (11), 十二 (12), 十五 (15), 二十 (20), 二十三 (23), 三十 (30)

中文名字: _____

生   日: _____ 年_____ 月_____日

中文地址: _____

Simplified and Traditional Characters

Read each character aloud. Write its simplified form. Then create a phrase and a sentence using the character.

For example, 學 → 学 → 学生 → 我是学生。

號 ( )   電 ( )   機 ( )   愛 ( )   從 ( )   來 ( )   紹 ( )

媽 ( )   間 ( )   碼 ( )

你认识不认识他?
Do You Know Him?

教学目标 OBJECTIVES

- More yes and no questions
- Make and respond to a plan

Do you know them?
(Yao Ming and Chairman Mao)

生词 VOCABULARY

核心词 Core Vocabulary

	SIMPLIFIED	TRADITIONAL	PINYIN		
1.	认识	認識	rènshi	V.	to know; to recognize
2.	去	去	qù	V.	to go
3.	上课	上課	shàngkè	V.O.	to attend class
4.	下课	下課	xiàkè	V.O.	to end class, class dismissed
5.	以后	以後	yǐhòu	N.	after, afterwards; later
6.	事儿	事兒	shèr	N.	matter, thing, business
7.	想	想	xiǎng	V.	to want *(expect, plan)*
8.	回	回	huí	V.	to return
9.	一起	一起	yìqǐ	Adv.	together *yǐhuàr (same)*
10.	吃	吃	chī	V.	to eat
11.	饭	飯	fàn	N.	cooked rice, meal
12.	吃饭	吃飯	chīfàn	V.O.	to eat, have a meal
13.	菜	菜	cài	N.	dish
14.	今天	今天	jīntiān	N.	today
15.	下次	下次	xiàcì		next time
16.	怎么样	怎麽樣	zěnmeyàng	Pron.	(used as a predicative or complement) how
17.	行	行	xíng	V.	to be all right, okay
18.	再见	再見	zàijiàn		see you again; goodbye
	再	再	zài	Adv.	again
	见	見	jiàn	V.	to see

专名 Proper Nouns

	SIMPLIFIED	TRADITIONAL	PINYIN		
1.	韩国	韓國	Hánguó	N.	Korea
2.	日本	日本	Rìběn	N.	Japan

补充词 Supplementary Vocabulary

	SIMPLIFIED	TRADITIONAL	PINYIN		
1.	名片	名片	míngpiàn	N.	name card (ID card)
2.	休息	休息	xiūxi	V.	to rest
3.	早饭	早飯	zǎofàn	N.	breakfast
4.	午饭 (中饭)	午飯 (中飯)	wǔfàn (zhōngfàn)	N.	lunch
5.	晚饭	晚飯	wǎnfàn	N.	dinner
6.	宵夜	宵夜	xiāoyè	N.	midnight snack

语文知识 LANGUAGE LINK

The Sentence Patterns provide models that will help you with the Language in Use section. In both sections, pay attention to the grammar points, vocabulary, and expressions.

句型 Sentence Patterns

A: 你去哪儿？ Where are you going?
Nǐ qù nǎr?

B: 我去上课。 I'm going to class
Wǒ qù shàngkè.

A: 你有事儿吗？   *Are you doing anything?*
   Nǐ yǒu shèr ma?

B: 我没有事儿。   *I'm not doing anything*
   Wǒ méiyǒu shèr.

A: 你认识不认识他？
   Nǐ rènshi bú rènshi tā?

B: 我认识他。
   Wǒ rènshi tā.

A: 我们吃韩国菜，怎么样？
   Wǒmen chī Hánguó cài, zěnmeyàng?

B: 行。
   Xíng.

课文   Language in Use: 你认识不认识他？ Nǐ rènshi bú rènshi tā?

张友朋： 爱文，你去哪儿？
         Àiwén, nǐ qù nǎr?

陈爱文： 是你，友朋，我去上课。你呢？
         Shì nǐ, Yǒupéng, wǒ qù shàngkè. Nǐ ne?

张友朋： 我也去上课。下课以后你有事儿吗？
         Wǒ yě qù shàngkè. Xiàkè yǐhòu nǐ yǒu shèr ma?

陈爱文： 我没有事儿。我想回宿舍。有什么事儿吗？
         Wǒ méiyǒu shèr. Wǒ xiǎng huí sùshè. Yǒu shénme shèr ma?

张友朋： 你认识不认识我的朋友小文？
         Nǐ rènshi bú rènshi wǒ de péngyou Xiǎowén?

陈爱文：　我认识他。我们一起上英国文学课。
　　　　　Wǒ rènshi tā. Wǒmen yìqǐ shàng Yīngguó wénxué kè.

张友朋：　下课以后我跟他一起去吃饭。你去不去？
　　　　　Xiàkè yǐhòu wǒ gēn tā yìqǐ qù chīfàn. Nǐ qù bú qù?

陈爱文：　太好了！去哪儿吃饭？
　　　　　Tài hǎo le! Qù nǎr chī fàn?

张友朋：　你想不想吃韩国菜？
　　　　　Nǐ xiǎng bù xiǎng chī Hánguó cài?

陈爱文：　想。可是我也想吃日本菜。
　　　　　Xiǎng. Kěshì wǒ yě xiǎng chī Rìběn cài.

张友朋：　我们今天吃韩国菜，
　　　　　Wǒmen jīntiān chī Hánguó cài,

　　　　　下次吃日本菜，怎么样？
　　　　　xiàcì chī Rìběn cài, zěnmeyàng?

陈爱文：　行。下课以后再见。
　　　　　Xíng. Xiàkè yǐhòu zàijiàn.

张友朋：　再见。
　　　　　Zàijiàn.

注释　LANGUAGE NOTES

事儿/事

事儿 means "matter, business." "我没有事儿" means "I have no business to attend to" or "I am free." 儿 can be omitted, as in "我没有事."

太好了！

"太好了！" is a phrase meaning "That's great!"

tài hǎo le

好，行

"好," "行" are both the expressions meaning "Good!" "Ok!" They are also used to indicate agreement with what others have just mentioned.

语法 GRAMMAR

Affirmative-Negative Questions ("A 不 A" Pattern)

The affirmative-negative question (also called "A 不 A" pattern) is a choice type of question. It requires a "yes" or "no" answer. It is formed by saying the positive and negative forms of a verb (or an adverb) together in the same sentence.

"A 不 A" pattern	
是不是	想不想
难不难	好不好
行不行	忙不忙
说不说	在不在
常不常	住不住
多不多	会不会
叫不叫	问不问
来不来	去不去
#认识不认识	有没有

Note: #"你认识不认识他？" ("Do you know him?") Some Chinese would use "你认不认识他？"

Note (1): Affirmative-negative question for 有 is 有没有.

Question ("A 不 A")	Reply "yes"	Reply "no"
你认识不认识他？	认识。(我认识他。)	不认识。(我不认识他。)
你想不想吃韩国菜？	想。(我想吃韩国菜。)	不想。(我不想吃韩国菜。)

Note (2): The "A 不 A" pattern functions in the same way as a question ending with 吗. For example,

Question with 吗	"A 不 A" pattern
你是中国人吗？	你是不是中国人？
你认识他吗？	你认识不认识他？

Note (3): In the "A 不 A" pattern, the object generally comes after the negative form of the predicate, but it may also be placed between the "A 不 A" form. For example,

你说不说中文？	Do you speak or not speak Chinese?
你说中文不说？	Do you speak Chinese or not?

Tag Question

The tag question is a short question that is attached to a statement. It is used for confirmation of the previous statement, or for making a suggestion. In Chinese, it is usually formed with "A 不 A" pattern or "是吗," "好吗," "行吗," "对吗" and "怎么样." For example,

你认识他，对不对？	You know him, right?
你想回宿舍，是不是？	You want to go back to the dorm, right?
你是学生，是吗？	You are a student, right?
我们今天吃韩国菜，好吗？	Let's go to eat Korean food today. How's that?
我们下次吃日本菜，行吗？	Let's eat Japanese food next time, all right?
我们一起去上课，怎么样？	Let's go to attend class together. How does that sound?

补充课文 ━◦◦◦ SUPPLEMENTARY PRACTICE

This selection will help you test your comprehension of the grammar and vocabulary you have learned in this lesson. Be prepared to answer questions about the meaning of the passage.

你们好！请问，你们认识不认识他？如果你们不认识他也没关系，现在我来给你们介绍一下儿，他是我的室友。他叫学友，他是韩国人，他学英国文学。他会说韩语，英文和一点儿中文。我们常常一起上课，下课。下课以后我们常一起回宿舍。

我们是好室友，好同学，也是好朋友。我们也常常一起去吃饭。今天我们想去吃日本菜，下次吃中国菜。你们呢？下课以后你们有事儿吗？你们想不想吃日本菜？跟我们一起去吃日本菜，怎么样？好，再见！

Notes: 如果 [rúguǒ]: if
没关系 [méiguānxi]: it doesn't matter

练习 ACTIVITIES

I. Pinyin Exercises

8-1 In each of following pairs, circle the one your instructor pronounces:

1. rènxi rènshi	2. shàngkè sàngkè	3. xiākè xiàkè
4. yǐhuò yǐhòu	5. yíqǐ yìqǐ	6. qīfàn chīfàn
7. jīntiān jiāntiān	8. sàcì xiàcì	9. zhàizhàn zàijiàn

8-2   Listen to the instructor and fill in the initial in the following Pinyin:

1. ___ù   2. ___iǎng   3. ___àng   4. ___ià

5. ___èr   6. ___ī   7. ___ài   8. ___íng

9. ___īn   10. ___ěn   11. ___ì   12. ___iàn

8-3   Form groups of three or four. Take turns reading the following tongue twister out loud, as quickly as you can. Each group will select one member to represent the group in a class competition.

Xiǎosì: 小四   Little Si (name of a person)

Xiǎoshí: 小十   Little Shi (name of a person)

lǎoshí: 老实   honest

Xiǎosì hé Xiǎoshí	**小四和小十**	**Little Si and Little Shi**
Xiǎosì shì lǎoshi rén,	小四是老实人，	Little Si is an honest man,
Xiǎoshí búshì lǎoshi rén.	小十不是老实人。	Little Shi is not an honest man.
Xiǎoshí qīfu Xiǎosì,	小十欺负小四，	Little Shi bullies Little Si,
Xiǎosì bèi Xiǎoshí qīfu.	小四被小十欺负。	Little Si is bullied by Little Shi.

II. Character Exercises

8-4   Read the following words and phrases:

课	去	一起
英文课	去宿舍	一起吃饭
中文课	去考试	一起去宿舍
上课	去中国	一起学中文
上日语课	去上课	一起上英国文学课
下课	去上工程课	跟朋友一起住

Now try to use the following characters to make words, phrases, and then sentences:

1. 认   2. 识   3. 以   4. 事   5. 想   6. 回

7. 今   8. 次   9. 样   10. 再   11. 饭   12. 菜

8-5   Write the Chinese characters for the following words, using one character for each blank:

1. know ___ ___   2. go ___   3. attend class ___ ___

4. after ___ ___   5. want ___   6. have a meal ___ ___

7. return ___   8. dish ___   9. goodbye ___ ___

10. today ___ ___   11. how ___ ___   12. next time ___ ___

III. Grammar Exercises

8-6 Substitution exercises:

1. 你去哪儿?
   我去<u>上课</u>。

上数学课 [shùxué] mathematics
考试
宿舍
吃饭
跟我室友吃日本菜

2. 下课以后你有事儿吗?
   <u>有</u>，<u>我有事儿</u>。<u>我去上英文课</u>。

有	有事儿	想跟朋友吃饭
有	有事儿	有一个考试
没有	没有事儿	

3. 你认识不认识<u>我的朋友小文</u>?
   我<u>认识</u>。

那个学生	认识
我的室友	不认识
他的哥哥	认识
[gēge] older brother	
我的中文老师	不认识

8-7 Ask questions on the underlined words, in three different ways:

I. A 不 A   II. 吗   III. Tag questions

For example,   <u>我学中文</u>。
Questions: 你学不学中文?
                你学中文吗?
                你学中文，对不对/是不是/对吗/是吗?

1. 下课以后我<u>有事儿</u>。
2. 我今天<u>想</u>吃日本菜。
3. 我<u>跟</u>小文一起上文学课。
4. 我的爸爸是<u>工程师</u>。
5. 我<u>学</u>法文。
6. 我的功课<u>很多</u>。

IV. Communicative Activities

8-8   Situational dialogue:

<u>Situation 1:</u>
Your high-school friend from another city is
visiting you. Please tell him/her some information
about the way you live and study right now.
Then ask your friend some similar questions.

Hints:
1. Topics to cover:
   - Greetings.
   - Chat about one of your common friends.
   - Ask about/describe where you live,
     your Chinese studies, courses, etc.

2. Words and expressions to use:

房间大不大？　　有没有电话？　　忙不忙？　　功课多不多？
对吗？　　　　　是吗？　　　　　怎么样？

<u>Situation 2:</u>
Your roommate brings a new friend to your dorm.
Please introduce yourself to the new friend and
ask him/her some questions. Then discuss what
to do in the evening.

Hints:
1. Topics to cover:
   - Greetings.
   - Recommend a restaurant for dinner together.
   - Exchange addresses and phone numbers.

2. Words and expressions to use:

介绍一下　　住在哪儿　　下课以后有事儿吗？
好吗？　　　行吗？　　　怎么样？

文化知识 ⊸⊙⊙⊙⊸ Culture Link

文化点滴　CULTURE NOTES

中国的名片文化
[Zhōngguó de míngpiàn wénhuà]
Business Cards in China
A Symbol of Social Position

Business cards in China, usually printed in both Chinese and English, not only show the owner's current position and responsibilities in a company or institution, but often list previous positions, roles of value, and even awards. Some business owners also like to use their name cards as advertisements to promote their business. With so much detail included, it is not uncommon to find Chinese business cards that are two-folded or even three-folded.

Often you might see on a business card someone's position as an adviser to a government institution, which indicates his/her strong connections with the government. However, top government officials do not usually present their business cards.

People are also becoming very particular about the decoration and selection of materials for their business cards. Many business cards have a colored background showing the city or the building where the card owner works. Some cards use special paper that cannot be torn easily by hand, and they are fireproof or waterproof. A few really wealthy people in China now have limited edition business cards made of pure gold. Those who are given gold business cards are usually guests of honor or trusted friends. In addition to its value as a precious gift, the card becomes a special pass for the recipient as well; if they need to see the card owner no one will prevent them from doing so.

Fancy card holders in leather used to be fashionable but these days gold-plated ones are preferred.

Questions:

1. How important are business cards in the U.S.?

2. How would you like your own business card to be designed?

121

Let's study the following Chinese business cards:

大中国科技有限公司
王美美
行销部经理

地址：上海市南京路21号3楼   邮编：200030

电话：021-32168688   宅电：(021) 68811688

传真：021-3213000   手机：13935356969

总机：021-3211111   直线：021-3211110

分机：021-3211112

传呼：128-223355   电邮：wangmeimei@dazhongguo_tech.com

真好吃快餐店

中餐西餐   便当外卖

电话：02-26886123   手机：(02) 922-886123

台北市忠孝东路三段25号

Useful words and expressions:

大中国(大中國) [Dàzhōngguó]: the great China
科技 [kējì]: technology
有限公司 [yǒuxiàn gōngsī]: limited-liability company
行销部(行銷部) [xíngxiāo bù]: marketing department
经理(經理) [jīnglǐ]: manager
楼(樓) [lóu]: floor
邮编(郵編) [yóubiān]: zip code
宅电(宅電) [zháidiàn]: home phone number
传真(傳真) [chuánzhēn]: fax
总机(總機) [zǒngjī]: switchboard
直线(直線) [zhíxiàn]: direct call
分机(分機) [fēnjī]: extension
传呼(傳呼) [chuánhū]: pager
快餐店 [kuàicāndiàn]: fast-food store
中餐 [zhōngcān]: Chinese food
西餐 [xīcān]: Western-style food
便当(便當) [biàndāng]: lunchbox
外卖(外賣) [wàimài]: deliver, take-away

趣味中文 FUN WITH CHINESE

一见钟情
to fall in love at first sight

yí	jiàn	zhōng	qíng
一	见	钟	情
one	see	concentrate	love

Question:

Can you think of any stories or movies which have an "一见钟情" scene? Do you believe in "一见钟情"? Why or why not? Would you like to experience this?

行动吧！ LET'S GO!

钞票上的大人物
Important Figures on Currency

Below are samples of currency in 人民币 [Rénmínbì] (人民幣) (RMB) and 新台币 [Xīntáibì] (NT) (新台幣)

Useful words and expressions:

钞票(鈔票) [chāopiào]: bill
有名 [yǒumíng]: famous
历史(歷史) [lìshǐ]: history
人物 [rénwù]: people
毛泽东(毛澤東) [Máo Zédōng]: Mao Zedong
孙逸仙(孫逸仙) [Sūn Yìxiān]: Sun Yat-sen
国父(國父) [guófù]: national father
蒋介石(蔣介石) [Jiǎng Jièshí]: Chiang Kai-shek
地位 [dìwèi]: status
知道 [zhīdào]: to know of
近代史 [jìndài shǐ]: modern history

Questions:

1. 他们是谁,你知道吗? 你知道不知道他们?
2. 你知道他们在中国近代史上的地位吗?

第九课
LESSON
9

他正在打电话
He Is Making a Phone Call

- Make a phone call
- Handle various phone situations
- Ask what someone is doing
- Explain what you are doing

Cell phones are very common in China.

Public telephones in China and Taiwan are commonly used by inserting a prepaid phone card.

jǐ extremely

生词 VOCABULARY

核心词 Core Vocabulary

	SIMPLIFIED	TRADITIONAL	PINYIN		
1.	正在	正在	zhèngzài	Adv.	(to indicate an action in progress) in the process of; in the course of
2.	打电话	打電話	dǎ diànhuà	V.O.	to make a phone call
3.	喂	喂	wèi (wéi)	Int.	(used in greeting or to attract attention) hello; hey
4.	等一下儿	等一下兒	děng yíxiàr		to wait for a moment; hang on (on the phone)
	等	等	děng	V.	to wait
5.	知道	知道	zhīdào	V.	to know; to be aware of; to realize
6.	了	了	le	Part.	(indicates assumption)
7.	谢谢	謝謝	xièxie		thanks
8.	吧	吧	ba	Part.	(indicates assumption or suggestion)
9.	对	對	duì	Adj.	correct; right
10.	忙	忙	máng	Adj.	busy
11.	看	看	kàn	V.	to look at; to see; to watch
12.	电视	電視	diànshì	N.	television
13.	做	做	zuò	V.	to do
14.	上网	上網	shàngwǎng	V.O.	to be online
15.	我就是	我就是	wǒ jiù shì		(on the phone) this is he/she speaking
16.	位	位	wèi	M.W.	(polite form, measure word for people)
17.	留言(留话)	留言(留話)	liúyán (liúhuà)	V.O.	to leave a message

Note: 留言 is used in Mainland China, while 留话 is also used in Taiwan.

	SIMPLIFIED	TRADITIONAL	PINYIN		
18.	对不起	對不起	duìbuqǐ		sorry
19.	时候	時候	shíhou	N.	(the duration of) time; (a point in) time
20.	回来	回來	huílai	V.	to return
21.	晚上	晚上	wǎnshàng	N.	evening
22.	要	要	yào	V.	to want, desire
23.	给	給	gěi	Prep. V.	for, to to give

补充词　Supplementary Vocabulary

	SIMPLIFIED	TRADITIONAL	PINYIN		
1.	占线	佔線	zhànxiàn	V.O.	to occupy a (phone) line, the line is busy
2.	打错了	打錯了	dǎcuòle		to dial a wrong number
3.	小说	小說	xiǎoshuō	N.	novel
4.	电影	電影	diànyǐng	N.	movie
5.	网络 (网路)	網絡 (網路)	wǎngluò (wǎnglù)	N.	Internet
6.	网吧 (网咖)	網吧 (網咖)	wǎngbā (wǎngkā)	N.	Internet cafe
7.	网站	網站	wǎngzhàn	N.	web site
8.	网页	網頁	wǎngyè	N.	web page
9.	聊天室	聊天室	liáotiānshì	N.	chat room
10.	电脑游戏	電腦遊戲	diànnǎoyóuxì	N.	computer game
11.	在线游戏 (线上游戏)	在線遊戲 (線上遊戲)	zàixiànyóuxì (xiànshàngyóuxì)	N.	online game
12.	病毒	病毒	bìngdú	N.	virus

	SIMPLIFIED	TRADITIONAL	PINYIN		
13.	软件 (软体)	軟件 (軟體)	ruǎnjiàn (ruǎntǐ)	N.	software
14.	硬件 (硬体)	硬件 (硬體)	yìngjiàn (yìngtǐ)	N.	hardware
15.	发短信 (送简讯)	發短信 (送簡訊)	fā duǎnxìn (sòng jiǎnxùn)	V.O.	to send a short (cell phone) message
16.	通	通	tōng	M.W.	(measure word for telephone conversation)
17.	休息	休息	xiūxi	V.	to rest
18.	睡觉	睡覺	shuìjiào	V.O.	to sleep
19.	不客气	不客氣	búkèqi		(in reply to thank you) you're welcome
20.	不谢	不謝	búxiè		(in reply to thank you) you're welcome

语文知识   LANGUAGE LINK

The Sentence Patterns provide models that will help you with the Language in Use section. In both sections, pay attention to the grammar points, vocabulary, and expressions.

句型   Sentence Patterns

A: 喂！
Wéi!

B: 喂！
Wéi!

A: 请问友朋在吗？
Qǐngwèn Yǒupéng zài ma?

B: <u>Situation 1:</u> 在，请等一下儿。
Zài, qǐng děng yíxiàr.

<u>Situation 2:</u> 我就是。
Wǒ jiù shì.

<u>Situation 3:</u> 对不起，他不在。
Duìbuqǐ, tā bú zài.

A: 你在做什么？
　　Nǐ zài zuò shénme?

B: 我在上网。
　　Wǒ zài shàngwǎng.

A: 你在忙吗？
　　Nǐ zài máng ma?

B: 没有，我正在看电视呢。
　　Méiyǒu, wǒ zhèngzài kàn diànshì ne.

课文　Language in Use: 他正在打电话 Tā zhèngzài dǎ diànhuà

Telephone Situation 1: 在，请等一下儿
　　　　　　　　　　　　Zài, qǐng děng yíxiār

陈爱文：　喂！我是爱文。请问友朋在吗？
　　　　　Wéi! Wǒ shì Àiwén. Qǐngwèn Yǒupéng zài ma?

方书程：　在，他在他的房间。请等一下儿。喂！友朋！你的电话。
　　　　　Zài, tā zài tā de fángjiān. Qǐng děng yíxiàr. Wèi! Yǒupéng, nǐ de diànhuà.

张友朋：　知道了！谢谢！
　　　　　Zhīdào le! Xièxie!

张友朋：　喂！我是友朋，你是爱文吧！
　　　　　Wéi! Wǒ shì Yǒupéng, nǐ shì Àiwén ba!

陈爱文：　对，是我。你在忙吗？
　　　　　Duì, shì wǒ. Nǐ zài máng ma?

张友朋：　没有。我正在看电视呢。你在做什么？
　　　　　Méiyǒu. Wǒ zhèngzài kàn diànshì ne. Nǐ zài zuò shénme?

陈爱文：　我在上网。
　　　　　Wǒ zài shàngwǎng.

Telephone Situation 2:　我就是
　　　　　　　　　　　　　Wǒ jiù shì

陈爱文：　　喂！
　　　　　　Wéi!

张友朋：　　喂！
　　　　　　Wéi!

陈爱文：　　请问友朋在吗？
　　　　　　Qǐngwèn Yǒupéng zài ma?

张友朋：　　我就是。请问您是哪位？
　　　　　　Wǒ jiù shì. Qǐngwèn nín shì nǎ wèi?

陈爱文：　　我是爱文。
　　　　　　Wǒ shì Àiwén.

Telephone Situation 3:　不在，请留言
　　　　　　　　　　　　　Bú zài, qǐng liúyán

陈爱文：　　喂！请问友朋在吗？
　　　　　　Wéi! Qǐngwèn Yǒupéng zài ma?

丁明：　　　对不起，他不在。他在上课。
　　　　　　Duìbuqǐ, tā bú zài. Tā zài shàngkè.

陈爱文：　　请问他什么时候回来？
　　　　　　Qǐngwèn tā shénme shíhou huílai?

丁明：　　　今天晚上。你要不要留言？
　　　　　　Jīntiān wǎnshàng. Nǐ yào bú yào liúyán?

陈爱文：　　好的。我是爱文。我的电话是(一四二)二六八九七五三。
　　　　　　Hǎo de. Wǒ shì Àiwén. Wǒ de diànhuà shì yī sì èr èr liù bā jiǔ qī wǔ sān.

　　　　　　请他回来以后给我打电话。谢谢！
　　　　　　Qǐng tā huílai yǐhòu gěi wǒ dǎ diànhuà. Xièxie!

丁明：　　　不谢。再见。
　　　　　　Búxiè. Zàijiàn.

注释　LANGUAGE NOTES

喂

喂 means "Hello!" It is generally used as a telephone greeting. When making or answering a phone call, it is pronounced as [wéi] to soften the tone and sound polite.

吧

吧 is a particle used at the end of a statement to indicate assumption on the part of the speaker.

你是爱文吧！　You must be Aiwen!

位

位 is a measure word for people. It is used for being polite. 哪位 means "which person."

你是哪位？　　May I know who is calling?

留言

留言 literally means "keep/stay words." In practice it means "leave a message." In Taiwan, people also use 留话 for "leave a message."

回来以后给我打电话(给我回电话/回电)

给 means "to give." "回来以后给我打电话" means "Give me a call (when person) comes back." Chinese people also use 回电话 or 回电 to refer to returning a phone call.

语法 GRAMMAR

The Progressive Aspect of an Action   在/正在

The progressive aspect of an action indicates that someone or something is currently in the process of doing something. This is similar to the English "-ing." The main structural pattern is "Subject + 在 + Verb Phrase + 呢." However, there are some options which are listed below:

Pattern				Example (I am watching TV.)
Subject	在	VP	(呢)	我在看电视 (呢) 。
	正			我正看电视 (呢) 。
	正在			我正在看电视 (呢) 。
			呢	我看电视呢。

- Negative pattern:

Pattern					Example (I am not watching TV.)
Subject	没有	在	VP	(呢)	我没有在看电视 (呢) 。
	没				我没在看电视 (呢) 。
	不				我不在看电视 (呢) 。

- Asking questions:

Pattern	Example	
	Question	Answer
Subject 在做什么 (呢)? *What is Subject doing?*	你哥哥在做什么 (呢)?	我哥哥 (正) 在看电视 (呢) 。 我哥哥看电视呢。 我哥哥没在做什么。
Subject 在 VP 吗? *Is Subject V-ing?*	你在看电视吗?	(是),我在看电视。 (没有),我没有在看电视。 (不),我不在看电视。

Summary: Ways of Asking Questions

Type of question	Structure	Usage	Example
Yes-no question	吗	turn a sentence into a question	你忙吗?
Affirmative-negative questions	A 不 A 有没有	a choice type of question	你忙不忙? 你有没有哥哥?
"Wh"-questions — request more specific questions what who which where when how . . .	什么 什么时候	What When	你叫什么名字? 他什么时候回来?
	谁	Who	他是谁?
	哪 哪国人 哪儿 哪位 哪年(L10)#	Which Which nationality Where Which year Which person (polite)	你是哪国人? 你住哪儿? 你是哪位? 今年是哪年?
	几 几点(L10) 几月几日/号 (L10)	How many (under 10) What time What month and day	你有几个室友? 你几点回来? 今天是几月几日/号?
	多少 多少号	How many (over 10)	你有多少书? 你的电话是多少号?
Tag question	A 不 A 是吗? 好吗? 行吗? 怎么样?	Ask for confirmation or making a suggestion	你是小美,对不对? 你是中国人,是吗? 你给我打电话,好吗? 我们去吃饭,行吗? 我们吃韩国菜,怎么样?
Other	呢	Information has been shared. "How about N?"	**A:** 你好吗? **B:** 我很好,你呢?

Note: # L10 means it will be introduced in Lesson 10.

补充课文 ⟶ SUPPLEMENTARY PRACTICE

This selection will help you test your comprehension of the grammar and vocabulary you have learned in this lesson. Be prepared to answer questions about the meaning of the passage.

今天我给小谢打电话的时候，他不在，他室友接了电话。他室友说他正在上课，他问我要不要留言，我说麻烦他回来以后给我打电话，我有事找他。晚上小谢回来了，他给我回电的时候，我正在看电视呢。我问他你在忙吗？你正在做什么呢？他说他正在上网呢！

Notes: 接 [jiē]: to receive
了 [le]: an aspect particle indicating an action completed
麻烦 [máfan]: trouble somebody to do something
回来 [huílai]: to return
有事 [yǒushì]: have some matters to attend to
找 [zhǎo]: to look for

练习   ACTIVITIES

I. Pinyin Exercises

9-1   Listen to the instructor. Mark "√" after the Pinyin if it is correct, or write in the correct Pinyin:

1. shíhuò _____   2. fángjiān _____   3. zhīdòu _____

4. diānhuà _____   5. diānsì _____   6. zhèngzài _____

7. shàngwáng _____   8. wǎngshàng _____   9. jīngtiān _____

10. liúyán _____   11. děn _____   12. zhàijiàn _____

9-2   Listen to the instructor, then fill in the Pinyin final for each of the following:

1. d _____   2. x _____   3. w _____   4. w _____

5. d _____   6. d _____   7. k _____   8. w _____

9. h _____   10. y _____   11. z _____   12. m _____

9-3　Read the following Chinese poem, paying special attention to the tones and rhythm:

Dēng Guànquèlóu (Wáng Zhīhuàn)	登鹳鹊楼 (王之涣)	On the Stork Pagoda (Wang, Zhihuan)
Báirì yī shān jìn,	白日依山尽，	White sun disappears from the mountains,
Huánghé rù hǎi liú.	黄河入海流。	Yellow River flows into the sea.
Yù qióng qiān lǐ mù,	欲穷千里目，	If one desires to expand the eye's view for a thousand miles,
Gèng shàng yì céng lóu.	更上一层楼。	Climb up another story of the pagoda.

II. Character Exercises

9-4　Read the following words and phrases:

看	正在
看书	正在上课
看电视	正在考试
看电脑	正在睡觉
看电影	正在看中文小说
看小说	正在学西班牙语

Now try to use the following characters to make words, phrases, and then sentences:

1. 打　　2. 电　　3. 等　　4. 知　　5. 忙　　6. 看

7. 做　　8. 位　　9. 时　　10. 晚　　11. 要　　12. 给

9-5　Indicate the number of strokes in each of the following characters, then create as many phrases as you can with each character:

	Number of strokes	Phrases
Example 有	6	有手机，没有电话，有事儿，没有事儿……
1. 在		
2. 上		
3. 要		

III. Grammar Exercises

9-6   Substitution exercises:

1. 你在做什么呢?
   我(正)在<u>打电话</u>呢。

休息
上网
看电视
做功课
看法国小说
跟朋友一起吃饭

2. 喂! 请问文中在吗?
   <u>我就是。请问你是哪位?</u>

在。请等一下儿。
喂! 文中,你的电话。
对不起,他不在。你要不要留言?
对不起,你打错了。
[dǎ cuò] dial a wrong number

9-7   Complete the sentences in their progressive forms with the phrases given, then change these sentences into their negative forms:

1. 我 _____ 。   (忙)
2. 他 _____ 。   (上课)
3. 她 _____ 。   (吃饭)
4. 文中 _____ 朋友 。   (介绍)
5. 小美 _____ 中文 。   (说)
6. 于英 _____ 功课 。   (做)

9-8 Look at the pictures below and describe what the people are doing.

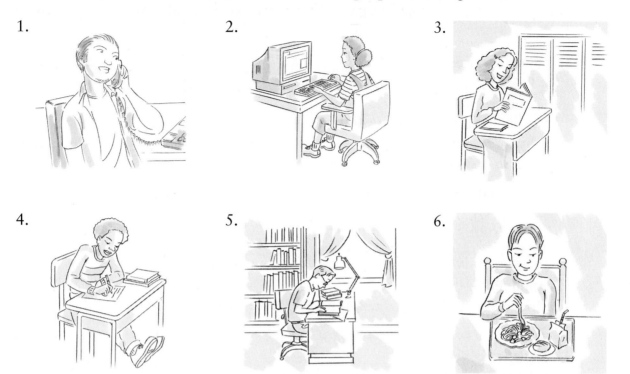

1.

2.

3.

4.

5.

6.

IV. Communicative Activities

9-9 Situational dialogue:

Situation 1:

You have a Chinese friend from Shanghai. She/He is a new student and is looking for an apartment/house. Please say a little bit about your apartment when she/he calls you on your cell phone.

Hints:

1. Topics to cover:
   - Greetings.
   - Ask about/Describe the apartment/house, rent, condition, and facilities.

2. Words and expressions to use:

请问是 …… 吗？ 住在哪儿？ 房间大吗？ 有电话吗？
我就是。 住在公寓。 房间很小。 有电话。

Situation 2:

You are going to have lunch with 小文. Call to invite another friend to join you.

Hints:

1. Topics to cover:
   - Greetings; ask about the friend's recent studies.
   - Talk about what you are doing right now.
   - Invite the friend to have lunch and discuss which restaurant you would like to go to.

2. Words and expressions to use:

正在做什么?　　认识不认识 ...?
去不去?　　　　跟 ... 一起

Situation 3:

The friend you are calling is not at home. Please leave a message.

Hints:

1. Topics to cover:
   - Greetings; ask where your friend is right now.
   - Leave a short message with the roommate (invite your friend to visit your teacher, to lunch, or to look for an apartment with you, etc.).
   - Chat about your studies with the roommate for a while.

2. Words and expressions to use:

请问......在吗?　　　　什么时候回来?　　谢谢。
对不起,他/她不在。　要不要留言?　　　不客气。

文化点滴   CULTURE LINK

手机在中国 [Shǒujī zài Zhōngguó]
Cell Phones in China
A Symbol of Fashion

Cell phones have become very popular recently in China. As well as being a status symbol, many children use them as a daily communication tool, and they are also status symbols.

Today you will see many different brands and styles of cell phones in China. The smaller in size and the newer in style, the more fashionable they are. They are especially popular among young girls and business people.

Many young people do not care too much about the features of their cell phones as long as they are small and stylish. It is very common to see young people wearing a small cell phone on a necklace. You may also see a cell phone with a tiny, artistically made light attached to a girl's shoulder bag or purse. Whenever there is an incoming call, the light flashes. What a sight!

Nowadays many business people have two or three cell phones and increasingly more young people have two cell phones turned on 24/7 for worldwide communication. The cost of cell phone calls in Mainland China is quite high, so many subscribers simply use the short messaging service, feature of the phone. They do not answer or call back directly from their phone, but wait until they get to a desk phone to do so. This is not as common in Hong Kong or Taiwan, where cell phone service is comparatively inexpensive.

If you don't have a cell phone while you are in China, look for a public telephone sign 公用电话 [gōngyòng diànhuà] such as this one. The sign above is for a public restroom 公共卫生间 [gōnggòng wèishēng jiān].

Questions:

1. What are the similarities and differences in the way cell phones are used in China and the U.S.?

2. What would you advise your professor to do when someone's cell phone rings in class?

趣味中文   FUN WITH CHINESE

不管三七二十一
no matter what

bù	guǎn	sān	qī	èrshíyī
不	管	三	七	二十一
don't	care	three	seven	twenty-one

不管三七二十一

This slang literally means "Don't care if three times seven is twenty-one."
It is used as a metaphor to show a determined mind.

Question:

Are there any sayings in English that include numbers? Can you give some examples?

行动吧！ LET'S GO!
电话卡   **Telephone Card**

明正 received a pager message from his friend. To call his friend back he will need to insert his prepaid telephone card (IC telephone card) into the slot on a public telephone.

Useful words and expressions:

卡 [kǎ]: card
电信(電信) [diànxìn]: telecommunications
磁卡 [cíkǎ]: magnetic card
换(換) [huàn]: to change
欣-欣喜 [xīnxǐ]: happy, joy
集团(集團) [jítuán]: organization
公司 [gōngsī]: company
发行(發行) [fāxíng]: issue, publish
技术(技術) [jìshù]: technology
更 [gèng]: even more
先进(先進) [xiānjìn]: advance and improve
正面 [zhèngmiàn]: the front side
反面 [fǎnmiàn]: the reverse side

(正面)

(反面)

Questions:

1. For what amount is 明正's prepaid phone card?

2. What company issued this IC telephone card?

3. What does the phrase 用心换欣 mean? What implications might it have on a telephone card?

4. What does the phrase 技术更先进 mean?

复习 Review

给朋友打电话

Call your Chinese friend and invite her/him to do something with you. Practice greetings, talking about somebody else, setting up the time, etc.

Useful words and expressions:

"A 不 A" pattern: e.g. 认识不认识，想不想
Tag question: e.g. 是吗，好吗，怎么样
正在 ...... 呢

Picture Description

Use 正在 to describe the pictures below (at least eight sentences).
Be creative!

(1)   (2)   (3)

(4)   (5)   (6)

(7)   (8)

Character Writing

Pay attention to stroke order.

<u>Situation:</u> 写便条 [xiě biàntiáo] Write a note

You would like to invite your friend, 小明, to eat out with you. You went to his dorm and he wasn't in. You would like to leave a note for him. (Use one character for each blank.)

小明:

你好，我是 _____ (your name) 。我来找你的 ____ ____ (When I came) ，你不 ____ (You were not in) 。你室友在，他 ____ 在 ____ 电 ____ 呢 (He was watching TV) 。他说你正在学校 ____ ____ (on the Internet) 。我问他你 什么时候 ____ ____ (when you would be back) ，他说今天 ____ ____ (tonight) 。

你 ____ 不 ____ 跟我 ____ ____ 去 ____ ____ (Do you want to go out to eat)? 我们去吃 ____ ____ ____ , ____ ____ ____ (Let's go eat Chinese food. How does that sound)? 请你回来 ____ ____ , ____ 我 ____ 电话 。(Please call me when you return) 。你 ____ ____ 我的 ____ ____ 号码吗 (Do you know my cell phone number)? 号码是 ____ ____ ____ ____ ____ ____ ____ ____ ____ ____ (142) 268-9753 。

_____ ____ (Thank you), ____ ____ (Bye-bye)!

_____ (Your name)

____ ____ 月 ____ 日 (Nov. 5) ____ ____ 点 ____ ____ ____ 分 (11:27)

我每天七点半起床
I Get Up at 7:30 Every Day

教学目标 OBJECTIVES

- Give times and dates in Chinese
- Describe your daily schedule
- Write letters in Chinese

University life is a time for learning, making friends, trying new things, having fun, and preparing for your future career.

生词 VOCABULARY

核心词 Core Vocabulary

	SIMPLIFIED	TRADITIONAL	PINYIN		
1.	每天	每天	měitiān		every day
2.	半	半	bàn	Adj.	half
3.	起床	起床	qǐchuáng	V.	to get up
4.	大学	大學	dàxué	N.	college, university
5.	生活	生活	shēnghuó	N.	life
6.	学期	學期	xuéqī	N.	semester
7.	门	門	mén	M.W.	(measure word for school courses)
8.	点	點	diǎn	M.W.	o'clock (point on clock)
9.	睡觉	睡覺	shuìjiào	V.O.	to go to bed; to sleep
10.	就	就	jiù	Adv.	as early as; already
11.	才	才	cái	Adv.	(used before a verb to indicate that something is rather late by general standards, or something has just happened)
12.	刻	刻	kè	M.W.	a quarter (of an hour)
13.	分	分	fēn	N.	minute
14.	然后	然後	ránhòu	Adv.	then, after that, afterwards
15.	图书馆	圖書館	túshūguǎn	N.	library
16.	下午	下午	xiàwǔ	N.	afternoon
17.	喜欢	喜歡	xǐhuān	V.	to like
18.	打球	打球	dǎqiú	V.O.	to play basketball/badminton/tennis/table tennis
19.	写	寫	xiě	V.	to write
20.	信	信	xìn	N.	letter
21.	电子邮件	電子郵件	diànzǐ yóujiàn	N.	e-mail

SIMPLIFIED	TRADITIONAL	PINYIN		
22. 地址	地址	dìzhǐ	N.	address
23. 祝	祝	zhù	V.	to wish
24. 年	年	nián	N.	year
25. 月	月	yuè	N.	month
26. 日	日	rì	N.	day

专名 Proper Nouns

SIMPLIFIED	TRADITIONAL	PINYIN		
1. 小明	小明	Xiǎomíng	N.	(name) Xiaoming
2. 学文	學文	Xuéwén	N.	(name) Xuewen

补充词 Supplementary Vocabulary

SIMPLIFIED	TRADITIONAL	PINYIN		
1. 点钟	點鐘	diǎnzhōng	M.W.	o'clock
2. 钟头	鐘頭	zhōngtóu	N.	hour
3. 小时	小時	xiǎoshí	N.	hour
4. 分钟	分鐘	fēnzhōng	N.	minute
5. 秒	秒	miǎo	M.W.	second
6. 过	過	guò	V.	to pass
7. 差	差	chà	V.	to lack, to be short of
8. 早	早	zǎo	Adj.	early
9. 晚	晚	wǎn	Adj.	late
10. 熬夜	熬夜	áoyè	V.O.	to burn the midnight oil
11. 刷牙	刷牙	shuāyá	V.O.	to brush your teeth
12. 洗脸	洗臉	xǐliǎn	V.O.	to wash your face
13. 洗澡	洗澡	xǐzǎo	V.O.	to take a bath

语文知识 LANGUAGE LINK

The Sentence Patterns provide models that will help you with the Language in Use section. In both sections, pay attention to the grammar points, vocabulary, and expressions.

句型 Sentence Patterns

A: 现在几点？
　　Xiànzài jǐdiǎn?

B: 十点五分。
　　Shídiǎn wǔ fēn.

Note: 现在 [xiànzài]: now

A: 你每天几点起床，
　　Nǐ měitiān jǐdiǎn qǐchuáng,

几点睡觉？
jǐdiǎn shuìjiào?

B: 我每天七点半起床，
　　Wǒ měitiān qīdiǎn bàn qǐchuáng,

十二点半睡觉。
shíèrdiǎn bàn shuìjiào.

A: 今天是几月几号？
　　Jīntiān shì jǐ yuè jǐ hào?

B: 十一月二十日。
　　Shíyī yuè èrshí rì.

NOVEMBER
20

A: 下课以后，你有事儿吗？
　　Xiàkè yǐhòu, nǐ yǒushèr ma?

B: 有，我有事儿，我去看书，
　　Yǒu, wǒ yǒushèr, wǒ qù kànshū,

然后去打球。
ránhòu qù dǎqiú.

课文　Language in Use: **我的大学生活 Wǒ de dàxué shēnghuó**

小明:
Xiǎomíng:

你好!
Nǐhǎo!

这个学期我很忙，有五门课。你知道我每天几点起床、
Zhège xuéqī wǒ hěnmáng, yǒu wǔ mén kè. Nǐ zhīdào wǒ měitiān jǐdiǎn qǐchuáng,

几点睡觉吗? 我七点半就起床，晚上十二点半以后才睡觉。
jǐdiǎn shuìjiào ma? Wǒ qīdiǎn bàn jiù qǐchuáng, wǎnshàng shíèrdiǎn bàn yǐhòu cái shuìjiào.

每天都很忙。九点一刻去上课，十点二十分下课。然后，
Měitiān dōu hěnmáng. Jiǔdiǎn yí kè qù shàngkè, shídiǎn èrshí fēn xiàkè. Ránhòu,

我去图书馆看书。下午下课以后，我喜欢去打球。每天都有
wǒ qù túshūguǎn kànshū. Xiàwǔ xiàkè yǐhòu, wǒ xǐhuān qù dǎqiú. Měitiān dōu yǒu

很多功课。
hěnduō gōngkè.

这是我的大学生活，你呢? 给我写信吧。我的电子邮件地址是:
Zhè shì wǒde dàxué shēnghuó, nǐ ne? Gěi wǒ xiěxìn ba. Wǒde diànzǐ yóujiàn dìzhǐ shì:

xuewen376@zhongwen.edu
xuewen376@zhongwen.edu

祝
Zhù

好
Hǎo

学文
Xuéwén

二〇〇三年十一月二十日
èr líng líng sān nián shí yī yuè èr shí rì

注释   LANGUAGE NOTES

五门课

The word 门 as a noun means "door." It is also used as a measure word for counting school courses. 五门课 means "five courses."

点

点 refers to the hour when expressing clock time. 点钟 [diǎnzhōng] is also used. For example,

三点   three o'clock
三点钟   three o'clock

钟 standing alone means "clock."
For example, "这个钟很好。" This clock is good.

吧   (For Suggestion)

吧 is a particle used at the end of a statement to turn it into a friendly suggestion: "You might . . ." or "Let's . . ." (When the subject is 我们 "we"). For example,

你学中文吧!   You might study Chinese.
我们一起去学中文吧!   Let's go study Chinese together!

Note that in Lesson 9 we learned that 吧 is also used for assumption.
For example, 你是爱文吧!   You must be Aiwen!

语法   GRAMMAR

How to Tell the Time

- The words 点 (hour), 分 (minute), 半 (half hour), and 刻 (quarter hour) are used to tell the time as illustrated below:

Time	Chinese expressions	Notes
9:00	九点(钟)	• For o'clock, 钟 [zhōng] can be used.
9:08	九点〇八分/九点八分/九点过八分	• 过 [guò] means "pass." It is only used when the time passed is within 10 minutes.
9:15	九点十五分/九点一刻	
9:30	九点三十分/九点半	
9:45	九点四十五分/九点三刻	
9:58	九点五十八分/差两分十点	• 差 [chà] means "lack." As with 过, it is used within 10 minutes of its reference time.

- Expressing A.M. and P.M.:

Morning	Noon	Afternoon	Night
早上 [zǎoshang] (around 7:00–9:00 A.M.) 7:00 A.M. 早上七点 上午 [shàngwǔ] (roughly after 9:00 A.M.) 10:15 A.M. 上午十点一刻	中午 [zhōngwǔ] 12:20 中午十二点二十分	下午 [xiàwǔ] 1:30 P.M. 下午一点半 4:10 P.M. 下午四点十分	晚上 [wǎnshang] 8:35 P.M. 晚上八点三十五分

- Expressing day and year:

The day before yesterday	Yesterday	Today	Tomorrow	The day after tomorrow
前天 qiántiān	昨天 zuótiān	今天 jīntiān	明天 míngtiān	后天 hòutiān
The year before last year	**Last year**	**This year**	**Next year**	**The year after next year**
前年 qiánnián	去年 qùnián	今年 jīnnián	明年 míngnián	后年 hòunián

Note: When giving the year, say the numbers individually. For example, 二〇〇五年 This is pronounced èr líng líng wǔ nián.

- Expressing months and days:

January 一月	February 二月	March 三月	April 四月
May 五月	June 六月	July 七月	August 八月
September 九月	October 十月	November 十一月	December 十二月
the first of the month 一号 (日)	the sixth 六号 (日)	October 17th 十月十七号 (日)	December 25th 十二月二十五号 (日)

Note: 日 means "day." 号 means "number." Both 日 and 号 can be used to refer to the day of the month. For example, October 3rd 十月三号/十月三日

号 is mostly used in speaking, while 日 is mostly used in writing.

- Pattern:

When telling the time, the Chinese always begins with the larger unit of time.
Time phrases can occur either before or after the subject.

二〇〇三年七月八日上午十点二十分。	It is 10:20 A.M., 8th July, 2003.
Subject　Time　VP	我　今天上午　十点半上课。 subject　time
Time　Subject　VP	昨天晚上　我　十一点五十分睡觉。 time　　subject

- Asking questions

Asking the time	现在几点? 现在是什么时候?	What time is it now?
	昨天你几点起床? 昨天你什么时候起床?	What time did you get up yesterday?
Asking the month and day	今天是几月几号?	What month and day is it today?
Asking the year	今年是哪年?	What year is it?

Adverbs　就　and　才

就 and 才 are adverbs that occur before a verb, stressing the time and expectation of an event. 就 is used when the speaker wants to say that an event was or will be carried out sooner than expected, 才 conveys the opposite feeling, that of "belatedness."

就 and 才 should be used after time expressions. For example,

(1) 我今天七点起床。　　I got up at 7:00 today.
(2) 我今天七点就起床。　I got up at 7:00 today.　　→ early
(3) 我今天七点才起床。　I didn't get up until 7:00 today.　→ too late

Example (1) is a simple statement. Example (2) indicates that I got up at 7 o'clock, which is early, while example (3) indicates that I got up at 7 o'clock, which is late.

The aspect 了 can only co-occur with 就, not with 才. 呢 and 的 can only occur with 才, not 就. For example,

(4) 他十二点四十分就来了。　　He came as early as 12:40.
(5) 他十二点四十分才来呢/的。　He didn't come until 12:40.

The action happened sooner than expected in example (4), but later than expected in example (5).

Grammar Summary   语法小结

1. Summary: Chinese word order

- **Modifier + Modified**
  Chinese sentences generally consist of a subject and a predicate. The basic rule of word order is that all modifiers, adjectives, adverbs, or relative clauses occur before the element they modify.

Subject		Predicate
我的 My **Modifier**	室友 roommates **Modified**	学中文。 studies Chinese **VP**

Subject			Predicate
我的 My **Modifier**	室友的 roommate's **Modifier**	哥哥 brother **Modified**	学中文。 studies Chinese **VP**

Subject			Predicate	
我的 My **Modifier**	室友的 roommate's **Modifier**	哥哥 brother **Modified**	也 also **Modifier**	学中文。 studies Chinese **VP**

Subject			Predicate	
我的 My **Modifier**	室友的 roommate's **Modifier**	哥哥 brother **Modified**	也在大学 also at the university **Modifier**	学中文。 studies Chinese **VP**

Subject			Predicate	
我的 My **Modifier**	室友的 roommate's **Modifier**	哥哥姐姐 brother and sister **Modified**	也都在大学 also all at the university **Modifier**	学中文。 studies Chinese **VP**

- Prepositional phrase (PP, as modifier) precedes the verb phrase (VP, modified). The places, objects, and recipients are specified before the action.

Pattern	Example		Meaning
在 + **place** + VP	我在图书馆 PP (Modifier)	看书 。 VP (Modified)	I study in the library.
跟 + **somebody** + VP	我跟他们 PP (Modifier)	说中文 。 VP (Modified)	I speak Chinese with them.
给 + **somebody** + VP	我给朋友 PP (Modifier)	写信 。 VP (Modified)	I write a letter to my friend.

- Wh- questions in Chinese:
  The word order of wh- questions in Chinese (e.g. 谁，什么，哪，几，少) is that the question word occurs where the expected answer would be.

Question word	Question	Answer
谁 什么 哪 几 多少	他是谁? 你学什么? 你是哪国人? 你几点上课? 你有多少中文书?	他是王老师 。 我学工程 。 我是美国人 。 我十点二十分上课 。 我有二十本中文书 。

- When talking about time, addresses, or places, Chinese progresses from larger units to smaller ones.

Larger unit → smaller unit	
Date	今天是二〇〇三年十一月二十日 。
Time	现在是下午五点十二分 。
Address	中国上海市100084中山路8号 他家在中国北京 。

- Subject + Time + VP/Time + Subject + VP

<u>我们</u>　　　<u>今天下午</u>　　去吃中国菜。
subject　　　time

<u>今天下午</u>　　<u>我们</u>　　去吃中国菜。
time　　　　　subject

2. Summary: Measure words

- Number + Measure word + Noun

Number	Measure word	Feature	Noun
一 二(两) 三 四 五 六 七 八 九 十	本	for bound items	书，杂志 [zázhì] (magazine)
	辆	for vehicles	车
	个	for people, buildings and characters	室友，图书馆，汉字 朋友，姐姐
	只	animals	狗，猫
	位	people (polite form)	老师
	门	courses	课

补充课文 ⚬⚬⚬ SUPPLEMENTARY PRACTICE

This selection will help you test your comprehension of the grammar and vocabulary you have learned in this lesson. Be prepared to answer questions about the meaning of the passage.

正生：　喂！请问欢欢在吗？

室友：　在，请等一下儿。喂，欢欢，你的电话。

欢欢：　知道了，谢谢。

　　　　喂！我是欢欢，请问你是哪位？

正生：　我是正生，好久没跟你联络了。怎么样？你最近都在忙
　　　　什么呢？

欢欢：　我这个学期很忙，我上五门课，每天都有很多功课。忙死了！

正生：　你每天几点起床，几点睡觉呢？

欢欢：　我每天七点半就起床，晚上十二点半以后才睡觉。你呢？
　　　　你的大学生活怎么样？

正生：　这个学期我有四门课，不太忙，我每天十点一刻去上课，
　　　　十一点二十分下课，然后，我喜欢去图书馆看书，下午下课
　　　　以后，我常和朋友一起去打球。

欢欢：　你常看你的电子邮件吗？

正生：　常看，我每天都看我的电子邮件。

欢欢：　我的电子邮件地址是：huanhuan@zhongwen.edu 。

　　　　有空常给我写电子邮件吧！

正生：　好，就这样，再见！

欢欢：　再见！

Notes: 好久 [hǎojiǔ]: long time
联络 [liánluò]: contact
最近 [zuìjìn]: recently
忙死了 [mángsǐle]: extremely busy
就这样 [jiùzhèyàng]: that's it; that's all

练习　ACTIVITIES

I. Pinyin Exercises

10-1 Draw lines between the matching items and read aloud:

1.

地址	diànzǐ
学期	yóujiàn
每天	ránhòu
起床	xǐhuān
睡觉	qǐchuáng
喜欢	xiěxìn
然后	dǎqiú
写信	dìzhǐ
电子	měitiān
邮件	xuéqī
打球	shuìjiào

2.

才	jiù
刻	zhù
几	bàn
日	mén
半	cái
就	jǐ
点	nián
祝	diǎn
门	kè
月	rì
年	yuè

10-2 Form groups of three or four. Take turns reading the following tongue twister out loud, as quickly as you can. Each group will select one member to represent the group in a class competition.

Notes: téng: 藤   vine

tóu: 头   end, head

tónglíng: 铜铃   bronze bell

tíng: 停   pause, stop

Téngtiáo Hé Tónglíng	藤条和铜铃
Gāogāo shān shàng yì tiáo téng,	高高山上一条藤，
Téngtiáo tóu shàng guà tóng líng.	藤条头上挂铜铃。
Fēng chuī téng dòng tónglíng dòng,	风吹藤动铜铃动，
Fēng tíng téng tíng tónglíng tíng.	风停藤停铜铃停。

The Vine and the Bronze Bell

High on the mountain hangs a vine,
On the vine end is tied a bronze bell.
The bronze bell sways with the vine when the breeze passes by,
The bronze bell halts with the vine when the breeze pauses.

II. Character Exercises

10-3 Read the following words and phrases:

两点	一个学期
两点十分	一门课
两点一刻	一位老师
两点半	一本书
两点三刻	一辆车
差十分两点	一只狗

Now try to use the following characters to make words, phrases, and then sentences:

1. 活   2. 每   3. 床   4. 睡   5. 然   6. 图
7. 喜   8. 球   9. 写   10. 邮   11. 地   12. 祝

10-4 Write out the following times and read aloud:

Morning: 早上 [zǎoshang], 上午 [shàngwǔ]

Noon: 中午 [zhōngwǔ]　　　Afternoon: 下午 [xiàwǔ]　　　Night: 晚上 [wǎnshang]

半　　刻　　　　　　　　Pass: 过 [guò]　　　　　　Lack: 差 [chà]

1. 3:00 P.M.　　　　2. 4:10 P.M.　　　　3. 5:15 A.M.　　　　4. 12:02 P.M.

_____　_____　_____　_____

5. 6:30 A.M.　　　　6. 9:45 P.M.　　　　7. 10:20 A.M.　　　　8. 1:59 P.M.

_____　_____　_____　_____

III. Grammar Exercises

10-5 Substitution exercises:

1. 你每天几点起床?
   我每天八点起床。

睡觉	12:30
去教室	8:15
去图书馆	3:45
做功课	4:30
吃晚饭	6:20

2. 下课以后你做什么?
   我去图书馆看书。

去打球
回宿舍休息
去朋友家
给朋友写电子邮件
去吃中国菜

10-6 Fill in the blanks with one or two versions of the following times:

_____   _____   _____   _____

_____   _____   _____   _____

_____   _____   _____   _____

_____   _____   _____   _____

10-7 Fill in the blanks with one of the following:

就   才   然后

1. 我常常在下午三点一刻去图书馆看书，____ 四点回宿舍。

2. 小明这个学期很忙，他没有空。他考试以后 ____ 可以给哥哥写信。

3. 文中每天很早 ____ 起床。他七点 ____ 起床，____ 八点去学校。

4. 今天我有事儿，一点半 ____ 吃午饭。

Note: 早 [zǎo]: early

IV. Communicative Activities

10-8 Situational dialogues:

Situation 1:

You want to play tennis with 李文中. There are two open times for the court right now. Ask for 文中's schedule to find out a suitable time to play together.

李文中   *Notes:* 网球 [wǎngqiú]: (tennis)

12:45–1:15	去吃中饭	2:30–3:30
1:30–2:20	上中文课	4:30–5:30
2:30–3:30	上数学课	

Hints:

1. Topics to cover:
   - Greetings.
   - Chat about this semester's courses, then suggest that you do some exercise together.

2. Words and expressions to use:

忙不忙?   功课多不多?
下课以后，我们一起......怎么样?
......吧。   是吗?   几点......?

Situation 2:

You are calling one of your good friends in another city to describe your current university life.

Hint:

Words and expressions to use:

就/才   每天...(睡觉、起床、上课)

Notes: 刷牙 [shuāyá]: to brush one's teeth
          洗脸 [xǐliǎn]: to wash one's face
          洗澡 [xǐzǎo]: to take a bath

从......到......   然后   早上   上午   中午   下午   过   差   半   刻

Situation 3:
Picture description: Talk about 小明's schedule on 22 November.

6:15 A.M.	6:20 A.M.	6:45 A.M.	7:02 A.M.

起床	刷牙	洗脸	吃早饭

8:30 A.M.–11:30 A.M.	12:00 P.M.	1:30 P.M.–4:15 P.M.	4:30 P.M.

上课	吃午饭	去图书馆	打球

6:55 P.M.	7:30 P.M.	8:05 P.M.	9:00 P.M.

洗澡	吃晚饭	看电视	上网

10:00 P.M.–1:00 A.M.	1:58 A.M.

做功课	睡觉

文化知识 ⟞∘∘∘⟝ Culture Link

文化点滴　CULTURE NOTES

中国的大学生活
[Zhōngguó de dàxué shēnghuó]
University Life in China
A Look into the Ivory Tower

Unlike in the United States, where university buildings are often integrated into the surrounding communities, many universities in China have their own exclusive land and buildings, surrounded by high walls. This setting provides a sense of exclusivity for the small number of young people who are lucky enough to live and study at the university.

Until recently students in China were required to live on campus, with separate buildings for male and female students. With larger numbers of students entering the universities, however, some students are required to live off campus. Since most on-campus dining rooms are subsidized, students can enjoy good food at a relatively low price. Some dining rooms on university campuses accept meal tickets, which are only available to students.

For new students, university life can be filled with wonder and enchantment. Despite all the excitement, the pressure of competition is ever present, because Chinese students work very hard. Academic performance plays a very significant role in their future success.

In recent years it has become common for students to have part-time jobs, especially during the long summer break. Bulletin boards, the Internet, and student service agencies are good sources for finding a summer internship. Popular jobs include tutor, interpreter, travel guide, and information technology positions.

University life provides an ideal environment for students to forge the foundation of their future. This occurs on multiple levels: through academic life, personal growth, and career development. University life is so highly valued by Chinese college students that they often document their college experiences in writings that they share with others, called 校园文学 [xiàoyuán wénxué] (campus literature), and write songs called 校园歌曲 [xiàoyuán gēqǔ] (campus songs).

163

Karaoke is a popular activity among college students.

Roommates and friends share a 火锅 [huǒguō] (hot pot) together in the dorm. This is a favorite activity during the winter months.

Questions:

1. Would you like your university to have walls to separate you from the outside world as many universities in China do? Why or why not?

2. How do you like the food at your university?

趣味中文 FUN WITH CHINESE

开夜车
to burn the midnight oil

kāi	yè	chē
开	夜	车
drive	night	car

开夜车

Question:

Do you think "开夜车" is the best way to achieve good results in your studies? Do you often "开夜车"?

行动吧！ LET'S GO!

电视节目时间表　TV Programming Schedule

王中 is visiting his relatives in Beijing for a week. During his stay, he would like to learn more about the following topics: Beijing news, preparations for the 2008 Olympics, Chinese food. Please help him to organise his TV viewing schedule.

Useful words and expressions:

节目(節目) [jiémù]: program for performing events

时间表(時間表) [shíjiān biǎo]: schedule list

可以 [kěyǐ]: may

筹备(籌備) [chóubèi]: prepare

奥运(奧運) [Ào yùn]: Olympics

报道(報道) [bàodào]: report, used in Mainland China. While 报道 (報導) [bàodǎo] report, used in Mainland China and Taiwan

体育新闻(體育新聞) [tǐyù xīnwén]: sports news

午间新闻(午間新聞) [wǔjiān xīnwén]: news at noon

三国演义(三國演義) [Sānguó Yǎnyì]: The Romance of Three Kingdoms

电视剧(電視劇) [diànshìjù]: TV series

播 [bō]: to broadcast

连续剧(連續劇) [liánxùjù]: TV series

从...到...(從...到...) [cóng . . . dào . . .]: from . . . to . . .

北京电视一台电视节目时间表						
	周一 (12/11)	周二 (12/12)	周三 (12/13)	周四 (12/14)	周五 (12/15)	周六 (12/16)	周日 (12/17)
7:00–9:00	新闻	新闻	新闻	新闻	新闻	新闻	新闻
10:50–12:00			中国菜	中国菜			
12:05–13:30	午间新闻	午间新闻	午间新闻	午间新闻	午间新闻	午间新闻	午间新闻
13:55–14:30	连续剧: 我爱我家		连续剧: 我爱我家		连续剧: 我爱我家		
16:45–18:00				奥运筹备 报道		奥运筹备 报道	
18:05–18:30	体育新闻	北京新闻	体育新闻	北京新闻	体育新闻	北京新闻	
20:00–21:00	电视剧: 三国演义	电视剧: 三国演义	电视剧: 三国演义	电视剧: 三国演义	电视剧: 三国演义		

Questions:

1. 他每天早上什么时候可以看新闻?

2. 介绍中国菜的节目是几月几号星期几?

3. 他也喜欢体育,有体育新闻吗? 每天都有吗?

4. 他想知道筹备奥运的新闻,他可以什么时候看呢?

5. 听说 [tīngshuō] (it is said that) 三国演义电视剧很不错,
   每天都播吗? 他可以什么时候看呢?

6. 他也想看看中国的连续剧,每天什么时候播?
   连续剧叫什么?

复习　**Review**

Conversation

Form groups. Ask the following questions, and then report the information you collect:

1. 你每天几点睡觉？几点起床？
2. 你喜欢吃哪国菜？
3. 你这个学期有几门课？什么课？功课多不多？难吗？
4. 昨天 [zuótiān] (yesterday) 晚上七点的时候，你正在做什么？
5. 你常给谁写电子邮件？
6. 你这个学期很忙，是吗？
7. 谁是你的好朋友，她/他在哪儿？她/他在大学学工程吗？
8. 你常给你的爸爸妈妈写信，对不对？
9. 你是不是从日本来的？
10. 下课以后，你有没有事儿？
11. 下午下课以后，你要不要打球？
12. 你有没有中文书？有几本？是在哪儿买的？
13. 你什么时候期末考试 [qīmò kǎoshì] (final exam)？有期末报告 [qīmò bàogào] (final term paper) 吗？什么时候学期结束 [jiéshù] (end)？
14. 寒假 [hánjià] (winter break) 你有什么计划 [jìhuà] (plan)？你想做什么？

Translation

<u>Situation:</u> You are 小文's roommate. This morning you received a phone call from 小文's older brother. He said he would be coming to visit 小文 for the Thanksgiving holidays. He will arrive this Saturday. Since you will be leaving to go home for Thanksgiving before 小文 returns, please leave a note for her.

New words:

感恩节 [Gǎn'ēnjié] (Thanksgiving Day)　　　快乐 [kuàilè] (happy)
过 [guò] (to spend time)　　　　　　　　走 [zǒu] (to leave)

小文：

_____

When I was sleeping at 9:15 this morning, your older brother called.

_____

You were not here. I told him you were in class.

_____

He asked me when you would be back. I said 4:30 in the afternoon.

_____

He left you a message, saying that he would come to visit you on Saturday.

_____

He will come to our dorm at 8:45 in the morning. He asked you to wait for him in the dorm.

_____

Then he wants to have Chinese food with you.

_____

Your brother asked you to call him back after you return. He said you know his phone number.

_____

I'll be leaving at 10:00 A.M. to go home to spend Thanksgiving with my family.

祝你感恩节快乐！再见！
Have a Happy Thanksgiving! Bye!

_____ Your name

_____ Nov. 23, 上午 _____ 9:42 A.M.

你要红茶还是绿茶?
Do You Want Black Tea or Green Tea?

- Order food at a restaurant
- Present/choose from alternatives
- Ask what someone wants
- Tell someone what you want

A fancy seafood restaurant in Hong Kong.

饺子 *[jiǎozi] (dumplings), a representative Chinese food.*

Traditional food stands are all along the street. Go get a treat!

生词 VOCABULARY

核心词 Core Vocabulary

	SIMPLIFIED	TRADITIONAL	PINYIN		
1.	红	紅	hóng	Adj.	red
2.	茶	茶	chá	N.	tea
3.	还是	還是	háishì	Conj.	or
4.	绿	綠	lǜ	Adj.	green
5.	服务员	服務員	fúwùyuán	N.	waiter/waitress
6.	坐	坐	zuò	V.	to sit
7.	小姐	小姐	xiǎojiě	N.	miss
8.	先生	先生	xiānsheng	N.	mister
9.	先	先	xiān	Adv.	first
10.	喝	喝	hē	V.	to drink
11.	杯	杯	bēi	M.W.	cup
12.	冰	冰	bīng	N.	ice
13.	可乐	可樂	kělè	N.	cola
14.	瓶	瓶	píng	M.W.	bottle
15.	啤酒	啤酒	píjiǔ	N.	beer
16.	面	面	miàn	N.	noodle
17.	饺子	餃子	jiǎozi	N.	dumpling (crescent shaped)
18.	盘	盤	pán	M.W.	plate
19.	炒	炒	chǎo	V.	to stir fry
20.	十	十	shí	Num.	ten
21.	碗	碗	wǎn	M.W.	bowl
22.	汤	湯	tāng	N.	soup
23.	双	雙	shuāng	M.W.	pair
24.	筷子	筷子	kuàizi	N.	chopstick

专名　Proper Nouns

SIMPLIFIED	TRADITIONAL	PINYIN		
1. 张正然	張正然	Zhāng Zhèngrán	N.	(name) Zhengran Zhang
2. 孙信美	孫信美	Sūn Xìnměi	N.	(name) Xinmei Sun
3. 杨欢	楊歡	Yáng Huān	N.	(name) Huan Yang

补充词　Supplementary Vocabulary

SIMPLIFIED	TRADITIONAL	PINYIN		
1. 饭馆	飯館	fànguǎn	N.	restaurant
2. 餐厅	餐廳	cāntīng	N.	restaurant
3. 餐馆	餐館	cānguǎn	N.	restaurant
4. 饭店	飯店	fàndiàn	N.	restaurant, hotel
5. 菜单	菜單	càidān	N.	menu
6. 白饭	白飯	báifàn	N.	steamed rice
7. 饮料	飲料	yǐnliào	N.	drink
8. 果汁	果汁	guǒzhī	N.	juice
9. 橙汁	橙汁	chéngzhī	N.	orange juice
10. 柳橙汁 (柳丁汁)	柳橙汁 (柳丁汁)	liǔchéngzhī (liǔdīngzhī)	N.	tangerine juice
11. 咖啡	咖啡	kāfēi	N.	coffee
12. 点菜	點菜	diǎncài	V.O.	to order food
13. 小费	小費	xiǎofèi	N.	tip
14. 买单	買單	mǎidān	V.O.	to pay the bill
15. 结账 (结帐)	結賬 (結帳)	jiézhàng	V.O.	to settle the account
16. 酸	酸	suān	Adj.	sour
17. 甜	甜	tián	Adj.	sweet

	SIMPLIFIED	TRADITIONAL	PINYIN		
18.	苦	苦	kǔ	Adj.	bitter
19.	辣	辣	là	Adj.	spicy
20.	咸	鹹	xián	Adj.	salty
21.	清淡	清淡	qīngdàn	Adj.	plain
22.	烫	燙	tàng	Adj.	burning hot
23.	凉	涼	liáng	Adj.	cool

常见食品 [Chángjiàn shípǐn]   **Common Foods**

	SIMPLIFIED	TRADITIONAL	PINYIN		
1.	馄饨	餛飩	húntun	N.	wonton
2.	春卷	春捲	chūnjuǎn	N.	spring roll
3.	鱼	魚	yú	N.	fish
4.	虾	蝦	xiā	N.	shrimp
5.	海鲜	海鮮	hǎixiān	N.	seafood
6.	青菜	青菜	qīngcài	N.	vegetable
7.	猪肉	豬肉	zhūròu	N.	pork
8.	牛肉	牛肉	niúròu	N.	beef
9.	鸡肉	雞肉	jīròu	N.	chicken
10.	豆腐	豆腐	dòufu	N.	bean curd
11.	甜点	甜點	tiándiǎn	N.	dessert
12.	饼干	餅乾	bǐnggān	N.	cracker
13.	蛋糕	蛋糕	dàngāo	N.	cake
14.	沙拉	沙拉	shālā	N.	salad
15.	面包	麵包	miànbāo	N.	bread

常见水果 [Chángjiàn shuǐguǒ]   Common Fruits

	SIMPLIFIED	TRADITIONAL	PINYIN		
1.	苹果	蘋果	píngguǒ	N.	apple
2.	香蕉	香蕉	xiāngjiāo	N.	banana
3.	桃子	桃子	táozi	N.	peach
4.	梨子	梨子	lízi	N.	pear
5.	西瓜	西瓜	xīguā	N.	watermelon
6.	草莓	草莓	cǎoméi	N.	strawberry
7.	葡萄	葡萄	pútao	N.	grape

语文知识   LANGUAGE LINK

The Sentence Patterns provide models that will help you with the Language in Use section. In both sections, pay attention to the grammar points, vocabulary, and expressions.

句型   Sentence Patterns

A: 你要红茶还是绿茶？
Nǐ yào hóngchá háishì lǜchá?

B: 我要红茶。
Wǒ yào hóngchá.

A: 你想点什么？
Nǐ xiǎng diǎn shénme?

B: 我们点一杯可乐、一瓶啤酒、
Wǒmen diǎn yìbēi kělè, yìpíng píjiǔ,

一盘炒饭、三碗汤和
yìpán chǎofàn, sānwǎn tāng hé

二十个饺子。
èrshíge jiǎozi.

课文   **Language in Use:** 你要红茶还是绿茶？
Nǐ yào hóngchá háishì lǜchá?

服务员：　请问，几位？
　　　　　Qǐngwèn, jǐ wèi?

张正然：　三位。
　　　　　Sān wèi.

服务员：　好，请跟我来。请坐。
　　　　　Hǎo, qǐng gēn wǒ lái. Qǐngzuò.

张正然、孙信美、杨欢：　谢谢！
　　　　　　　　　　　　　Xièxie!

服务员：　小姐，先生，请问，你们想先喝点儿什么？
　　　　　Xiǎojiě, xiānsheng, qǐngwèn, nǐmen xiǎng xiān hē diǎr shénme?

孙信美：　我喜欢喝茶。
　　　　　Wǒ xǐhuān hē chá.

服务员：　你要红茶还是绿茶？
　　　　　Nǐ yào hóngchá háishì lǜchá?

孙信美：　我要一杯冰红茶。
　　　　　Wǒ yào yìbēi bīng hóngchá.

杨欢：　　我要一杯可乐。
　　　　　Wǒ yào yìbēi kělè.

张正然：　我要一瓶啤酒。
　　　　　Wǒ yào yìpíng píjiǔ.

服务员：　好，一杯冰红茶、一杯可乐、一瓶啤酒。请等一下。
　　　　　Hǎo, yìbēi bīng hóngchá, yìbēi kělè, yìpíng píjiǔ. Qǐng děng yíxià.

张正然：　对了，你们喜欢吃饭还是吃面？
　　　　　Duì le, nǐmen xǐhuān chīfàn háishì chīmiàn?

孙信美：　我都喜欢。
　　　　　Wǒ dōu xǐhuān.

杨欢：　　我想吃饺子。
　　　　　Wǒ xiǎng chī jiǎozi.

服务员：　这是您的冰红茶、可乐、还有啤酒。你们要点菜吗?
　　　　　Zhè shì nín de bīng hóngchá, kělè, háiyǒu píjiǔ. Nǐmen yào diǎncài ma?

张正然：　好，我们点一盘炒饭、一盘炒面和二十个饺子吧。
　　　　　Hǎo, wǒmen diǎn yìpán chǎofàn, yìpán chǎomiàn hé èrshí ge jiǎozi ba.

孙信美：　我们还要三碗汤。对了，我们也要三双筷子，谢谢!
　　　　　Wǒmen háiyào sānwǎn tāng. Duìle, wǒmen yě yào sānshuāng kuàizi, xièxie!

注释　LANGUAGE NOTES

服务员

In Mainland China, this term is used for anyone who provides service, mainly waiters and waitresses. In Taiwan, people use 服务生 instead of 服务员.

位

As was explained previously, 位 is another measure word for people. It is usually used to be courteous to guests or to show respect. In a restaurant, the waiter/waitress usually politely asks "几位?" and the customers reply with a phrase, such as "三位" (three of us) or "五位" (five of us). In this situation, the word "位" is only a response to the question and has nothing to do with courtesy or politeness.

点

点 is used to order (dishes, wine, music pieces, etc.)
Similar to点, 要 can also be used to order food.

饺子

Instead of 饺子, 水饺 is more commonly used in Taiwan.

语法   GRAMMAR

还是

还是 is a conjunction corresponding to "or" in English. It is used to connect two alternatives in an alternative question (a question of the form "A or B"?). These two alternatives can be noun phrases, verb phrases, adjective phrases, etc., for example,

你要红茶还是绿茶？	Would you like black tea or green tea?
你想打电话还是写信？	Do you want to make a phone call or write a letter?
你今天上午上课还是下午上课？	Do you have class in the morning or in the afternoon?
谁是中国人，你还是他？	Who is Chinese, you or he?

量词   (Measure Words/Classifiers) (3)

Words identifying containers can also be used as measure words. Here are some examples,

Measure word	Example		
杯	一杯冰红茶	yìbēi bīnghóngchá	a *glass* of iced tea
瓶	两瓶啤酒	liǎngpíng píjiǔ	two *bottles* of beer
盘	三盘炒饭	sānpán chǎofàn	three *plates* of fried rice
碗	四碗酸辣汤	sìwǎn suānlàtāng	four *bowls* of hot and sour soup

Also,

Measure word	Example		
壶	一壶咖啡	yìhú kāfēi	a *pot* of coffee
盒	两盒巧克力	liǎnghé qiǎokèlì	two *boxes* of chocolate
桶	三桶水	sāntǒng shuǐ	three *buckets* of water
罐	四罐可乐	sìguàn kělè	four *cans* of Coke
箱	五箱书	wǔxiāng shū	five *cases* of books
袋	六袋花生	liùdài huāshēng	six *bags* of peanuts

补充课文 ━◦○◦━ SUPPLEMENTARY PRACTICE

This selection will help you test your comprehension of the grammar and vocabulary you have learned in this lesson. Be prepared to answer questions about the meaning of the passage.

今天我们下课以后都饿了，我们就约了几个朋友一起去中国饭馆吃饭。服务员小姐看到我们很亲切地说"欢迎光临"，然后问我们想喝点儿什么饮料。我要了一杯冰红茶，杨欢要了一杯可乐，正然喜欢喝啤酒，他要了一瓶啤酒。

服务员小姐还问我们想吃面还是想吃饭，我们看了看菜单，有很多好吃的东西，最后我们点了一盘炒饭，一盘炒面，二十个饺子和三碗汤。我们不太习惯用叉子，比较喜欢用筷子，我们就跟服务员小姐要了三双筷子。我们一面吃饭一面聊天，大家吃得又饱又高兴。

Notes: 饿 [è]: hungry
了 [le]: an aspect particle indicating completion of an action
约 [yuē]: to make an appointment, invite
看到 [kàndào]: to see; to catch sight of
亲切 [qīnqiè]: cordial; warm
欢迎光临 [huānyíng guānglín]: welcome
然后 [ránhòu]: then
饮料 [yǐnliào]: beverage
还 [hái]: also
菜单 [càidān]: menu
好吃 [hǎochī]: yummy; delicious
最后 [zuìhòu]: finally
习惯 [xíguàn]: to get used to
叉子 [chāzi]: fork
一面 … 一面 … [yímiàn … yímiàn …]: adverb indicating two simultaneous actions
聊天 [liáotiān]: chat
又 … 又 … [yòu]: both . . . and
得 [de]: 得 is used in the "degree of complement" sentence to tell how an action is performed
饱 [bǎo]: to be full
高兴 [gāoxìng]: happy

练习   ACTIVITIES

I. Pinyin Exercises

11-1 Listen to the instructor pronounce the Pinyin below. Mark "√" after the Pinyin if correct, or write in the correct Pinyin:

1. fānguǎn _____   2. lùchá _____   3. píjǔ _____

4. kuāzi _____   5. kěliè _____   6. xiānsheng _____

7. kēchá_____   8. fúwùyuán _____   9. jīwéi _____

10. jiǎozǐ _____   11. bīnhóngchá _____   12. chǎofàn _____

11-2 Listen to the instructor and fill in each blank with the correct Pinyin:

1. qǐng _____   2. _____ shì   3. _____ chá   4. _____ cài

5. liǎng _____ chá   6. sān _____ fàn   7. xiǎo _____   8. yǐn _____

9. yì _____ kuàizi   10. sìwǎn _____   11. kā _____   12. bái _____

13. chǎo _____   14. _____ yào   15. cài _____   16. _____ cài

11-3 Read the following Chinese poem, paying special attention to the tones and rhythm:

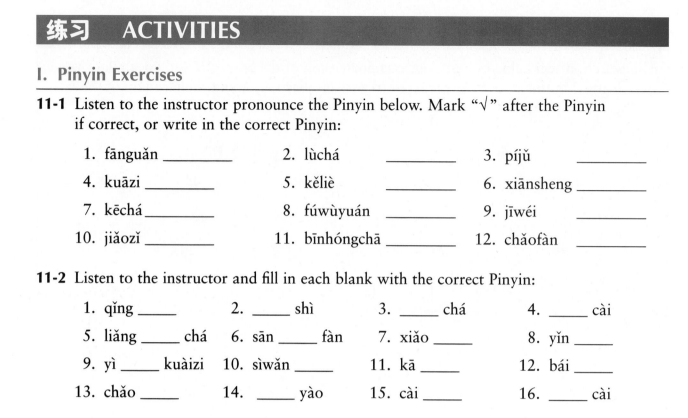

Mǐn Nóng **(Lǐ Shēn)**	**悯农** **(李绅)**
Chú hé rì dāng wǔ, Hàn dī hé xià tǔ. Shéi zhī pán zhōng cān, Lìlì jiē xīnkǔ.	除禾日当午， 汗滴禾下土。 谁知盘中餐， 粒粒皆辛苦。

Gratefulness to Peasants
(Li, Shen)

Hoeing the crops under the hot sun,
Sweat drips onto the soil beneath the crops.
Who realizes the rice in the bowl
Is every grain produced from hard labor?

II. Character Exercises

11-4 Read the following words, phrases, and sentences:

茶	想
红茶	想吃饭
冰红茶	想吃炒饭
一杯冰红茶	他想吃一盘炒饭
喝一杯冰红茶	他想吃一盘虾炒饭
她要喝一杯冰红茶	他想吃一盘还是两盘虾炒饭

Note: 虾 [xiā]: shrimp

Now try to use the following characters to make words, phrases, and then sentences:

1. 馆　　2. 服　　3. 坐　　4. 喝　　5. 红　　6. 绿

7. 可　　8. 瓶　　9. 酒　　10. 面　　11. 汤　　12. 筷

11-5 Insert the proper measure word into the phrases below:

1. 三　小　说　　2. 两　车　　3. 那　啤　酒

4. 这　炒　饭　　5. 多　少　饺　子　　6. 三　狗

7. 两　绿　茶　　8. 一　老　师　　9. 一　工　程　课

10. 一　啤　酒　　11. 四　馄　饨　汤　　12. 几　筷　子

III. Grammar Exercises

11-6 Substitution exercises:

1. 你想喝茶还是喝咖啡？
   我想喝茶。

喝红茶	喝绿茶
喝可乐	喝啤酒
吃炒饭	吃炒面
看小说	看电视
做功课	上网
学工程	学电脑

2. 请问，你想喝什么？
   我要一杯可乐。

吃	二十个饺子
点	一盘炒面
喝	一瓶啤酒
喝	一杯冰红茶
喝	一杯绿茶

11-7 Fill in the blanks with the words below. Some words may be used more than once.

跟　想　要　还是

1. 你喜欢吃饭 _____ 吃面？
2. 请 ____ 我来。
3. 你 ____ 喝什么？
4. 我 ____ 二十个饺子。
5. 李文中常 ____ 丁明说中文。
6. 吃晚饭以后，你 ____ 上网 _____ 看电视？

11-8 Combine the words or phrases in parentheses with the sentences and the word "还是" to make alternative questions:

For example,　　今天下午他有课。　　　　　（法语　　　　工程）
　　　　　　　→ 今天下午他有法语课还是工程课？

1. 他喜欢学习。　　　　　　　　　　　（在图书馆　　在宿舍）
2. 杨欢要去图书馆。　　　　　　　　　（六点半　　　七点）
3. 李先生是老师。　　　　　　　　　　（日文　　　　中文）
4. 她要一杯茶。　　　　　　　　　　　（红　　　　　绿）

IV. Communicative Activities

11-9 Situational dialogues:

<u>Situation 1:</u>
Your classmates are visiting you in your apartment. Please act as a good host.

Hints:
1. Topics to cover:
   • Greetings.
   • Ask what your friends would like to eat and drink.
   • Chat about your hobbies, your apartment, your studying schedule, etc.

2. Words and expressions to use:

喜欢…　　　　　…还是…
想吃/喝…　　　　…吧

<u>Situation 2:</u>
You and several international students are eating together in a Korean restaurant.

Hints:
1. Topics to cover:
   - Greetings.
   - Discuss what kinds of food and drink you like and place an order.
   - Get to know some new friends.
   - Ask about foods in other countries.

2. Words and expressions to use:

喜欢…	…还是…	想吃/喝…
您贵姓?	哪国人?	学什么?
有没有…?	是不是…?	

<u>Situation 3:</u>
Discuss with your friend what to do after class.

Hints:
1. Topics to cover:
   - Meet the friend on campus and greet each other.
   - Chat for a while about each other's courses this semester and ask about your mutual friends.
   - Discuss what you want to do after class: practice Chinese, visit friends, go to a restaurant, etc.

2. Words and expressions to use:

你好吗?	忙吗?	是…还是…?
…难吗?	喜欢	看朋友

文化点滴 CULTURE NOTES

中国菜系介绍 [Zhōngguó càixì jièshào]
Chinese Food (1)

Chinese food is among the best-known cuisines in the world. It is abundant in variety, delicious in taste, and pleasing to the eye. Chinese food is also considered to be healthy.

Chinese people have studied the art of cooking for over 3,000 years. It would not be surprising today if you were served at a restaurant in China with 一鸡三味 [yìjī sānwèi] (one chicken with three different flavors), 一鸭四吃 [yìyā sìchī] (one Peking roast duck in four or five courses) or 一鱼二烧 [yìyú èrshāo] (one fish served in two cooking styles). Chinese cooking places emphasis on 色 [sè], 香 [xiāng], and 味 [wèi] (color, flavor, and taste). From simple family meals to the most elaborate banquets (usually over 18 courses), every mouthful manages to combine nutrition, aesthetics, and history.

There are eight styles of Chinese cuisine. They are 鲁菜 [Lǔcài] (Shandong style), 川菜 [Chuāncài] (Sichuan style), 淮阳菜 [Huáiyángcài] (Yangzhou style), 粤菜 [Yuècài] (Cantonese style), 闽菜 [Mǐncài] (Fujian style), 浙菜 [Zhècài] (Zhejiang style), 皖菜 [Wǎncài] (Anhui style), and 湘菜 [Xiāngcài] (Hunan style). Both the 川菜 and 湘菜 are hot and spicy, whereas 淮阳菜 and 浙菜 are a sweet and

A common Chinese breakfast, 粥 [zhōu] (porridge), 酱菜 [jiàngcài] (pickles) and 蛋 [dàn] (eggs).

A banquet feast with fancy decorations.

**At Chinese traditional markets
菜市场 [càishìchǎng] you can find
processed meat, chicken, pickles,
fish balls, baked goods, desserts,
vegetables, and seafood.**

light in flavor with fresh, tender ingredients. The characteristics of
粤菜 are very special and unique ingredients, consisting mostly of
fresh seafood with an emphasis on the "original flavor." 点心 [diǎnxīn]
(dim sum), a Cantonese-style brunch with dozens of varieties of light
appetizers, is very popular among Chinese both at home and abroad.

Chinese food commonly uses a lot of ingredients with purported healing
properties, including ginger, green onion, garlic, cinnamon, yam, eggs,
vinegar, mung beans, and rice wine. All ingredients are categorized into
groups of three different nature — hot, cold, and neutral. The combination
of ingredients is based on Daoist yin-yang theory to strive for balance.
Chinese people are interested in 食疗 [shíliáo] (medical treatment
with food). They have known for centuries that sea cucumbers strengthen
bones and protect against aging. Bitter melon clears the blood. Carp is
good for the gallbladder and spleen, as well as for pregnant women and
their fetuses. Pig's feet and chicken broth help blood circulation. With these
ideas in mind, Chinese people often use herbal medicine together with
certain ingredients in their stir-fry dishes and soups to help meet the
body's needs.

Food is an extremely important part of people's lives in China. In the Qing Dynasty, there were approximately 2,000 people working to provide food for the emperor and his family. Dining partners have always been a symbol of one's social status. Today, food still plays a great role in the social life of Chinese people. "Business is done at the dining table" is a common saying in China.

Dining in China is often associated with hospitality as well. Chinese usually treat their guests to abundant food of great variety.

Questions:

1. What kind of food do you like best? What do you think are the major differences between Chinese food and Western food?
2. Do you often go to Chinese restaurants? Describe one of your favorite Chinese dishes.

Chinese Food (2)

Western-brand foods are also popular in China, Taiwan, and Hong Kong:

麦当劳	[Màidāngláo]	McDonald's
肯德基 炸鸡	[Kěndéjī zhájī]	Kentucky Fried Chicken
必胜客 匹萨	[Bìshèngkè pǐsà]	Pizza Hut
星巴克 咖啡	[Xīngbākè kāfēi]	Starbucks Coffee

趣味中文 FUN WITH CHINESE

> 饭后百步走，活到九十九。
> Take a walk after each meal and you will live to be 99 years old.

fàn	hòu	bǎi	bù	zǒu	huó	dào	jiǔshíjiǔ
饭	后	百	步	走	活	到	九十九
meal	after	hundred	step	walk	live	to	ninety-nine

Questions:

1. Do you know any similar sayings in a language other than Chinese?
2. Can you give an example?

行动吧！ LET'S GO!

小吃 Chinese Snacks

1. While traveling in China, 小中 saw the following interesting shop signs. Read the signs and answer the following questions.

Useful words and expressions:

小吃 [xiǎochī]: snacks
左边 (左邊) [zuǒbiān]: left side
右边 (右邊) [yòubiān]: right side
馅 (餡) [xiàn]: food filling
熊 [xióng]: bear
之父 [zhīfù]: father of
快餐 [kuàicān]: fast food
店名 [diànmíng]: name of a shop

Question:

左边的店名叫什么，卖什么？右边的店呢？

2. 小中 also visited Taiwan. During his stay there his Chinese friends took him out to eat at the following places. They ate several dishes at each place.

Useful words and expressions:

发财(發財) [fācái]: get rich
排骨 [páigǔ]: ribs or pork chop
香菇 [xiānggū]: mushroom
炸酱面(炸醬麵) [zhájiàng miàn]:
　　noodles with spicy bean sauce

锅贴(鍋貼) [guōtiē]:
　　fried dumpling
鱼丸(魚丸) [yúwán]:
　　fish ball

十二月十八日星期一　　十二月二十二日星期日

Questions:

1. 左边的店名叫什么？

2. 他们十二月十八日星期一吃什么？十二月二十二日星期日呢？

3. 你想点些什么？

生词表　VOCABULARY LIST

Lesson 1

你	好	是	学生	学	吗	我	呢
也	他	不	老师				

Lesson 2

您	贵	姓	请问	请	问	的	英文
名字	中文	叫	什么	她	谁	同学	

专名

李文中　吴小美　于英

补充词

汉语　英语

Lesson 3

哪	国	人	很	对了	法国	美国	英国
中国	说	会	一点儿	儿	法文	和	

补充词

德国	德国人	德语(德文)		韩国	韩国人	韩语(韩文)
加拿大	加拿大人			泰国	泰国人	泰语(泰文)
日本	日本人	日语(日文)				
西班牙	西班牙人		西班牙语(西班牙文)			

Lesson 4

那	书	这	本	文学	工程	难	太
可是	功课	多	我们	们	少		

补充词

系	数学	计算机(电脑)	专业(主修)		辅修	容易
忙	累	作业	考试	有点儿	还好	

Lesson 5

朋友	来	介绍	一下	室友	有	几	两
个	他们	都	常	跟			

专名

王红	丁明	方小文

补充词

没有	女朋友	男朋友	认识

Lesson 6

家	大家	从	在	一	四	爸爸	妈妈
姐姐	工作	工程师	男	男朋友	没有	辆	车
只	狗	爱					

专名

纽约

补充词

自我介绍		自己	兄弟姐妹		哥哥	妹妹	弟弟
女	女朋友	孩子	宠物	猫			

Lesson 7

住	哪儿	宿舍	多少	号	房间	大	电话
小	号码	二	三	五	六	七	八
九	手机	校外					

专名

陈爱文	张友朋

补充词

校内	公寓	房子	十	〇

Lesson 8

认识	去	上课	下课	以后	事儿	想	回
一起	吃	饭	吃饭	菜	今天	下次	怎么样
行	再见	再	见				

专名

韩国	日本

补充词

名片	休息	早饭	午饭(中饭)	晚饭	宵夜

Lesson 9

正在	打电话	喂	等一下儿	等	知道	了
谢谢	吧	对	忙	看	电视	做	上网
我就是	位	留言(留话)	对不起	时候	回来	晚上
要	给					

补充词

占线	打错了	小说	电影	网络(网路)	网吧(网咖)
网站	网页	聊天室	电脑游戏	在线游戏(线上游戏)
病毒	软件(软体)	硬件(硬体)	发短信(送简信)
通	休息	睡觉	不客气	不谢

Lesson 10

每天	半	起床	大学	生活	学期	门	点
睡觉	就	才	刻	分	然后	图书馆	下午
喜欢	打球	写	信	电子邮件	地址	祝
年	月	日				

专名

小明	学文

补充词

点钟	钟头	小时	分钟	秒	过	差	早
晚	熬夜	刷牙	洗脸	洗澡			

Lesson 11

红	茶	还是	绿	服务员	坐	小姐	先生
先	喝	杯	冰	可乐	瓶	啤酒	面
饺子	盘	炒	十	碗	汤	双	筷子

专名

张正然　孙信美　杨欢

补充词

饭馆	餐厅	餐馆	饭店	菜单	白饭	饮料	果汁
橙汁	柳橙汁(柳丁汁)		咖啡	点菜	小费	买单	
结账(结帐)		酸	甜	苦	辣	咸	清淡
烫	凉						

Lesson 12

可以	借	明天	用	得	机场	接	妹妹
玩	飞机	到	手排挡(手排)		开	应该	问题
白	色	停	停车场	这次	练习	这样	就
能	进步						

专名

于影　　王本乐　上海　　洛杉矶

补充词

自动排挡(自排)

Lesson 13

买	件	衬衫	店员	条	裙子	或者	裤子
黄	不错	比较	穿	黑	试试	帮	好看
让	觉得	钱	块	张	电影	票	

专名

毛爱红　方子英

补充词

贵	便宜	卖	号	几号	特大	大	中
小	特小						

Lesson 14

岁	有空	星期	过	生日	为	舞会	参加
一定	做	蛋糕	送	棒	不客气	多大	地图

补充词

日历	月历	庆生	礼物	蜡烛	祝你生日快乐

Lesson 15

前边	参观	欢迎	里边	厨房	公用	旁边	客厅
走	对面	餐厅	洗澡间	卧室	中间	桌子	上边
后边	公园	真					

专名

田进	梁园生	包志中

补充词

左边	右边	门	书桌	窗户	椅子	衣橱	床
教室	杂志	乱	整齐	干净	脏	整理	

Lesson 16

篮球	得	俩	教练	教	游泳	非常	快
体育馆	游泳池	健身房	锻炼	现在	昨天	球赛	作业
包	慢						

补充词

社团	俱乐部	球季

Lesson 17

春天	久	时间	过	放	春假	气候	夏
秋	冬	其中	最	暖和	短	有时候	热
华氏	百	度	极	刮风	下雨	冷	雪
见面							

专名

小玲

补充词

天气	四季	放假	寒假	暑假	假期	摄氏	长
气温	上升	下降				

Lesson 18

火车	旅行	离	学校	远	只要	分钟	骑
自行车	公共汽车		走路	近	西部	先	风景
船	南部	听说	海边	景色	一共	租	

专名

季长风　白秋影　加拿大

补充词

海滩	东	北	旺季	淡季	单车(脚踏车)	汽车
机车(摩拖车)	出租汽车(计程车)	火车	公车(巴士)		
面包车(包型车)	吉普车	跑车	大货车	四轮驱动(四轮传动)	
越野车	车站	捷运	地铁	磁浮铁路	天桥	马路
地下道	隧道	码头	司机			

Lesson 19

感冒	饿	好像	舒服	头疼	发烧	咳嗽	生病
考试	复习	所以	医生	吃药	地	休息	准备
笔记	感谢					

专名

欧阳迎　唐志信

补充词

医务室(医护室)	打针	护士	医院	诊所	严重	厉害
体温	流感(流行性感冒)		预防针	流感疫苗	

Lesson 20

把	带来	啊	进	搬	出	出去	过来
做饭	吸烟	没关系	以前	但是	女朋友	必须	第一天
付	房租	楼上	马上				

专名

常天	夏中明	谢进学

补充词

房东	房客	签约	租屋

Lesson 21

暑假	毕业	决定	申请	研究生院	国外	留学
找	打工	家	公司	实习	电脑	暑期	班
一面	有意思	愉快	一路平安	好运		

专名

程海华	白秋雨	加州

补充词

大学生	研究生	博士生	学位	学士	硕士	博士
简历(履历表)					

Lesson 22

对不起	因为	不过	认真	已经	美丽	城市	到处
新	大楼	地方	活动	比如	京剧	书法	东西
最	小笼包	机会	尝尝	开始	高兴	收到	看来
开心	同事	热心	老板	一些	学到	来信	保重

补充词

心想事成	健康	顺利

简繁体字对照表
SIMPLIFIED/TRADITIONAL CHARACTER TABLE

简体字：[jiǎn tǐ zì]　simplified character
繁体字：[fán tǐ zì]　traditional character (or: complex character)

第一课　Lesson 1

简：	学	吗	师
繁：	學	嗎	師

第二课　Lesson 2

简：	贵	请	问	么	谁
繁：	貴	請	問	麼	誰

第三课　Lesson 3

简：	国	对	说	会	点	儿
繁：	國	對	說	會	點	兒

第四课　Lesson 4

简：	书	这	难	课	们
繁：	書	這	難	課	們

第五课　Lesson 5

简：	来	绍	几	两	个
繁：	來	紹	幾	兩	個

第六课　Lesson 6

简：	从	妈	没	辆	车	只	爱
繁：	從	媽	沒	輛	車	隻	愛

第七课　Lesson 7

简：	号	间	电	话	码	机
繁：	號	間	電	話	碼	機

第八课　Lesson 8

简：	认	识	后	饭	样	见
繁：	認	識	後	飯	樣	見

第九课　Lesson 9

简：	谢	视	网	时	给
繁：	謝	視	網	時	給

第十课　Lesson 10

简：	门	觉	图	馆	欢	写	邮
繁：	門	覺	圖	館	歡	寫	郵

第十一课　Lesson 11

简：	红	还	绿	务	员	乐	面	饺	盘	汤	双
繁：	紅	還	綠	務	員	樂	麵	餃	盤	湯	雙

第十二课　Lesson 12

简：	场	飞	挡	开	应	该	题	练	习	进
繁：	場	飛	擋	開	應	該	題	練	習	進

第十三课　Lesson 13

简：	买	衬	条	裤	黄	错	较	试	帮	让	钱
繁：	買	襯	條	褲	黃	錯	較	試	幫	讓	錢

简：	块	张
繁：	塊	張

第十四课　Lesson 14

简：	岁	过	为	参	气
繁：	歲	過	為	參	氣

第十五课　Lesson 15

简：	边	观	里	厨	厅	卧	园
繁：	邊	觀	裡	廚	廳	臥	園

第十六课 Lesson 16

简：	篮	俩	体	锻	炼	现	赛	业
繁：	籃	倆	體	鍛	煉	現	賽	業

第十七课 Lesson 17

简：	热	华	极	风
繁：	熱	華	極	風

第十八课 Lesson 18

简：	离	远	钟	骑	听
繁：	離	遠	鐘	騎	聽

第十九课 Lesson 19

简：	饿	头	发	烧	复	医	药	准	备	笔	记
繁：	餓	頭	發	燒	復	醫	藥	準	備	筆	記

第二十课 Lesson 20

简：	带	烟	关	系	须	楼	马
繁：	帶	煙	關	係	須	樓	馬

第二十一课 Lesson 21

简：	毕	决	实	脑	运
繁：	畢	決	實	腦	運

第二十二课 Lesson 22

简：	经	丽	处	动	剧	东	笼	尝	兴	板
繁：	經	麗	處	動	劇	東	籠	嚐	興	闆

第一课　你好!

Mary:	你好!
John:	你好!
Mary:	你是学生吗?
John:	我是学生。你呢?
Mary:	我也是学生。
John:	他呢? 他是学生吗?
Mary:	他不是学生。他是老师。

第一課　你好!

Mary:	你好!
John:	你好!
Mary:	你是學生嗎?
John:	我是學生。你呢?
Mary:	我也是學生。
John:	他呢? 他是學生嗎?
Mary:	他不是學生。他是老師。

第二课　您贵姓?

Mary:	你好! 请问您贵姓?
John:	我姓李, 我的英文名字是 John Lee, 中文名字是李文中。你呢, 请问你叫什么名字?
Mary:	我叫 Mary, 我的英文名字是 Mary Wood, 中文名字是吴小美。
John:	她呢? 她是谁?
Mary:	她是我的同学于英。

第二課　您貴姓?

Mary:	你好! 請問您貴姓?
John:	我姓李, 我的英文名字是 John Lee, 中文名字是李文中。你呢, 請問你叫什麼名字?
Mary:	我叫 Mary, 我的英文名字是 Mary Wood, 中文名字是吳小美。
John:	她呢? 她是誰?
Mary:	她是我的同學于英。

第三课　你是哪国人？

李文中：小美，你好吗？
吴小美：我很好。对了，文中，你是哪国人？
李文中：我是法国人，你呢？你是美国人吗？
吴小美：不是，我不是美国人，我是英国人。
李文中：老师呢？
吴小美：他是中国人。他说中文。
李文中：你会说中文吗？
吴小美：我会说一点儿中文，我也会说法文和英文。

第三課　你是哪國人？

李文中：小美，你好嗎？
吴小美：我很好。對了，文中，你是哪國人？
李文中：我是法國人，你呢？你是美國人嗎？
吴小美：不是，我不是美國人，我是英國人。
李文中：老師呢？
吴小美：他是中國人。他說中文。
李文中：你會說中文嗎？
吴小美：我會說一點兒中文，我也會說法文和英文。

第四课　你学什么？

吴小美：文中，那是你的书吗？
李文中：那是我的书。
吴小美：那是一本什么书？
李文中：那是一本英文书。
吴小美：这本呢？这是一本什么书？
李文中：这是一本中文书。
吴小美：对了，你学什么？
李文中：我学英国文学，你呢？
吴小美：我学工程。
李文中：工程难吗？
吴小美：不太难，可是功课很多。
李文中：我们的功课也不少。

第四課　你學什麼?

吳小美: 文中, 那是你的書嗎?
李文中: 那是我的書。
吳小美: 那是一本什麼書?
李文中: 那是一本英文書。
吳小美: 這本呢? 這是一本什麼書?
李文中: 這是一本中文書。
吳小美: 對了, 你學什麼?
李文中: 我學英國文學, 你呢?
吳小美: 我學工程。
李文中: 工程難嗎?
吳小美: 不太難, 可是功課很多。
李文中: 我們的功課也不少。

第五课　这是我朋友

吳小美: 文中, 来! 我来介绍一下。这是我室友, 王红。这是我朋友,
　　　　文中。
李文中: 你好!
王　红: 你好! 你有室友吗?
李文中: 有, 我有室友。
王　红: 你有几个室友?
李文中: 我有两个室友。
王　红: 他们都是谁?
李文中: 他们是丁明和方小文。他们都是中国人。我常跟他们说中文。

第五課　這是我朋友

吳小美: 文中, 來! 我來介紹一下。這是我室友, 王紅。這是我朋友,
　　　　文中。
李文中: 你好!
王　紅: 你好! 你有室友嗎?
李文中: 有, 我有室友。
王　紅: 你有幾個室友?
李文中: 我有兩個室友。
王　紅: 他們都是誰?
李文中: 他們是丁明和方小文。他們都是中國人。我常跟他們說中文。

第六课   我的家

　　大家好! 我叫吴小美。我是从纽约来的。我学工程。我来介绍一下我的家。我家在纽约，有四个人：爸爸、妈妈、姐姐和我。爸爸是英国人，妈妈是美国人，他们都在纽约工作。爸爸是工程师，妈妈是老师，我和姐姐都是学生。姐姐有男朋友，我没有。我们有两辆车，一只狗。我的家很好。我很爱我的家。

第六課   我的家

　　大家好! 我叫吳小美。我是從紐約來的。我學工程。我來介紹一下我的家。我家在紐約，有四個人：爸爸、媽媽、姐姐和我。爸爸是英國人，媽媽是美國人，他們都在紐約工作。爸爸是工程師，媽媽是老師，我和姐姐都是學生。姐姐有男朋友，我沒有。我們有兩輛車，一隻狗。我的家很好。我很愛我的家。

第七课   你住哪儿?

陈爱文：友朋，你住在哪儿?
张友朋：我住宿舍。
陈爱文：多少号?
张友朋：三一四号。
陈爱文：你的房间大吗? 有没有电话?
张友朋：房间很小。有电话。
陈爱文：你的电话号码是多少?
张友朋：(一四二)二六八九三七五。
陈爱文：你有手机吗?
张友朋：有。号码是(一四二) 五一二六八三七。你也住宿舍吗?
陈爱文：不，我不住宿舍，我住校外。

第七課   你住哪兒?

陳愛文：友朋，你住在哪兒?
張友朋：我住宿舍。
陳愛文：多少號?
張友朋：三一四號。
陳愛文：你的房間大嗎? 有沒有電話?
張友朋：房間很小。有電話。
陳愛文：你的電話號碼是多少?
張友朋：(一四二)二六八九三七五。
陳愛文：你有手機嗎?
張友朋：有。號碼是(一四二) 五一二六八三七。你也住宿舍嗎?
陳愛文：不，我不住宿舍，我住校外。

第八课　你认识不认识他?

张友朋: 爱文, 你去哪儿?
陈爱文: 是你, 友朋, 我去上课。你呢?
张友朋: 我也去上课。下课以后你有事儿吗?
陈爱文: 我没有事儿。我想回宿舍, 有什么事儿吗?
张友朋: 你认识不认识我的朋友小文?
陈爱文: 我认识他。我们一起上英国文学课。
张友朋: 下课以后我跟他一起去吃饭, 你去不去?
陈爱文: 太好了! 去哪儿吃饭?
张友朋: 你想不想吃韩国菜?
陈爱文: 想。可是我也想吃日本菜。
张友朋: 我们今天吃韩国菜, 下次吃日本菜, 怎么样?
陈爱文: 行。下课以后再见。
张友朋: 再见。

第八課　你認識不認識他?

張友朋: 愛文, 你去哪兒?
陳愛文: 是你, 友朋, 我去上課。你呢?
張友朋: 我也去上課。下課以後你有事兒嗎?
陳愛文: 我沒有事兒。我想回宿舍, 有什麼事兒嗎?
張友朋: 你認識不認識我的朋友小文?
陳愛文: 我認識他。我們一起上英國文學課。
張友朋: 下課以後我跟他一起去吃飯, 你去不去?
陳愛文: 太好了! 去哪兒吃飯?
張友朋: 你想不想吃韓國菜?
陳愛文: 想。可是我也想吃日本菜。
張友朋: 我們今天吃韓國菜, 下次吃日本菜, 怎麼樣?
陳愛文: 行。下課以後再見。
張友朋: 再見。

第九课　他正在打电话

<u>Situation 1:</u>　在，请等一下儿

陈爱文：喂！我是爱文。请问友朋在吗?
方书程：在，他在他的房间。请等一下儿。喂！友朋！你的电话。
张友朋：知道了！谢谢！
张友朋：喂！我是友朋，你是爱文吧！
陈爱文：对，是我。你在忙吗?
张友朋：没有。我正在看电视呢。你在做什么?
陈爱文：我在上网。

<u>Situation 2:</u>　我就是

陈爱文：喂！
张友朋：喂！
陈爱文：请问友朋在吗?
张友朋：我就是。请问您是哪位?
陈爱文：我是爱文。

<u>Situation 3:</u>　不在，请留言

陈爱文：喂！请问友朋在吗?
丁　明：对不起，他不在。他在上课。
陈爱文：请问他什么时候回来?
丁　明：今天晚上。你要不要留言?
陈爱文：好的。我是爱文。我的电话是(一四二)二六八九七五三。请他
　　　　回来以后给我打电话。谢谢！
丁　明：不谢。再见。

第九課　他正在打電話

Situation 1: 在，請等一下兒

陳愛文：喂！我是愛文。請問友朋在嗎?
方书程：在，他在他的房間。請等一下兒。喂！友朋！你的電話。
張友朋：知道了！謝謝!
張友朋：喂！我是友朋，你是愛文吧!
陳愛文：對，是我。你在忙嗎?
張友朋：沒有。我正在看電視呢。你在做什麼?
陳愛文：我在上網。

Situation 2: 我就是

陳愛文：喂!
張友朋：喂!
陳愛文：請問友朋在嗎?
張友朋：我就是。請問您是哪位?
陳愛文：我是愛文。

Situation 3: 不在，請留言

陳愛文：喂！請問友朋在嗎?
丁　明：對不起，他不在。他在上課。
陳愛文：請問他什麼時候回來?
丁　明：今天晚上。你要不要留言?
陳愛文：好的。我是愛文。我的電話是(一四二)二六八九七五三。請他
　　　　回來以後給我打電話。謝謝!
丁　明：不謝。再見。

第十课　我每天七点半起床

小明：

　　你好！

　　这个学期我很忙，有五门课。你知道我每天几点起床、几点睡觉吗？我七点半就起床，晚上十二点半以后才睡觉。每天都很忙。九点一刻去上课，十点二十分下课。然后，我去图书馆看书。下午下课以后，我喜欢去打球。每天都有很多功课。

　　这是我的大学生活，你呢？给我写信吧。我的电子邮件地址是：xuewen376@zhongwen.edu

　　　祝

好

　　　　　　　　　　　　　　　　　　　　　　　　学文
　　　　　　　　　　　　　　　　　　　　　二〇〇三年十一月二十日

第十課　我每天七點半起床

小明：

　　你好！

　　這個學期我很忙，有五門課。你知道我每天幾點起床、幾點睡覺嗎？我七點半就起床，晚上十二點半以後才睡覺。每天都很忙。九點一刻去上課，十點二十分下課。然後，我去圖書館看書。下午下課以後，我喜歡去打球。每天都有很多功課。

　　這是我的大學生活，你呢？給我寫信吧。我的電子郵件地址是：xuewen376@zhongwen.edu

　　　祝

好

　　　　　　　　　　　　　　　　　　　　　　　　學文
　　　　　　　　　　　　　　　　　　　　　二〇〇三年十一月二十日

第十一课　你要红茶还是绿茶?

服务员：请问，几位?
张正然：三位。
服务员：好，请跟我来。请坐。
张正然，孙信美，杨欢：　谢谢!
服务员：小姐，先生，请问，你们想先喝点儿什么?
孙信美：我喜欢喝茶。
服务员：你要红茶还是绿茶?
孙信美：我要一杯冰红茶。
杨　欢：我要一杯可乐。
张正然：我要一瓶啤酒。
服务员：好，一杯冰红茶、一杯可乐、一瓶啤酒。请等一下。
张正然：对了，你们喜欢吃饭还是吃面?
孙信美：我都喜欢。
杨　欢：我想吃饺子。
服务员：这是您的冰红茶、可乐、还有啤酒。你们要点菜吗?
张正然：好，我们点一盘炒饭、一盘炒面和二十个饺子吧。
孙信美：我们还要三碗汤。对了，我们也要三双筷子，谢谢!

第十一課　你要紅茶還是綠茶?

服務員：請問，幾位?
張正然：三位。
服務員：好，請跟我來。請坐。
張正然，孫信美，楊歡：　謝謝!
服務員：小姐，先生，請問，你們想先喝點兒什麼?
孫信美：我喜歡喝茶。
服務員：你要紅茶還是綠茶?
孫信美：我要一杯冰紅茶。
楊　歡：我要一杯可樂。
張正然：我要一瓶啤酒。
服務員：好，一杯冰紅茶、一杯可樂、一瓶啤酒。請等一下。
張正然：對了，你們喜歡吃飯還是吃麵?
孫信美：我都喜歡。
楊　歡：我想吃餃子。
服務員：這是您的冰紅茶、可樂、還有啤酒。你們要點菜嗎?
張正然：好，我們點一盤炒飯、一盤炒麵和二十個餃子吧。
孫信美：我們還要三碗湯。對了，我們也要三雙筷子，謝謝!

第十二课　我可以借你的车吗?

于　　影: 本乐，明天下午你用不用车?
王本乐: 我不用。你有什么事儿吗?
于　　影: 我得去机场接人，可以借你的车吗?
王本乐: 可以。你要去接谁?
于　　影: 我妹妹和她男朋友。他们从上海坐飞机去洛杉矶玩儿，
　　　　　明天会到我这儿来。
王本乐: 我的车是手排挡的，你会不会开?
于　　影: 应该没问题。我爸爸的车也是手排挡的，我常开他的车。
王本乐: 我的车是白色的，车号是BD5730,停在五号停车场。
于　　影: 知道了。谢谢!
王本乐: 不谢。你妹妹他们会说英文吗?
于　　影: 会一点儿，这次他们想多学习一点儿英文。
王本乐: 太好了，我得跟他们多练习一点儿中文。这样，我的中文就能
　　　　　进步了。

第十二課　我可以借你的車嗎?

于　　影: 本樂，明天下午你用不用車?
王本樂: 我不用。你有什麼事兒嗎?
于　　影: 我得去機場接人，可以借你的車嗎?
王本樂: 可以。你要去接誰?
于　　影: 我妹妹和她男朋友。他們從上海坐飛機去洛杉磯玩兒，
　　　　　明天會到我這兒來。
王本樂: 我的車是手排擋的，你會不會開?
于　　影: 應該沒問題。我爸爸的車也是手排擋的，我常開他的車。
王本樂: 我的車是白色的，車號是BD5730,停在五號停車場。
于　　影: 知道了。謝謝!
王本樂: 不謝。你妹妹他們會說英文嗎?
于　　影: 會一點兒，這次他們想多學習一點兒英文。
王本樂: 太好了，我得跟他們多練習一點兒中文。這樣，我的中文就能
　　　　　進步了。

第十三课　我想买一件衬衫

店　员：两位小姐想买什么?
毛爱红：我想买一件衬衫。
方子英：我想买一条裙子或者裤子。
店　员：这件黄衬衫怎么样?
毛爱红：还不错。可是我比较喜欢穿黑色的, 有没有黑色的?
店　员：有, 在这儿, 你试试!
方子英：爱红, 来, 你帮我看看, 我穿裙子好看还是穿裤子好看?
毛爱红：你穿穿, 让我看看。我觉得你穿这条裙子好看。
方子英：请问, 这条裙子多少钱?
店　员：十五块。
方子英：好, 我买了。
毛爱红：我要买这件黑衬衫。
店　员：对了, 小姐, 这张电影票是你的吗?
方子英：是的, 这张电影票是我的。谢谢! 我们等一下要去看电影。

第十三課　我想買一件襯衫

店　員：兩位小姐想買什麼?
毛愛紅：我想買一件襯衫。
方子英：我想買一條裙子或者褲子。
店　員：這件黃襯衫怎麼樣?
毛愛紅：還不錯。可是我比較喜歡穿黑色的, 有沒有黑色的?
店　員：有, 在這兒, 你試試!
方子英：愛紅, 來, 你幫我看看, 我穿裙子好看還是穿褲子好看?
毛愛紅：你穿穿, 讓我看看。我覺得你穿這條裙子好看。
方子英：請問, 這條裙子多少錢?
店　員：十五塊。
方子英：好, 我買了。
毛愛紅：我要買這件黑襯衫。
店　員：對了, 小姐, 這張電影票是你的嗎?
方子英：是的, 這張電影票是我的。謝謝! 我們等一下要去看電影。

第十四课　我今年二十岁

方子英：爱红，二月十八日你有没有空？
毛爱红：二月十八日那天是星期几？
方子英：星期六。
毛爱红：我有空。有什么事儿吗？
方子英：那天我过生日，我男朋友要为我开一个生日舞会，我想请你参加。
毛爱红：谢谢你，我一定去。还有谁会去？
方子英：我们想请我们的同学和朋友都参加。
毛爱红：我会做蛋糕。我送你一个生日蛋糕，怎么样？
方子英：太棒了！谢谢你！
毛爱红：不客气。你今年多大？
方子英：我今年二十岁。你呢？你的生日是几月几号？
毛爱红：我的生日是十月三号，我今年二十二岁。你的舞会在哪儿开？
方子英：在我男朋友的家，这是他的地址。你知道怎么去吗？
毛爱红：没问题！我有地图。星期六下午五点见。
方子英：再见。

第十四課　我今年二十歲

方子英：愛紅，二月十八日你有沒有空？
毛愛紅：二月十八日那天是星期幾？
方子英：星期六。
毛愛紅：我有空。有什麼事兒嗎？
方子英：那天我過生日，我男朋友要為我開一個生日舞會，我想請你參加。
毛愛紅：謝謝你，我一定去。還有誰會去？
方子英：我們想請我們的同學和朋友都參加。
毛愛紅：我會做蛋糕。我送你一個生日蛋糕，怎麼樣？
方子英：太棒了！謝謝你！
毛愛紅：不客氣。你今年多大？
方子英：我今年二十歲。你呢？你的生日是幾月幾號？
毛愛紅：我的生日是十月三號，我今年二十二歲。你的舞會在哪兒開？
方子英：在我男朋友的家，這是他的地址。你知道怎麼去嗎？
毛愛紅：沒問題！我有地圖。星期六下午五點見。
方子英：再見。

第十五课　图书馆在宿舍前边

(<u>Situation</u>: 今天是宿舍参观日，在学生宿舍)

田　进：你们好！欢迎你们来看我的宿舍。请跟我来。

梁园生：田进，你的宿舍里边有没有厨房?

田　进：有厨房，是公用的。

包志中：你的房间在哪儿?

田　进：我的房间在旁边，从这儿走。来，请进。这是客厅，客厅的对面是一个餐厅。

梁园生：洗澡间呢?

田　进：洗澡间在客厅和卧室的中间。你看，这是我的卧室。

包志中：桌子上边的中文书都是你的吗?

田　进：有的是我的，有的是我朋友的。

包志中：你常在宿舍学习吗?

田　进：不，我不常在宿舍学习，我常去图书馆学习。

梁园生：图书馆在哪儿?

田　进：图书馆在宿舍前边。图书馆的后边还有一个公园。我常去那儿打球。

梁园生，包志中：你们的宿舍真不错。

第十五課　圖書館在宿舍前邊

(<u>Situation</u>: 今天是宿舍參觀日，在學生宿舍)

田　進：你們好！歡迎你們來看我的宿舍。請跟我來。

梁園生：田進，你的宿舍裡邊有沒有廚房?

田　進：有廚房，是公用的。

包志中：你的房間在哪兒?

田　進：我的房間在旁邊，從這兒走。來，請進。這是客廳，客廳的對面是一個餐廳。

梁園生：洗澡間呢?

田　進：洗澡間在客廳和臥室的中間。你看，這是我的臥室。

包志中：桌子上邊的中文書都是你的嗎?

田　進：有的是我的，有的是我朋友的。

包志中：你常在宿舍學習嗎?

田　進：不，我不常在宿舍學習，我常去圖書館學習。

梁園生：圖書館在哪兒?

田　進：圖書館在宿舍前邊。圖書館的後邊還有一個公園。我常去那兒打球。

梁園生，包志中：你們的宿舍真不錯。

第十六课　她打篮球打得很好

张正然：你们俩要去哪儿？
孙信美，杨欢：　我们去打篮球。
张正然：你们篮球打得怎么样？
孙信美：杨欢篮球打得很好。我还不太会打篮球，她是我的教练，她教
　　　　得很好。
杨　欢：不行，我还打得不太好。
张正然：我不常打篮球，我常常和我室友去游泳，他游泳游得非常快。
杨　欢：你们常去哪儿游泳？
张正然：我们常去体育馆里边的游泳池游泳，我们也常去健身房锻炼。
孙信美：你现在要不要跟我们去打篮球？
张正然：现在不行。我昨天看球赛看得太晚了，今天起得很晚，
　　　　现在得去做作业。
杨　欢：昨天我们那儿包饺子、做中国菜。你晚上到我们那儿吃饺子
　　　　吧。
张正然：太好了！我很喜欢吃饺子。你们包饺子包得快不快？
孙信美：我们包得很慢。
杨　欢：信美很会做饭。她做饭做得很好。

第十六課　她打籃球打得很好

張正然：你們倆要去哪兒？
孫信美，楊歡：　我們去打籃球。
張正然：你們籃球打得怎麼樣？
孫信美：楊歡籃球打得很好。我還不太會打籃球，她是我的教練，她教
　　　　得很好。
楊　歡：不行，我還打得不太好。
張正然：我不常打籃球，我常常和我室友去游泳，他游泳游得非常快。
楊　歡：你們常去哪兒游泳？
張正然：我們常去體育館裡邊的游泳池游泳，我們也常去健身房鍛煉。
孫信美：你現在要不要跟我們去打籃球？
張正然：現在不行。我昨天看球賽看得太晚了，今天起得很晚，
　　　　現在得去做作業。
楊　歡：昨天我們那兒包餃子、做中國菜。你晚上到我們那兒吃餃子
　　　　吧。
張正然：太好了！我很喜歡吃餃子。你們包餃子包得快不快？
孫信美：我們包得很慢。
楊　歡：信美很會做飯。她做飯做得很好。

第十七课　春天就要来了

小玲：

好久不见。

你现在怎么样? 时间过得真快，春天就要来了，我们也快要放春假了。

我们这儿的气候春夏秋冬都有。其中我最喜欢春天，很暖和，可是很短。夏天有时候很热，最热的时候，会到华氏一百度，热极了。秋天有时候会刮风、下雨。这儿的冬天非常冷，常常下雪。

放春假的时候我想去你那儿玩玩，我们很快就要见面了!

　　　祝

好!

　　　　　　　　　　　　　　　　　　　　　　　　大中
　　　　　　　　　　　　　　　　　　　　　　二〇〇四年三月十日

第十七課　春天就要來了

小玲：

好久不見。

你現在怎麼樣? 時間過得真快，春天就要來了，我們也快要放春假了。

我們這兒的氣候春夏秋冬都有。其中我最喜歡春天，很暖和，可是很短。夏天有時候很熱，最熱的時候，會到華氏一百度，熱極了。秋天有時候會刮風、下雨。這兒的冬天非常冷，常常下雪。

放春假的時候我想去你那兒玩玩，我們很快就要見面了!

　　　祝

好!

　　　　　　　　　　　　　　　　　　　　　　　　大中
　　　　　　　　　　　　　　　　　　　　　　二〇〇四年三月十日

第十八课　我们要坐火车去旅行

季长风：秋影，你住在校外吗? 离学校远不远?
白秋影：不太远，开车只要五分钟。
季长风：你每天怎么来学校?
白秋影：我常骑自行车，下雨下雪的时候就坐公共汽车，有时候我也走路，可以锻炼锻炼。你呢?
季长风：我住在宿舍，离学校很近，我每天走路来学校。
白秋影：对了，这个春假你要做什么?
季长风：我要跟我的室友一起去西部旅行。
白秋影：你们怎么去?
季长风：我们想先坐火车去，路上看看风景。然后坐船去加拿大，再从加拿大坐飞机回来。你呢?
白秋影：我很想我爸爸、妈妈和妹妹，我要先回家。然后再跟朋友开车去玩儿。
季长风：你们要去哪儿玩儿?
白秋影：我们想去南部玩儿。听说那儿的海边景色很美。
季长风：你们有几个人去?
白秋影：我们一共有五个人去，我们想租一辆车。

第十八課　我們要坐火車去旅行

季長風：秋影，你住在校外嗎? 離學校遠不遠?
白秋影：不太遠，開車只要五分鐘。
季長風：你每天怎麼來學校?
白秋影：我常騎自行車，下雨下雪的時候就坐公共汽車，有時候我也走路，可以鍛煉鍛煉。你呢?
季長風：我住在宿舍，離學校很近，我每天走路來學校。
白秋影：對了，這個春假你要做什麼?
季長風：我要跟我的室友一起去西部旅行。
白秋影：你們怎麼去?
季長風：我們想先坐火車去，路上看看風景。然後坐船去加拿大，再從加拿大坐飛機回來。你呢?
白秋影：我很想我爸爸、媽媽和妹妹，我要先回家。然後再跟朋友開車去玩兒。
季長風：你們要去哪兒玩兒?
白秋影：我們想去南部玩兒。聽說那兒的海邊景色很美。
季長風：你們有幾個人去?
白秋影：我們一共有五個人去，我們想租一輛車。

第十九课　我感冒了

唐志信：欧阳迎，你吃饭了吗？
欧阳迎：还没有呢。我不饿。
唐志信：你怎么了？好像不舒服。
欧阳迎：我感冒了。我头疼发烧，还有一点儿咳嗽。
唐志信：你怎么生病了呢？
欧阳迎：这几天我有很多考试，每天都在复习，睡觉睡得太少，所以就
　　　　病了。
唐志信：你看医生了没有？
欧阳迎：看了。我也吃药了。可是还没有好呢。
唐志信：你应该在家好好地休息。不应该来上课。
欧阳迎：你说得很对，可是我有很多考试。我得好好地准备。
唐志信：这是我上课的笔记，借给你看看。
欧阳迎：非常感谢！好吧，我现在就回家休息。
唐志信：好，我开车送你回去。你得好好地睡觉。

第十九課　我感冒了

唐志信：歐陽迎，你吃飯了嗎？
歐陽迎：還沒有呢。我不餓。
唐志信：你怎麼了？好像不舒服。
歐陽迎：我感冒了。我頭疼發燒，還有一點兒咳嗽。
唐志信：你怎麼生病了呢？
歐陽迎：這幾天我有很多考試，每天都在復習，睡覺睡得太少，所以就
　　　　病了。
唐志信：你看醫生了沒有？
歐陽迎：看了。我也吃藥了。可是還沒有好呢。
唐志信：你應該在家好好地休息。不應該來上課。
歐陽迎：你說得很對，可是我有很多考試。我得好好地準備。
唐志信：這是我上課的筆記，借給你看看。
歐陽迎：非常感謝！好吧，我現在就回家休息。
唐志信：好，我開車送你回去。你得好好地睡覺。

第二十课　我把小谢带来了 . . .

常　　天：中明，我回来了。我把车开回来了，还把小谢也带来了。
夏中明：是小谢啊！快请他进来。
谢进学：我听说你们这儿有一个人搬出去了，我想搬进来，所以过来看
　　　　看。
常　　天：你不想住宿舍了，是不是？
谢进学：是的。宿舍太小了，我想搬出来住。这儿可以不可以做饭？
夏中明：可以，我们有厨房。
谢进学：太好了！我很喜欢做饭。搬出来以后就可以常常做饭了。
常　　天：你吸烟吗？我们这儿不能吸烟。
谢进学：没关系。以前我吸烟，但是我女朋友说我不应该吸烟，所以我
　　　　现在不吸烟了。
夏中明：还有，我们必须在每个月的第一天付房租。
谢进学：没问题！
常　　天：喂，小谢，我在楼上，你要不要上来看看？中明，你把小谢带
　　　　上来看看吧。
夏中明：常天，我们现在还不能上去，你得先下来帮我把这张桌子搬上
　　　　去。
常　　天：好的，我马上下去。

第二十課　我把小謝帶來了 . . .

常　　天：中明，我回來了。我把車開回來了，還把小謝也帶來了。
夏中明：是小謝啊！快請他進來。
謝進學：我聽說你們這兒有一個人搬出去了，我想搬進來，所以過來看
　　　　看。
常　　天：你不想住宿舍了，是不是？
謝進學：是的。宿舍太小了，我想搬出來住。這兒可以不可以做飯？
夏中明：可以，我們有廚房。
謝進學：太好了！我很喜歡做飯。搬出來以後就可以常常做飯了。
常　　天：你吸煙嗎？我們這兒不能吸煙。
謝進學：沒關係。以前我吸煙，但是我女朋友說我不應該吸煙，所以我
　　　　現在不吸煙了。
夏中明：還有，我們必須在每個月的第一天付房租。
謝進學：沒問題！
常　　天：喂，小謝，我在樓上，你要不要上來看看？中明，你把小謝帶
　　　　上來看看吧。
夏中明：常天，我們現在還不能上去，你得先下來幫我把這張桌子搬上
　　　　去。
常　　天：好的，我馬上下去。

第二十一课　暑假你要做什么？

程海华：秋雨，我问你，你明年就要毕业了，毕业以后你想做什么？
白秋雨：我还没有决定呢。可是我很喜欢学习，我可能会申请研究生院，
　　　　或者去国外留学。你呢？你什么时候毕业？
程海华：我还有两年才毕业呢。毕业以后我想去找工作。
白秋雨：我们就要放暑假了，今年暑假你要做什么？
程海华：我要去打工。我要去一家公司实习。
白秋雨：在哪儿？是什么工作？
程海华：在加州，是一家电脑公司。你呢？暑假你要做什么？
白秋雨：我要去中国，我申请了去上海的暑期班学习，我想一面学中文，
　　　　一面在中国旅行。
程海华：那一定很有意思。你什么时候去？
白秋雨：下个星期。
程海华：这么快！你到中国以后要常常给我写电子邮件。
白秋雨：没问题。我祝你工作愉快！
程海华：我也祝你一路平安！祝你好运！

第二十一课　暑假你要做什麼？

程海華：秋雨，我問你，你明年就要畢業了，畢業以後你想做什麼？
白秋雨：我還沒有決定呢。可是我很喜歡學習，我可能會申請研究生院，
　　　　或者去國外留學。你呢？你什麼時候畢業？
程海華：我還有兩年才畢業呢。畢業以後我想去找工作。
白秋雨：我們就要放暑假了，今年暑假你要做什麼？
程海華：我要去打工。我要去一家公司實習。
白秋雨：在哪兒？是什麼工作？
程海華：在加州，是一家電腦公司。你呢？暑假你要做什麼？
白秋雨：我要去中國，我申請了去上海的暑期班學習，我想一面學中文，
　　　　一面在中國旅行。
程海華：那一定很有意思。你什麼時候去？
白秋雨：下個星期。
程海華：這麼快！你到中國以後要常常給我寫電子郵件。
白秋雨：沒問題。我祝你工作愉快！
程海華：我也祝你一路平安！祝你好運！

第二十二课　我到上海了

海华:

　　你好! 今天是六月十五号, 我一个星期以前就到上海了。对不起, 因为太忙了, 所以今天才给你写电子邮件。

　　我们每天都有很多课, 功课也不少, 不过老师教得很好, 也很认真。我们每天都说中文, 我的中文进步得很快, 现在我已经能说很多中文了。

　　上海是一个非常美丽的城市, 到处都是新的大楼。我们参观了一些地方, 也参加了一些活动, 比如: 看京剧、写书法等等, 都很有意思。还有, 上海有很多好吃的东西, 其中我最喜欢吃的是小笼包, 你有机会应该尝尝。

　　你开始实习了吗? 忙不忙? 有空请给我写电子邮件。

　　　祝

好!

秋雨
二〇〇四年六月十五日

秋雨:

　　你好! 很高兴收到你的电子邮件。看来你在上海过得很开心。

　　我现在在洛杉矶, 已经开始实习了。这儿的同事都很好, 也很热心, 常常教我很多东西, 老板也不错。我的工作有时候忙, 有时候不太忙, 我想我得认真地工作, 才能学到一些东西。

　　好了, 不多写了。有空请多来信, 多保重。

　　　祝

好!

海华
二〇〇四年六月十七日

第二十二課　我到上海了

海華：

　　你好！今天是六月十五號，我一個星期以前就到上海了。對不起，因為太忙了，所以今天才給你寫電子郵件。

　　我們每天都有很多課，功課也不少，不過老師教得很好，也很認真。我們每天都說中文，我的中文進步得很快，現在我已經能說很多中文了。

　　上海是一個非常美麗的城市，到處都是新的大樓。我們參觀了一些地方，也參加了一些活動，比如：看京劇、寫書法等等，都很有意思。還有，上海有很多好吃的東西，其中我最喜歡吃的是小籠包，你有機會應該嚐嚐。

　　你開始實習了嗎？忙不忙？有空請給我寫電子郵件。

　　　祝

好！

　　　　　　　　　　　　　　　　　　　　　　　　秋雨
　　　　　　　　　　　　　　　　　　　　二〇〇四年六月十五日

秋雨：

　　你好！很高興收到你的電子郵件。看來你在上海過得很開心。

　　我現在在洛杉磯，已經開始實習了。這兒的同事都很好，也很熱心，常常教我很多東西，老闆也不錯。我的工作有時候忙，有時候不太忙，我想我得認真地工作，才能學到一些東西。

　　好了，不多寫了。有空請多來信，多保重。

　　　祝

好！

　　　　　　　　　　　　　　　　　　　　　　　　海華
　　　　　　　　　　　　　　　　　　　　二〇〇四年六月十七日

Lesson 1   Hello!

Mary: Hello!
John: Hello!
Mary: Are you a student?
John: I'm a student. How about you?
Mary: I'm also a student.
John: How about him? Is he a student?
Mary: He is not a student. He is a teacher.

Lesson 2   What's Your Surname?

Mary: Hello. May I ask your surname?
John: My family name is Lee. My English name is John Lee. My Chinese name is Wenzhong Li. What's your name?
Mary: I'm Mary. My English name is Mary Wood. My Chinese name is Xiaomei Wu.
John: How about her? Who is she?
Mary: She is my classmate Ying Yu.

Lesson 3   Which Country Are You From?

Wenzhong Li: Xiaomei, how are you?
Xiaomei Wu: I'm fine. By the way, Wenzhong, which country are you from?
Wenzhong Li: I'm French. How about you? Are you American?
Xiaomei Wu: No, I'm not American. I'm British.
Wenzhong Li: How about the teacher?
Xiaomei Wu: He is Chinese. He speaks Chinese.
Wenzhong Li: Can you speak Chinese?
Xiaomei Wu: I can speak a little Chinese. I can also speak French and English.

Lesson 4   What Do You Study?

Xiaomei Wu: Wenzhong, is that your book?
Wenzhong Li: That is my book.
Xiaomei Wu: What book is that?
Wenzhong Li: That is an English book.
Xiaomei Wu: How about this book? What book is this?
Wenzhong Li: This is a Chinese book.
Xiaomei Wu: Well, what do you study?

Wenzhong Li:	I study English literature. How about you?
Xiaomei Wu:	I study engineering.
Wenzhong Li:	Is engineering difficult?
Xiaomei Wu:	Not very difficult. But there is a lot of homework.
Wenzhong Li:	We have a lot of homework too.

Lesson 5　This Is My Friend

Xiaomei Wu:	Wenzhong, come here! Let me introduce you. This is my roommate Hong Wang. This is my friend Wenzhong.
Wenzhong Li:	Hello!
Hong Wang:	Hello! Do you have roommates?
Wenzhong Li:	Yes.
Hong Wang:	How many roommates do you have?
Wenzhong Li:	I have two roommates.
Hong Wang:	Who are they?
Wenzhong Li:	They are Ming Ding and Xiaowen Fang. They are both Chinese. I often speak with them in Chinese.

Lesson 6　My Family

Hi everybody! I'm Xiaomei Wu. I'm from New York. I study engineering. Let me introduce my family. My home is in New York. There are four people in my family: father, mother, elder sister, and I. My father is British. My mother is American. They both work in New York. My father is an engineer. My mother is a teacher. My elder sister and I are both students. She has a boyfriend; I don't. We have two cars and a dog. My family is very nice. I love my family.

Lesson 7　Where Do You Live?

Aiwen Chen:	Youpeng, where do you live?
Youpeng Zhang:	I live in the dorm.
Aiwen Chen:	What's your room number?
Youpeng Zhang:	No. 314.
Aiwen Chen:	Is your room big? Is there a phone?
Youpeng Zhang:	My room is very small. There is a phone.
Aiwen Chen:	What's your phone number?
Youpeng Zhang:	(142) 268-9375
Aiwen Chen:	Do you have a cell phone?
Youpeng Zhang:	Yes. My number is (142) 512-6037. Do you live in the dorm too?
Aiwen Chen:	No, I don't live in the dorm. I live off campus.

Lesson 8 Do You Know Him?

Youpeng Zhang:	Aiwen, where are you going?
Aiwen Chen:	It's you, Youpeng. I'm going to class. How about you?
Youpeng Zhang:	I'm going to class too. Do you have any plans for after class?
Aiwen Chen:	No. I'd like to go back to the dorm. What's up?
Youpeng Zhang:	Do you know my friend Xiao Wen?
Aiwen Chen:	I know him. We take English literature together.
Youpeng Zhang:	I'm going to have dinner with him after class. Will you come?
Aiwen Chen:	Great! Where are we going?
Youpeng Zhang:	Do you want to have Korean food?
Aiwen Chen:	Yes. But I also want to have Japanese food.
Youpeng Zhang:	Let's have Korean food today. Next time we'll have Japanese food. How is that?
Aiwen Chen:	OK. See you after class.
Youpeng Zhang:	See you.

Lesson 9 He Is Making a Phone Call

Situation 1 Please Hold

Aiwen Chen:	Hello! This is Aiwen. Is Youpeng in now?
Shucheng Fang:	Yes, he is in his room. Please hold. Hey, Youpeng, the phone is for you.
Youpeng Zhang:	Got it! Thank you!
Youpeng Zhang:	Hello! This is Youpeng. You must be Aiwen!
Aiwen Chen:	Right, it's me. Are you busy?
Youpeng Zhang:	No. I'm watching TV. What are you doing?
Aiwen Chen:	I'm online.

Situation 2 Speaking

Aiwen Chen:	Hello!
Youpeng Zhang:	Hello!
Aiwen Chen:	Is Youpeng in?
Youpeng Zhang:	Speaking. May I ask who is calling?
Aiwen Chen:	It's Aiwen.

Situation 3 Please Leave a Message

Aiwen Chen:	Hello! Is Youpeng in?
Ding Ming:	Sorry, he is not here. He is in class.
Aiwen Chen:	When will he be back?
Ding Ming:	Tonight. Do you want to leave a message?
Aiwen Chen:	OK. I'm Aiwen. My phone number is (142) 268-9753. Please ask him to call back when he returns. Thank you!
Ding Ming:	My pleasure. Goodbye.

Lesson 10   I Get Up at 7:30 Every Day

Xiao Ming,

   How are you?

   I'm very busy this semester. I have five classes. Can you guess when I get up and go to bed every day? I get up at 7:30, and go to bed after 12:00. I'm very busy every day. I walk from the dorm to class at 9:15 every morning. Class is over at 10:20. Then I go to the library to study. In the afternoon after class, I like to play basketball. I have lots of homework every day.

   This is my college life. How about you? Send me a letter. My e-mail address is xuewen376@zhongwen.edu.

   Wish you all the best.

Xuewen
Nov. 20, 2003

Lesson 11   Do You Want Black Tea or Green Tea?

Waitress:	How many?
Zhenran Zhang:	Three.
Waitress:	OK. Please follow me. Sit down, please.
Zhenran Zhang, Xinmei Sun, Huan Yang:	Thank you.
Waitress:	Miss, sir, what would you like to drink?
Xinmei Sun:	I would like tea.
Waitress:	Black tea or green tea?
Xinmei Sun:	Iced black tea, please.
Huan Yang:	Coke for me, please.
Zhenran Zhang:	I'd like to have a bottle of beer.
Waitress:	OK, iced tea, Coke, and a bottle of beer. Won't be a moment.
Zhenran Zhang:	Well. Do you want to have rice or noodles?
Xinmei Sun:	I like both.
Huan Yang:	I want to have dumplings.
Waitress:	These are your iced tea, Coke, and beer. Would you like to order food?
Zhenran Zhang:	OK. Let's have one fried rice, one fried noodles, and twenty dumplings.
Xinmei Sun:	We also want soup for three. And we would like to have three pairs of chopsticks too. Thanks.

Lesson 12   May I Borrow Your Car?

Xin Yu:	Benle, will you use your car tomorrow afternoon?
Benle Wang:	No. What's up?
Xin Yu:	I need to go to the airport to pick somebody up. May I borrow your car?
Benle Wang:	Sure. Who are you picking up?
Xin Yu:	My younger sister and her boyfriend. They are flying to Los Angeles from Shanghai to do some sightseeing. They arrive tomorrow.

Benle Wang:	My car has a manual transmission. Do you know how to drive it?
Xin Yu:	There should be no problem. My dad's car also has a manual transmission. I often drove his car.
Benle Wang:	My car is white. The plate number is BD5730, and it is parked at the parking lot No. 5.
Xin Yu:	I see. Thanks!
Benle Wang:	You are welcome. Does your sister speak English?
Xin Yu:	A little bit. This time they want to learn some English.
Benle Wang:	Great! I should practice some Chinese with them. That way, my Chinese will make progress.

Lesson 13　I Want to Buy a Shirt

Sales:	What would you like to buy?
Aihong Mao:	I want to buy a shirt.
Ziying Fang:	I want to buy a skirt or pants.
Sales:	How about this yellow shirt?
Aihong Mao:	Good. But I like black better. Do you have black ones?
Sales:	Yes, here. Have a try.
Ziying Fang:	Aihong, come and have a look. Would I look good in this shirt or pants?
Aihong Mao:	Put them on and let me have a look. I think you look good in this shirt.
Ziying Fang:	How much is this shirt?
Sales:	Fifteen dollars.
Ziying Fang:	OK, I'll buy it.
Aihong Mao:	I'll take this shirt too.
Sales:	Well, miss, is this movie ticket yours?
Ziying Fang:	Yes, thank you! The ticket is mine. We are going to see a movie later.

Lesson 14　I Am 20 This Year

Ziying Fang:	Aihong, will you be free on February 18?
Aihong Mao:	What day of the week is February 18?
Ziying Fang:	It's a Saturday.
Aihong Mao:	I'll be free. Do you have anything in mind?
Ziying Fang:	It's my birthday. My boyfriend is having a party for me. I'd like to invite you.
Aihong Mao:	Thank you. I'll definitely come. Who else is coming?
Ziying Fang:	We want to invite all our classmates and friends.
Aihong Mao:	I know how to make cake. I'll make a cake for you, how's that?
Ziying Fang:	Great! Thank you!
Aihong Mao:	You're welcome. How old are you?
Ziying Fang:	I'll be twenty this year. How about you? When's your birthday?
Aihong Mao:	My birthday is October 3. I'm twenty-two. Where will the party be held?
Ziying Fang:	At my boyfriend's place. This is his address. Do you know how to get there?
Aihong Mao:	No problem. I have a map. See you at 5:00 Saturday afternoon.
Ziying Fang:	See you.

Lesson 15　The Library Is in Front of the Dorm

(At the students' dorm)

Jin Tian:	Hello! Welcome to my dorm. Please follow me.
Yuansheng Liang:	Jin Tian, is there a kitchen in your dorm?
Jin Tian:	Yes, it's shared.
Zhizhong Bao:	Where is your room?
Jin Tian:	My room is on that side. Go this way. Come, please come in! This is the living room. The dining room is on the opposite side.
Yuansheng Liang:	Where is the bathroom?
Jin Tian:	The bathroom is between the living room and the bedroom. Look, this is my bedroom.
Zhizhong Bao:	Are all the Chinese books on the table yours?
Jin Tian:	No. Some are mine, some are my friends'.
Zhizhong Bao:	Do you often study in your dorm?
Jin Tian:	No, I don't often study in the dorm. I usually go to study in the library.
Yuansheng Liang:	Where is the library?
Jin Tian:	The library is in front of the dorm. At the back of the library there is a park. I often go there to play ball.
Yuansheng Liang and Zhizhong Bao:	Your dorm is very nice.

Lesson 16　She Plays Basketball Very Well

Zhengran Zhang:	Where are you going?
Xinmei Sun and Huan Yang:	We are going to play basketball.
Zhengran Zhang:	Are you good at it?
Xinmei Sun:	Huan Yang plays very well. I'm not very good at it. She is my coach. She coaches me very well.
Huan Yang:	No, I don't play very well.
Zhengran Zhang:	I don't play basketball often. I usually go swimming with my roommate. He swims really fast!
Huan Yang:	Where do you usually go?
Zhengran Zhang:	The swimming pool in the gym. And we also exercise often in the gym.
Xinmei Sun:	Do you want to come to play basketball with us?
Zhengran Zhang:	Not now. I stayed up too late watching the game last night, so I got up very late this morning. Now I have to do homework.
Huan Yang:	Yesterday we made dumplings and Chinese food. Come to our place to eat dumplings tonight.
Zhengran Zhang:	Great. I like dumplings very much. Do you make dumplings quickly?
Xinme Sun:	No, we are very slow.
Huan Yang:	Xinmei is very good at cooking. She cooks very well.

Lesson 17   Spring Is Coming Soon

Xiao Ling:

Long time no see. How are you? Time is flying by. Spring is coming. And we will have spring break soon.

We have four seasons here. I like spring most. It's warm, but very short. In the summer, sometimes it's very hot. On the hottest days, the temperature usually reaches 100°F. So hot! In the fall, sometimes it is rainy and windy. Winter is very cold here, with lots of snow.

I plan to go to your place during spring break. We'll meet soon.

Best wishes.

Dazhong
Mar. 10, 2004

Lesson 18   We Are Going to Take a Train Trip

Ji Changfeng:	Qiuying, do you live off campus? Is it far from school?
Bai Qiuying:	Not too far. Only a five-minute drive.
Ji Changfeng:	How do you get to school each day?
Bai Qiuying:	I usually ride a bike. When it is raining or snowing, I take the bus. Sometimes I walk, which gives me some exercise. How about you?
Ji Changfeng:	I live in the dorm, which is very close to school. I walk to school every day.
Bai Qiuying:	Well, what will you do during the spring break?
Ji Changfeng:	I'll travel to the West with my roommates.
Bai Qiuying:	How will you go?
Ji Changfeng:	We want to go by train. We would like to do some sightseeing on the road. Then we'll go to Canada by boat. Finally, from Canada, we'll take a plane back home. How about you?
Bai Qiuying:	I miss my parents and sister very much. I'll go home first. Then I'll drive somewhere with my friends.
Ji Changfeng:	Where do you want to go?
Bai Qiuying:	We'd like to go to the South. It is said that the shore is beautiful there.
Ji Changfeng:	How many people will go with you?
Bai Qiuying:	There are five people. We want to rent a car.

Lesson 19   I Caught a Cold

Zhixin Tang:	Ouyang Ying, have you eaten yet?
Ouyang Ying:	Not yet. I'm not hungry.
Zhixin Tang:	What's wrong? You look sick.
Ouyang Ying:	I have a cold. I have a headache, a fever, and a bit of a cough.
Zhixin Tang:	How did you get sick?
Ouyang Ying:	I had lots of exams these past few days. Every day I revised a lot and didn't get enough sleep. So I'm sick.

Zhixin Tang:	Did you see the doctor?
Ouyang Ying:	Yes. I took pills. But it's not over yet.
Zhixin Tang:	You should stay at home and get some rest. You shouldn't come to class.
Ouyang Ying:	You are right. But I have lots of exams. I have to be well prepared.
Zhixin Tang:	These are my class notes. You may borrow them.
Ouyang Ying:	Thanks a lot. I'd better go home and get some rest.
Zhixin Tang:	OK, I'll drive you home. You should sleep well.

Lesson 20　　I've Brought Xiao Xie Over . . .

Tian Chang:	Zhongming, I'm back. I drove the car back, and I also brought Xiao Xie over.
Zhongming Xia:	Oh, it's Xiao Xie! Ask him to come in.
Jinxue Xie:	I heard that one of your roommates moved out. I want to move in. So here I am to have a look.
Tian Chang:	You don't want to live in the dorm any more, right?
Jinxue Xie:	Yes. The dorm is too small. I want to move out. Can you cook here?
Zhongming Xia:	Yes. We have a kitchen.
Jinxue Xie:	Great. I like to cook. After moving out of the dorm, I could cook often.
Tian Chang:	Do you smoke? It's non-smoking here.
Jinxue Xie:	It's OK. I used to smoke, but my girlfriend said I shouldn't, so I quit.
Zhongming Xia:	And, we have to pay the rent on the 1st of each month.
Jinxue Xie:	No problem.
Tian Chang:	Hi, Xiao Xie, I'm upstairs. Don't you want to come up to have a look? Zhongming, bring Xiao Xie up here.
Zhongming Xia:	Tian Chang, we can't come up now. You'd better come down to help me move the table up first.
Tian Chang:	OK. I will come down immediately.

Lesson 21　　What Will You Do During the Summer Vacation?

Haihua Cheng:	Qiuyu, let me ask you, you'll graduate next year. What will you do after graduation?
Qiuyu Bai:	I haven't decided yet. But I love to study. I'll probably apply for graduate school, or go to study abroad. How about you? When will you graduate?
Haihua Cheng:	I still have two more years to go. After graduation, I want to find a job.
Qiuyu Bai:	We'll have summer vacation soon. What will you do this summer?
Haihua Cheng:	I'll work. I have a summer internship with a company.
Qiuyu Bai:	Where? What kind of job?
Haihua Cheng:	In California, a computer company. How about you? What will you do this summer?
Qiuyu Bai:	I'll go to China. I applied for a summer class in Shanghai. I want to learn some Chinese, and at the same time do some traveling in China.
Haihua Cheng:	It must be very interesting. When will you leave?
Qiuyu Bai:	Next week.

Haihua Cheng: So fast! E-mail me often after you arrive in China.
Qiuyu Bai: No problem. Have a good time working!
Haihua Cheng: Have a safe journey, and good luck!

Lesson 22   I Have Arrived in Shanghai

Haihua,

　　How are you? Today is June 15. I arrived in Shanghai a week ago. Sorry, I've been too busy to write you an e-mail before today.

　　We have many classes every day, and lots of homework too. The instructor is good and very conscientious. We speak Chinese every day. My Chinese has improved greatly. Now I can speak lots of Chinese.

　　Shanghai is a beautiful city, with new buildings everywhere. We visited some places, as well as attending some activities, including watching Peking Opera, writing calligraphy, etc. All very interesting! And, there is a lot of good food here. Of all the food, I love the little steamed buns the best. You should have a taste some time.

　　Have you begun your internship yet? Are you busy? When you have time, please e-mail me.

　　Best wishes.

Qiuyu
June 15, 2004

Qiuyu:

　　How are you? I was so glad to get your e-mail. It seems you are very happy in Shanghai.

　　I've begun my internship in Los Angeles. My colleagues here are all very nice and warmhearted. They are teaching me many things. The boss is nice too. I'm busy from time to time. I believe I will work hard to learn more things.

　　OK, I should stop here. Write to me more when you have time. Take care.

　　Best wishes.

Haihua
June 17, 2004

Each entry lists Pinyin, simplified character, traditional character, part of speech, English meaning, and lesson number.

Note: The letter "s" means that the entry occurs in the supplementary vocabulary to that lesson.

A

a	啊	啊	*Int.*	(used at the end of a sentence to indicate surprise)	20
āyí	阿姨	阿姨	*N.*	aunt (mother's sister)	6s
ài	爱	愛	*V.*	to love	6
áoyè	熬夜	熬夜	*V.O.*	to burn the midnight oil	10s

B

ba	吧	吧	*Part.*	(indicates an assumption or suggestion)	9
bā	八/捌	八/捌	*Num.*	eight	7
bǎ	把	把	*Prep.*	(introduces the object of a verb)	20
bàba	爸爸	爸爸	*N.*	father	6
bái	白	白	*Adj.*	white	12
báifàn	白饭	白飯	*N.*	steamed rice	11s
báisè	白色	白色	*Adj.*	white	13s
bǎi	百	百	*Num.*	hundred	17
bān	搬	搬	*V.*	to move	20
	班	班	*N.*	class	21
bàn	半	半	*Adj.*	half	10
bāng	帮	幫	*V.*	to help	13
bàng	棒	棒	*Adj.*	wonderful	14
bàngqiú	棒球	棒球	*N.*	baseball	16s
bāo	包	包	*V.*	to wrap	16
bǎozhòng	保重	保重		Take care.	22s
bēi	杯	杯	*M.W.*	cup	11
běi	北	北	*N.*	north	18s
bèixīn	背心	背心	*N.*	vest	13s
běn	本	本	*M.W.*	(measure word for book)	4
bǐjì	笔记	筆記	*N.*	notes	19
bǐjiào	比较	比較	*Adv.*	relatively	13
bǐrú	比如	比如	*Conj.*	for example	22
bìxū	必须	必須	*Aux.*	must	20

bìyè	毕业	畢業	*V.*	to graduate	21
biǎodì	表弟	表弟	*N.*	cousin (son of parents' sister or mother's brother) (younger than the speaker)	6s
biǎodìmèi	表弟妹	表弟妹	*N.*	cousin (wife of 表弟)	6s
biǎogē	表哥	表哥	*N.*	cousin (son of parents' sister or mother's brother) (older than the speaker)	6s
biǎojiě	表姐	表姐	*N.*	cousin (daughter of parents' sister or mother's brother) (older than the speaker)	6s
biǎojiěfu	表姐夫	表姐夫	*N.*	cousin (husband of 表姐)	6s
biǎomèi	表妹	表妹	*N.*	cousin (daughter of parents' sister or mother's brother) (younger than the speaker)	6s
biǎomèifu	表妹夫	表妹夫	*N.*	cousin (husband of 表妹)	6s
biǎosǎo	表嫂	表嫂	*N.*	cousin (wife of 表哥)	6s
bīng	冰	冰	*N.*	ice	11
bīngqiú	冰球	冰球	*N.*	ice hockey	16s
bǐnggān	饼干	餅乾	*N.*	cracker	11s
bìngdú	病毒	病毒	*N.*	virus	9s
bóbo	伯伯	伯伯	*N.*	uncle (father's elder brother)	6s
bómǔ	伯母	伯母	*N.*	aunt (wife of father's elder brother)	6s
bóshì	博士	博士	*N.*	doctoral degree	21s
bóshìshēng	博士生	博士生	*N.*	doctoral students	21s
bù	不	不	*Adv.*	not, no (used to form a negative)	1
búcuò	不错	不錯		not bad; pretty good	13
búguò	不过	不過	*Conj.*	but, however	22
búkèqi	不客气	不客氣		you're welcome; don't mention it (in reply to thank you)	9s, 14
búxiè	不谢	不謝		you're welcome; don't mention it (in reply to thank you)	9s

C

cái	才	才	*Adv.*	(used before a verb to indicate that something is rather late by general standards or something has just happened)	10
cǎisè	彩色	彩色	*Adj.*	multicolor	13s
cài	菜	菜	*N.*	dish	8
càidān	菜单	菜單	*N.*	menu	11s

cānguān	参观	參觀	*V.*	to visit	15
cānguǎn	餐馆	餐館	*N.*	restaurant	11s
cānjiā	参加	參加	*V.*	to participate, join	14
cāntīng	餐厅	餐廳	*N.*	restaurant, dining room	11s, 15
cǎoméi	草莓	草莓	*N.*	strawberry	11s
chá	茶	茶	*N.*	tea	11
chà	差	差	*V.*	to lack	10s
cháng	常	常	*Adv.*	often; frequently	5
	长	長	*Adj.*	long	17s
chángchang	尝尝	嚐嚐	*V.*	to have a try, taste	22
chángjiàn	常见	常見	*Adj.*	common	11s
chángkù	长裤	長褲	*N.*	long pants	13s
chǎo	炒	炒	*V.*	to stir fry	11
chē	车	車	*N.*	car	6
chēzhàn	车站	車站	*N.*	stop, station	18s
chènshān	衬衫	襯衫	*N.*	shirt	13
chēngwèi	称谓	稱謂	*N.*	form of address	6s
chéngsè	橙色	橙色	*Adj.*	orange	13s
(júsè)	(橘色)	(橘色)			
chéngshì	城市	城市	*N.*	city	22
chéngxùyuán	程序员	程序員	*N.*	computer programmer	6s
(chéngshì shèjìshī)	(程式设计师)	(程式設計師)			
chéngzhī	橙汁	橙汁	*N.*	orange juice	11s
chī	吃	吃	*V.*	to eat	8
chīfàn	吃饭	吃飯	*V.O.*	to eat, have a meal	8
chīyào	吃药	吃藥	*V.O.*	to take medicine	19
chǒngwù	宠物	寵物	*N.*	pet	6s
chū	出	出	*V.*	to be out	20
chūqù	出去	出去	*V.C.*	to go out	20
chūzūqìchē	出租汽车	出租汽車	*N.*	taxi	18s
(jìchéngchē)	(计程车)	(計程車)			
chúfáng	厨房	廚房	*N.*	kitchen	15
chuān	穿	穿	*V.*	to wear, put on (regular clothes)	13, 13s
chuānshàng	穿上	穿上	*V.C.*	to put on (regular clothes)	13s
chuán	船	船	*N.*	ship	18
chuānghu	窗户	窗戶	*N.*	window	15s
chuáng	床	床	*N.*	bed	15s
chūnjià	春假	春假	*N.*	spring break	17
chūnjuǎn	春卷	春捲	*N.*	spring roll	11s
chūntiān	春天	春天	*N.*	spring	17
cífú tiělù	磁浮铁路	磁浮鐵路	*N.*	magnetic railway	18s
cóng	从	從	*Prep.*	from	6

D

dǎ diànhuà	打电话	打電話	V.O.	to make a phone call	9
dǎcuòle	打错了	打錯了		to dial a wrong number	9s
dǎgōng	打工	打工	V.O.	to work for others, be employed	21
dǎqiú	打球	打球	V.O.	to play basketball/badminton/ tennis/table tennis	10
dǎzhēn	打针	打針	V.O.	to give or receive an injection	13s, 19s
dà	大	大	Adj.	big, large	7, 13s
dàhuòchē	大货车	大貨車	N.	truck	18s
dàjiā	大家	大家	Pron.	all, everybody	6
dàlóu	大楼	大樓	N.	tall building	22
dàxué	大学	大學	N.	college; university	10
dàxuéshēng	大学生	大學生	N.	college student(s)	6s, 21s
dàyī	大衣	大衣	N.	overcoat	13s
dài	戴	戴	V.	to wear, put on (accessories)	13s
dàilái	带来	帶來	V.C.	to bring over	20
dàishàng	戴上	戴上	V.C.	to put on (accessories)	13s
dānchē (jiǎotàchē)	单车 (脚踏车)	單車 (腳踏車)	N.	bicycle	18s
dàngāo	蛋糕	蛋糕	N.	cake	11s, 14
dànjì	淡季	淡季	N.	off-season	18s
dànshì	但是	但是	Conj.	but	20
dǎoyóu	导游	導遊	N.	tourist guide	6s
dào	到	到	V.	to arrive	12
dàochù	到处	到處	Adv.	everywhere	22
de	的	的	Part.	(a structural particle)	2
	得	得	Part.	(used between a verb or an adjective and its complement to indicate result, possibility or degree)	16
	地	地	Part.	(attached to an adjective to transform the whole unit into an adverb)	19
Déguó	德国	德國	N.	Germany	3s
Déguórén	德国人	德國人	N.	German (person)	3s
Déyǔ (Déwén)	德语 (德文)	德語 (德文)	N.	German (language)	3s
děi	得	得	Aux.	must; have to	12
děng	等	等	V.	to wait	9
děng yíxiàr	等一下儿	等一下兒		to wait for a moment	9
dìdi	弟弟	弟弟	N.	younger brother	6s

dìfang	地方	地方	N.	place	22
dìtú	地图	地圖	N.	map	14
dìtiě	地铁	地鐵	N.	subway	18s
dìxiàdào	地下道	地下道	N.	underground passage	18s
dìyītiān	第一天	第一天	N.	first day	20
dìzhǐ	地址	地址	N.	address	10
diǎn	点	點	M.W.	o'clock (point on clock)	10
diǎncài	点菜	點菜	V.O.	to order food	11s
diǎnzhōng	点钟	點鐘	M.W.	hour	10s
diànhuà	电话	電話	N.	phone	7
diànnǎo	电脑	電腦	N.	computer	21
diànnǎo yóuxì	电脑游戏	電腦遊戲	N.	computer game	9s
diànshì	电视	電視	N.	television	9
diànyǐng	电影	電影	N.	movie	9s, 13
diànyuán	店员	店員	N.	salesman; saleswoman	13
diànzǐ yóujiàn	电子邮件	電子郵件	N.	email	10
diàoyú	钓鱼	釣魚	V.O.	to fish	16s
dōng	冬	冬	N.	winter	17
	东	東	N.	east	18s
dōngxi	东西	東西	N.	thing	22
dòngzuò	动作	動作	N.	action	13s
dōu	都	都	Adv.	all; both	5
dòufu	豆腐	豆腐	N.	bean curd	11s
dù	度	度	N.	degree	17
duǎn	短	短	Adj.	short	17
duǎnkù	短裤	短褲	N.	shorts	13s
duànliàn	锻炼	鍛煉	V.	to exercise	16
duì	对	對	Adj.	correct, right	9
duìbuqǐ	对不起	對不起		sorry, I'm sorry; Excuse me.	9, 22
duìle	对了	對了		by the way (a phrase used to start a new topic)	3
duìmiàn	对面	對面	N.	opposite	15
duō	多	多	Adj.	many, much	4
duōdà	多大	多大		how old	14
duōshǎo	多少	多少	Pron.	how many, how much	7

E

è	饿	餓	Adj.	hungry	19
			V.	to starve	3
ér	儿	兒		(retroflex ending)	3
ěrhuán	耳环	耳環	N.	earrings	13s
èr	二/贰	二/貳	Num.	two	7

F

fā duǎnxìn	发短信	發短信	*V.O.*	to send a short (cell phone)	9s
(sòng jiǎnxùn)	(送简讯)	(送簡訊)		message	
fāshāo	发烧	發燒	*V.O.*	to have a fever	19
Fǎguó	法国	法國	*N.*	France	3
Fǎwén	法文	法文	*N.*	French (language)	3
fàn	饭	飯	*N.*	cooked rice; meal	8
fàndiàn	饭店	飯店	*N.*	restaurant	11s
fànguǎn	饭馆	飯館	*N.*	restaurant	11s
fángdìchǎn gùwèn	房地产顾问	房地產顧問	*N.*	real estate agent	6s
fángdōng	房东	房東	*N.*	landlord	20s
fángjiān	房间	房間	*N.*	room	7
fángkè	房客	房客	*N.*	tenant	20s
fángzū	房租	房租	*N.*	rent	20
fángzi	房子	房子	*N.*	house; room	7s
fàng	放	放	*V.*	to have, start (a vacation)	17
fàngjià	放假	放假	*V.O.*	to have vacation	17s
fēicháng	非常	非常	*Adv.*	very	16
fēijī	飞机	飛機	*N.*	airplane	12
fēixíngyuán	飞行员	飛行員	*N.*	pilot	6s
fēn	分	分	*N.*	minute; 100 fen = 10 jiao/ 10 mao = 1 yuan/1 kuai	10, 13s
fēnzhōng	分钟	分鐘	*N.*	minute	10s, 18
fěnhóngsè	粉红色	粉紅色	*Adj.*	pink	13s
fēngjǐng	风景	風景	*N.*	scenery	18
fúwùyuán	服务员	服務員	*N.*	waiter/waitress	11
fǔxiū	辅修	輔修	*N.*	minor	4s
fù	付	付	*V.*	to pay	20
fùxí	复习	復習	*V.*	to review	19

G

gānjìng	干净	乾淨	*Adj.*	clean	15s
gǎnlǎnqiú	橄榄球	橄欖球	*N.*	football	16s
gǎnmào	感冒	感冒	*N.*	cold, flu	19
gǎnxiè	感谢	感謝	*V.*	to thank, be grateful	19
Gǎngbì	港币	港幣	*N.*	currency of Hong Kong	13s
gāo'ěrfūqiú	高尔夫球	高爾夫球	*N.*	golf	16s
gāoxìng	高兴	高興	*Adj.*	happy	22
gēge	哥哥	哥哥	*N.*	elder brother	6s
gè	个	個	*M.W.*	(the most commonly used measure word for cups, buildings, characters, etc.)	5

gěi	给	給	*Prep.*	for, to	9
			V.	to give	
gēn	跟	跟	*Prep.*	with	5
gōngchē	公车	公車	*N.*	bus	18s
(bāshì)	(巴士)	(巴士)			
gōngchéng	工程	工程	*N.*	engineering	4
gōngchéngshī	工程师	工程師	*N.*	engineer	6, 6s
gōnggòngqìchē	公共汽车	公共汽車	*N.*	bus	18
gōngkè	功课	功課	*N.*	homework; assignment	4
gōngsī	公司	公司	*N.*	company	21
gōngyù	公寓	公寓	*N.*	apartment	7s
gōngyòng	公用	公用	*Adj.*	for public use, communal	15
gōngyuán	公园	公園	*N.*	park	15
gōngzuò	工作	工作	*N.*	job	6
			V.	to work	6
gǒu	狗	狗	*N.*	dog	6
gūfù	姑父	姑父	*N.*	uncle (husband of father's sister)	6s
gūgu	姑姑	姑姑	*N.*	aunt (father's sister)	6s
gūmā	姑妈	姑媽	*N.*	aunt (father's sister)	6s
gūzhàng	姑丈	姑丈	*N.*	uncle (husband of father's sister)	6s
gùwèn	顾问	顧問	*N.*	consultant	6s
guāfēng	刮风	刮風	*V.O.*	to blow (wind)	17
guānyuán	官员	官員	*N.*	government official	6s
guì	贵	貴	*Adj.*	noble, honored; expensive	2, 13s
guó	国	國	*N.*	country	3
guówài	国外	國外	*N.*	overseas, abroad	21
guǒzhī	果汁	果汁	*N.*	juice	11s
guò	过	過	*V.*	to pass, to spend (life, time); celebrate (e.g., birthday)	10s, 14, 17
guòlái	过来	過來	*V.C.*	to come over	20

H

hái hǎo	还好	還好		not bad; okay	4s
háishì	还是	還是	*Conj.*	or	11
háizi	孩子	孩子	*N.*	child	6s
hǎibiān	海边	海邊	*N.*	seaside	18
hǎitān	海滩	海灘	*N.*	seashore	18s
hǎixiān	海鲜	海鮮	*N.*	seafood	11s
Hánguó	韩国	韓國	*N.*	Korea	3s, 8
Hánguórén	韩国人	韓國人	*N.*	Korean (person)	3s
hánjià	寒假	寒假	*N.*	winter vacation	17s
Hányǔ	韩语	韓語	*N.*	Korean (language)	3s
(Hánwén)	(韩文)	(韓文)			

Hànyǔ	汉语	漢語	*N.*	Chinese (language)	2s
hǎo	好	好	*Adj.*	good; well	1
hǎokàn	好看	好看	*Adj.*	good looking	13
hǎoxiàng	好像	好像	*V.*	to be like, seem	19
hǎoyùn	好运	好運		Good luck.	21
hào	号	號	*N.*	number, size	7, 13s
hàomǎ	号码	號碼	*N.*	number	7
hē	喝	喝	*V.*	to drink	11
hé	和	和	*Conj.*	and	3
hēi	黑	黑	*Adj.*	black	13
hēisè	黑色	黑色	*Adj.*	black	13s
hěn	很	很	*Adv.*	very, quite	3
hóng	红	紅	*Adj.*	red	11
hóngsè	红色	紅色	*Adj.*	red	13s
hòubiān	后边	後邊	*N.*	behind, at the back	15
hùshi	护士	護士	*N.*	nurse	6s, 19s
huábīng	滑冰	滑冰	*V.O.*	to skate	16s
huáchuán	划船	划船	*V.O.*	to row	16s
huáshì	华氏	華氏	*N.*	Fahrenheit	17
huáxuě	滑雪	滑雪	*V.O.*	to snow ski	16s
huānyíng	欢迎	歡迎	*V.*	to welcome	15
huáng	黄	黃	*Adj.*	yellow	13
huángsè	黄色	黃色	*Adj.*	yellow	13s
huīsè	灰色	灰色	*Adj.*	gray	13s
huí	回	回	*V.*	to return	8
huílai	回来	回來	*V.C.*	to return	9
huì	会	會	*Aux.*	can, be able to	3
húntun	馄饨	餛飩	*N.*	wonton	11s
huódòng	活动	活動	*N.*	activity	22
huǒchē	火车	火車	*N.*	train	18, 18s
huòbì	货币	貨幣	*N.*	currency	13s
huòzhě	或者	或者	*Conj.*	or; either . . . or . . .	13

J

jīchǎng	机场	機場	*N.*	airport	12
jīhuì	机会	機會	*N.*	opportunity	22
jīròu	鸡肉	雞肉	*N.*	chicken	11s
jí	极	極	*Adv.*	extremely	17
jípǔchē	吉普车	吉普車	*N.*	jeep	18s
jǐ	几	幾		how many	5
jǐ hào	几号	幾號		which size	13s
jìsuànjī (diànnǎo)	计算机 (电脑)	計算機 (電腦)	*N.*	computer	4s
jiā	家	家	*N.*	home; family	6

			M.W.	(measure word for company, enterprises, store, etc.)	21
Jiānádà	加拿大	加拿大	N.	Canada	3s
Jiānádàrén	加拿大人	加拿大人	N.	Canadian (person)	3s
jiātíng zhǔfù	家庭主妇	家庭主婦	N.	housewife	6s
Jiāzhōu	加州	加州	N.	California (state)	21
jiákèshān (jiákè)	夹克衫 (夹克)	夾克衫 (夾克)	N.	jacket	13s
jiàqī	假期	假期	N.	holiday	17s
jiǎnlì (lǚlìbiǎo)	简历 (履历表)	簡歷 (履歷表)	N.	resume	21s
jiàn	见	見	V.	to see	8
	件	件	M.W.	(measure word for clothes)	13
jiànkāng	健康	健康	Adj.	healthy	22s
jiànmiàn	见面	見面	V.O.	to meet each other	17
jiànshēnfáng	健身房	健身房	N.	gym	16
jiànzhùshī	建筑师	建築師	N.	architect	6s
jiāo	教	教	V.	to teach, coach	16
jiǎo	角	角	N.	(10 角 = 1 元)	13s
jiǎozi	饺子	餃子	N.	dumpling (crescent shaped)	11
jiào	叫	叫	V.	to call	2
jiàoliàn	教练	教練	N.	coach, trainer	16
jiàoshì	教室	教室	N.	classroom	15s
jiàoshòu	教授	教授	N.	professor	6s
jiàoyù gōngzuòzhě	教育工作者	教育工作者	N.	educator	6s
jiē	接	接	V.	to pick up	12
jiéyùn	捷运	捷運	N.	MRT (Mass Rapid Transportation) in Taiwan	18s
jiézhàng (jiézhàng)	结账 (结帐)	結賬 (結帳)	V.O.	to settle the account	11s
jiějie	姐姐	姐姐	N.	older sister	6
jiè	借	借	V.	to borrow	12
jièshào	介绍	介紹	V.	to introduce	5
			N.	introduction	5
jièzhi	戒指	戒指	N.	ring	13s
jīnhuángsè	金黄色	金黃色	Adj.	gold	13s
jīntiān	今天	今天	N.	today	8
jìn	近	近	Adj.	near	18
	进	進	V.	to enter	20
jìnbù	进步	進步	V.	to improve	12
jīngjìrén	经纪人	經紀人	N.	agent	6s
jīngjìshī	经济师	經濟師	N.	economist	6s
jīngjù	京剧	京劇	N.	Peking opera	22
jīnglǐ	经理	經理	N.	manager	6s
jǐngsè	景色	景色	N.	scenery; view	18

lǎolao	姥姥	姥姥	*N.*	maternal grandmother	6s
lǎoshī	老师	老師	*N.*	teacher	1, 6s
lǎoye	姥爷	老爺	*N.*	maternal grandfather	6s
le	了	了	*Part.*	(indicates assumption)	9
lèi	累	累	*Adj.*	tired	4s
lěng	冷	冷	*Adj.*	cold	17
lí	离	離	*V.*	to be off, away, from	18
lízi	梨子	梨子	*N.*	pear	11s
lǐbiān	里边	裡邊	*N.*	inside	15
lǐwù	礼物	禮物	*N.*	gift	14s
lìhài	厉害	厲害	*Adj.*	severely, very much	19s
liǎ	俩	倆		two people (colloquial)	16
liànxí	练习	練習	*V.*	to practice	12
liáotiānshì	聊天室	聊天室	*N.*	chat room	9s
liáng	凉	涼	*Adj.*	cool	11s
liángxié	凉鞋	涼鞋	*N.*	sandles	13s
liǎng	两	兩	*Num.*	two	5
liàng	辆	輛	*M.W.*	(measure word for vehicles)	6
líng	〇/零	〇/零	*Num.*	zero	7s
lǐngdài	领带	領帶	*N.*	necktie	13s
liúgǎn (liúxíngxìng gǎnmào)	流感 (流行性感冒)	流感 (流行性感冒)	*N.*	flu	19s
liúgǎn yìmiáo	流感疫苗	流感疫苗	*N.*	flu shot	19s
liú xuéshēng	留学生	留學生	*N.*	international students	6s
liúxué	留学	留學	*V.O.*	to study abroad	21
liúyán (liúhuà)	留言 (留话)	留言 (留話)	*V.O.*	to leave a message	9
liǔchéngzhī (liǔdīngzhī)	柳橙汁 (柳丁汁)	柳橙汁 (柳丁汁)	*N.*	tangerine juice	11s
liù	六/陆	六/陸	*Num.*	six	7
lóushàng	楼上	樓上	*N.*	upstairs	20
luàn	乱	亂	*Adj.*	messy	15s
lǚxíng	旅行	旅行	*V.*	to travel	18
lǜ	绿	綠	*Adj.*	green	11
lǜsè	绿色	綠色	*Adj.*	green	13s
lǜshī	律师	律師	*N.*	lawyer	6s

M

ma	吗	嗎	*Part.*	(used at the end of a sentence to transform it into a question)	1
māma	妈妈	媽媽	*N.*	mother	6
mǎlù	马路	馬路	*N.*	road, street	18s
mǎshàng	马上	馬上	*Adv.*	immediately	20

mǎtóu	码头	碼頭	N.	wharf, dock, pier	18s
mǎi	买	買	V.	to buy	13
mǎidān	买单	買單	V.O.	to pay the bill	11s
mài	卖	賣	V.	to sell	13s
màn	慢	慢	Adj.	slow	16
máng	忙	忙	Adj.	busy	4s, 9
māo	猫	貓	N.	cat	6s
máo	毛	毛	N.	(10 毛 = 1 块)	13s
máoyī	毛衣	毛衣	N.	sweater	13s
màozi	帽子	帽子	N.	hat	13s
méiguānxi	没关系	沒關係		No problem.	20
méiyǒu	没有	沒有	V.	to not have; be without	5s, 6
Měiguó	美国	美國	N.	the United States	3
Měijīn	美金	美金	N.	U.S. dollar	13s
měilì	美丽	美麗	Adj.	beautiful	22
měitiān	每天	每天	N.	every day	10
mèimei	妹妹	妹妹	N.	younger sister	6s, 12
men	们	們		(used after a personal pronoun or noun to show plural number)	4
mén	门	門	M.W.	(measure word for school course)	10
			N.	door	15s
mínǐqún	迷你裙	迷你裙	N.	miniskirt	13s
mìshū	秘书	祕書	N.	secretary	6s
miàn	面	麵	N.	noodle	11
miànbāo	面包	麵包	N.	bread	11s
miànbāochē (bāoxíngchē)	面包车 (包型车)	麵包車 (包型車)	N.	minibus, van	18s
miǎo	秒	秒	N.	second	10s
míngpiàn	名片	名片	N.	name card	8s
míngtiān	明天	明天	N.	tomorrow	12
míngzi	名字	名字	N.	name	2
mótuōchē (jīchē)	摩托车 (机车)	摩托車 (機車)	N.	scooter, motorcycle	18s

N

nǎ	哪	哪	Pron.	which	3
nà	那	那	Pron.	that	4
nǎinai	奶奶	奶奶	N.	grandmother	6s
nán	难	難	Adj.	difficult	4
	男	男	N.	male	6
nánbù	南部	南部	N.	south	18
nánpéngyou	男朋友	男朋友	N.	boyfriend	5s, 6
nǎr	哪儿	哪兒	Pron.	where	7

ne	呢	呢	*Part.*	(used at the end of an interrogative sentence)	1
nèikù	内裤	內褲	*N.*	underpants	13s
nèiyī	内衣	內衣	*N.*	underwear	13s
néng	能	能	*Aux.*	can	12
nǐ	你	你	*Pron.*	you	1
nián	年	年	*N.*	year	10
nín	您	您	*Pron.*	you (polite)	2
niúròu	牛肉	牛肉	*N.*	beef	11s
niúzǎikù	牛仔裤	牛仔褲	*N.*	jeans	13s
Niǔyuē	纽约	紐約	*N.*	New York	6
nuǎnhuo	暖和	暖和	*Adj.*	warm	17
nǚ	女	女	*N.*	female	6s
nǚpéngyou	女朋友	女朋友	*N.*	girlfriend	5s, 6s, 20

O

| Ōuyuán | 欧元 | 歐元 | *N.* | Euro | 13s |

P

páshān	爬山	爬山	*N.*	mountain climbing	16s
			V.O.	to climb a mountain	
páiqiú	排球	排球	*N.*	volleyball	16s
pán	盘	盤	*M.W.*	plate	11
pángbiān	旁边	旁邊	*N.*	nearby	15
pǎobù	跑步	跑步	*V.O.*	to run	16s
pǎochē	跑车	跑車	*N.*	sports car	18s
péngyou	朋友	朋友	*N.*	friend	5
píjiǔ	啤酒	啤酒	*N.*	beer	11
píxié	皮鞋	皮鞋	*N.*	leather shoes	13s
piányi	便宜	便宜	*Adj.*	inexpensive	13s
piào	票	票	*N.*	ticket	13
píng	瓶	瓶	*M.W.*	bottle	11
píngguǒ	苹果	蘋果	*N.*	apple	11s
pútao	葡萄	葡萄	*N.*	grape	11s

Q

qī	七/柒	七/柒	*Num.*	seven	7
qí	骑	騎	*V.*	to ride	18
qí zìxíngchē	骑自行车	騎自行車	*V.O.*	to ride a bike	16s
qízhōng	其中	其中		among (whom, which)	17
qǐchuáng	起床	起床	*V.O.*	to get up	10
qìchē	汽车	汽車	*N.*	car	18s

qìhòu	气候	氣候	N.	climate	17
qìwēn	气温	氣溫	N.	temperature	17s
qiānyuē	签约	簽約	V.O.	to sign a contract	20s
qián	钱	錢	N.	money	13
qiánbiān	前边	前邊	N.	in front of	15
qiánshuǐ	潜水	潛水	V.O.	to dive	16s
qiǎnlǜsè	浅绿色	淺綠色	Adj.	light green	13s
qiǎnsè	浅色	淺色	Adj.	light	13s
qīnshǔ	亲属	親屬	N.	relatives	6s
qiū	秋	秋	N.	autumn	17
qiújì	球季	球季	N.	season (of a sport)	16s
qiúsài	球赛	球賽	N.	ball game, match	16
qiúxié	球鞋	球鞋	N.	sneakers	13s
qīngcài	青菜	青菜	N.	vegetable	11s
qīngdàn	清淡	清淡	Adj.	plain	11s
qìngshēng	庆生	慶生	V.O.	to celebrate a birthday	14s
qǐng	请	請		please (polite)	2
qǐng wèn	请问	請問		may I ask	2
qù	去	去	V.	to go	8
qúnzi	裙子	裙子	N.	skirt	13

R

ránhòu	然后	然後	Adv.	then; after that; afterwards	10
ràng	让	讓	V.	to let, allow	13
rè	热	熱	Adj.	hot	17
rèxīn	热心	熱心	Adj.	warm-hearted	22
rén	人	人	N.	person	3
Rénmínbì	人民币	人民幣	N.	currency of the People's Republic of China	13s
rènshi	认识	認識	V.	to know, recognize	5s, 8
rènzhēn	认真	認真	Adj.	conscientious; serious	22
rì	日	日	N.	day	10
Rìběn	日本	日本	N.	Japan	3s, 8
Rìběnrén	日本人	日本人	N.	Japanese (person)	3s
Rìyǔ (Rìwén)	日语 (日文)	日語 (日文)	N.	Japanese (language)	3s
róngyì	容易	容易	Adj.	easy	4s
ruǎnjiàn (ruǎntǐ)	软件 (软体)	軟件 (軟體)	N.	sorftware	9s

S

sān	三/叁	三/叁	Num.	three	7
sè	色	色	N.	color	12

shālā	沙拉	沙拉	N.	salad	11s
shǎo	少	少	Adj.	few, little	4
shāngrén	商人	商人	N.	businessman	6s
shàngbiān	上边	上邊	N.	on top of, above, over	15
shàngkè	上课	上課	V.O.	to begin class; attend class	8
shàngshēng	上升	上升	V.C.	to increase	17s
shàngwǎng	上网	上網	V.O.	to be online	9
shàngyī	上衣	上衣	N.	upper clothing	13s
shèshì	摄氏	攝氏	N.	Centigrade	17s
shètuán	社团	社團	N.	organization	16s
shéi	谁	誰	Pron.	who, whom	2
shēnlánsè	深蓝色	深藍色	Adj.	dark blue	13s
shēnqǐng	申请	申請	V.	to apply	21
shēnsè	深色	深色	Adj.	dark	13s
shénme	什么	什麼	Pron.	what	2
shěnshen	婶婶	嬸嬸	N.	aunt (wife of father's younger brother)	6s
shēngbìng	生病	生病	V.O.	to fall ill	19
shēnghuó	生活	生活	N.	life	10
shēngrì	生日	生日	N.	birthday	14
shèr	事儿	事兒	N.	matter, thing, business	8
shí	十/拾	十/拾	Num.	ten	7s, 11
shíhou	时候	時候	N.	time (the duration of time); (a point in)	9
shíjiān	时间	時間	N.	time	17
shípǐn	食品	食品	N.	food	11s
shíxí	实习	實習	N.	internship	21
shì	是	是	V.	to be; yes (affirmative answer)	1
shìpǐn	饰品	飾品	N.	accessory	13s
shìshi	试试	試試	V.	to try	13
shìyǒu	室友	室友	N.	roommate	5
shōudào	收到	收到	V.C.	to receive	22
shǒubiǎo	手表	手錶	N.	watch	13s
shǒujī	手机	手機	N.	cellular phone	7
shǒujuàn	手绢	手絹	N.	handkerchief	13s
shǒupáidǎng (shǒupái)	手排挡 (手排)	手排擋 (手排)	N.	manual transmission	12
shǒutào	手套	手套	N.	gloves	13s
shǒuzhuó	手镯	手鐲	N.	bracelet	13s
shū	书	書	N.	book	4
shūfǎ	书法	書法	N.	calligraphy	22
shūfu	舒服	舒服	Adj.	comfortable, be well	19
shūshu	叔叔	叔叔	N.	uncle (father's younger brother)	6s
shūzhuō	书桌	書桌	N.	desk	15s
shǔjià	暑假	暑假	N.	summer vacation	17s, 21
shǔqī	暑期	暑期	N.	summer	21

shùxué	数学	數學	N.	mathematics	4s
shuāyá	刷牙	刷牙	V.O.	to brush teeth	10s
shuāng	双	雙	M.W.	pair	11
shuìjiào	睡觉	睡覺	V.O.	to sleep; to go to bed	9s, 10
shùnlì	顺利	順利	Adj.	smooth	22s
shuō	说	說	V.	to speak	3
shuòshì	硕士	碩士	N.	master's degree	21s
sījī	司机	司機	N.	driver	18s
sījīn	丝巾	絲巾	N.	handkerchief	13s
sì	四/肆	四/肆	Num.	four	6
sìjì	四季	四季	N.	four seasons	17s
sìlúnqūdòng	四轮驱动	四輪驅動	N.	four-wheel drive	18s
(sìlúnchuándòng)	(四轮传动)	(四輪傳動)			
sòng	送	送	V.	to give as a present	14
sùshè	宿舍	宿舍	N.	dorm	7
suān	酸	酸	Adj.	sour	11s
suì	岁	歲	N.	age, years	14
suìdào	隧道	隧道	N.	tunnel	18s
suǒyǐ	所以	所以	Conj.	therefore, consequently	19

T

tā	他	他	Pron.	he, him	1
	她	她	Pron.	she, her	2
tāmen	他们	他們	Pron.	they, them	5
tài	太	太	Adv.	too	4
Tàiguó	泰国	泰國	N.	Thailand	3s
Tàiguórén	泰国人	泰國人	N.	Thai (person)	3s
Tàiyǔ	泰语	泰語	N.	Thai (language)	3s
(Tàiwén)	(泰文)	(泰文)			
tāng	汤	湯	N.	soup	11
tángdì	堂弟	堂弟	N.	cousin (son of father's brother) (younger than the speaker)	6s
tángdìmèi	堂弟妹	堂弟妹	N.	cousin (wife of 堂弟)	6s
tánggē	堂哥	堂哥	N.	cousin (son of father's brother) (older than the speaker)	6s
tángjiě	堂姐	堂姐	N.	cousin (daughter of father's brother) (older than the speaker)	6s
tángjiěfu	堂姐夫	堂姐夫	N.	cousin (husband of 堂姐)	6s
tángmèi	堂妹	堂妹	N.	cousin (daughter of father's brother) (younger than the speaker)	6s
tángmèifu	堂妹夫	堂妹夫	N.	cousin (husband of 堂妹)	6s
tángsǎo	堂嫂	堂嫂	N.	cousin (wife of 堂哥)	6s
tàng	烫	燙	Adj.	burning hot	11s

táozi	桃子	桃子	*N.*	peach	11s
tè dà	特大	特大	*Adj.*	extra large	13s
tè xiǎo	特小	特小	*Adj.*	extra small	13s
tiānqì	天气	天氣	*N.*	weather	17s
tiānqiáo	天桥	天橋	*N.*	overhead bridge	18s
tián	甜	甜	*Adj.*	sweet	11s
tiándiǎn	甜点	甜點	*N.*	dessert	11s
tiáo	条	條	*M.W.*	(measure word for skirt/pants)	13
tīxùshān	T-恤衫	T-恤衫	*N.*	T-shirt	13s
(tīxù)	(T-恤)	(T-恤)			
tǐwēn	体温	體溫	*N.*	body temperature	19s
tǐyùguǎn	体育馆	體育館	*N.*	gymnasium	16
tīngshuō	听说	聽說	*V.*	to be told; hear of; it is said	18
tíng	停	停	*V.*	to park	12
tíngchēchǎng	停车场	停車場	*N.*	parking lot	12
tōng	通	通	*M.W.*	(measure word for telephone conversation)	9s
tóngshì	同事	同事	*N.*	colleague	22
tóngxué	同学	同學	*N.*	classmate, student	2
tóuténg	头疼	頭疼	*V.*	to have a headache	19
túshūguǎn	图书馆	圖書館	*N.*	library	10
tuīxiāoyuán	推销员	推銷員	*N.*	salesman	6s
tuō	脱	脫	*V.*	to take off (regular clothes)	13s
tuōxià	脱下	脫下	*V.C.*	to take off (regular clothes)	13s
tuōxié	拖鞋	拖鞋	*N.*	slippers	13s

W

wàzi	袜子	襪子	*N.*	socks	13s
wàigōng	外公	外公	*N.*	maternal grandfather	6s
wàipó	外婆	外婆	*N.*	maternal grandmother	6s
wàisheng	外甥	外甥	*N.*	nephew (sister's son)	6s
wàishengnǚ	外甥女	外甥女	*N.*	niece (sister's daughter)	6s
wàitào	外套	外套	*N.*	coat	13s
wàizǔfù	外祖父	外祖父	*N.*	maternal grandfather	6s
wàizǔmǔ	外祖母	外祖母	*N.*	maternal grandmother	6s
wán	玩	玩	*V.*	to play, have fun	12
wǎn	晚	晚	*Adj.*	late	10s
	碗	碗	*M.W.*	bowl	11
wǎnfàn	晚饭	晚飯	*N.*	dinner	8s
wǎnshàng	晚上	晚上	*N.*	evening, night	9
wǎngbā	网吧	網吧	*N.*	Internet cafè	9s
(wǎngkā)	(网咖)	(網咖)			
wǎngluò	网络	網絡	*N.*	Internet	9s
(wǎnglù)	(网路)	(網路)			

wǎngqiú	网球	網球	N.	tennis	16s
wǎngyè	网页	網頁	N.	Web page	9s
wǎngzhàn	网站	網站	N.	Web site	9s
wàngjì	旺季	旺季	N.	busy season	18s
wéijīn	围巾	圍巾	N.	scarf	13s
wèi	位	位	M.W.	(polite form, measure word for people)	9
	为	為	Prep.	(indicates the object of one's act of service)	14
(wéi)	喂	喂	Int.	hello; hey (used in greeting or to attract attention)	9
wénxué	文学	文學	N.	literature	4
wèn	问	問	V.	to ask	2
wèntí	问题	問題	N.	problem, question	12
wǒ	我	我	Pron.	I, me	1
wǒjiùshì	我就是	我就是		this is he/she speaking (on the phone)	9
wǒmen	我们	我們	Pron.	we, us	4
wòshì	卧室	臥室	N.	bedroom	15
wǔ	五/伍	五/伍	Num.	five	7
wǔfàn (zhōngfàn)	午饭 (中饭)	午飯 (中飯)	N.	lunch	8s
wǔhuì	舞会	舞會	N.	dance party	14

X

xībù	西部	西部	N.	west	18
Xībānyá	西班牙	西班牙	N.	Spain	3s
Xībānyárén	西班牙人	西班牙人	N.	Spanish (person)	3s
Xībānyáyǔ (Xibānyáwén)	西班牙语 (西班牙文)	西班牙語 (西班牙文)	N.	Spanish (language)	3s
xīguā	西瓜	西瓜	N.	watermelon	11s
xīyān	吸烟	吸煙	V.O.	to smoke	20
xīzhuāng	西装	西裝	N.	suit	13s
xǐhuān	喜欢	喜歡	V.	to like	10
xǐliǎn	洗脸	洗臉	V.O.	to wash face	10s
xǐzǎo	洗澡	洗澡	V.O.	to take a bath	10s
xǐzǎojiān	洗澡间	洗澡間	N.	bathroom, restroom	15
xì	系	系	N.	department	4s
xiā	虾	蝦	N.	shrimp	11s
xià	夏	夏	N.	summer	17
xiàcì	下次	下次		next time	8
xiàjiàng	下降	下降	V.C.	to decrease	17s
xiàkè	下课	下課	V.O.	to end class	8
xiàwǔ	下午	下午	N.	afternoon	10

xiàyǔ	下雨	下雨	V.O.	to rain	17
xiān	先	先	Adv.	first	11, 18
xiānsheng	先生	先生	N.	mister	11
xián	咸	鹹	Adj.	salty	11s
xiànzài	现在	現在	Adv.	now	16
xiāngjiāo	香蕉	香蕉	N.	banana	11s
xiǎng	想	想	V.	to want	8
xiàngliàn	项链	項鏈	N.	necklace	13s
xiāoyè	宵夜	宵夜	N.	midnight snack	8s
xiǎo	小	小	Adj.	small	7, 13s
xiǎofèi	小费	小費	N.	tip	11s
xiǎojiě	小姐	小姐	N.	miss	11
xiǎolóngbāo	小笼包	小籠包	N.	little steamed buns with stuffing	22
xiǎoshí	小时	小時	N.	hour	10s
xiǎoshuō	小说	小說	N.	novel	9s
xiàonèi	校内	校內	N.	on campus	7s
xiàowài	校外	校外	N.	off campus	7
xiézi	鞋子	鞋子	N.	shoes	13s
xiě	写	寫	V.	to write	10
xièxie	谢谢	謝謝		thank you, thanks	9
xīn	新	新	Adj.	new	22
Xīntáibì	新台币	新台幣	N.	currency of Taiwan	13s
xīnxiǎngshìchéng	心想事成	心想事成		Every wish comes true.	22s
xìn	信	信	N.	letter	10
xīngqī	星期	星期	N.	week	14
xíng	行	行	V.	to be all right, okay	8
xìng	姓	姓	N.	surname, family	2
			V.	to be surnamed	2
xiōngdìjiěmèi	兄弟姐妹	兄弟姐妹	N.	siblings	6s
xiūxi	休息	休息	V.	to rest	8s, 9s, 19
xuēzi	靴子	靴子	N.	boots	13s
xué	学	學	V.	to study, learn	1
xuédào	学到	學到	V.C.	to learn and master	22
xuéqī	学期	學期	N.	semester	10
xuésheng	学生	學生	N.	student	1
xuéshì	学士	學士	N.	bachelor's degree	21s
xuéwèi	学位	學位	N.	degree	21s
xuéxiào	学校	學校	N.	school	18
xuě	雪	雪	N.	snow	17

Y

yánjiūshēng	研究生	研究生	N.	graduate students	21s
yánjiūshēngyuàn	研究生院	研究生院	N.	graduate school	21
yánsè	颜色	顏色	N.	color	13s

yánzhòng	严重	嚴重	Adj.	severe	19s
yǎnjìng	眼镜	眼鏡	N.	glasses	13s
yào	要	要	V.	to want, desire	9
yéye	爷爷	爺爺	N.	grandfather	6s
yě	也	也	Adv.	also, too	1
yī	一/壹	一/壹	Num.	one	6
yīchú	衣橱	衣櫥	N.	wardrobe	15s
yīfu	衣服	衣服	N.	clothes	13s
yīshēng	医生	醫生	N.	doctor	6s, 19
yīwùshì (yīhùshì)	医务室 (医护室)	醫務室 (醫護室)	N.	clinic	19s
yīyuàn	医院	醫院	N.	hospital	19s
yídìng	一定	一定	Aux.	certainly, surely	14
yífù	姨父	姨父	N.	uncle (husband of mother's sister)	6s
yígòng	一共	一共	Adv.	altogether; in all	18
yílùpíng'ān	一路平安	一路平安		Have a pleasant journey.	21
yímā	姨妈	姨媽	N.	aunt (mother's sister)	6s
yímiàn	一面	一面	Adv.	at the same time	21
yíxià	一下	一下		(used after a verb to indicate a brief action)	5
yízhàng	姨丈	姨丈	N.	uncle (husband of mother's sister)	6s
yǐhòu	以后	以後	N.	after; afterwards; later	8
yǐjīng	已经	已經	Adv.	already	22
yǐnliào	饮料	飲料	N.	drink	11s
yǐqián	以前	以前	N.	before; previously	20
yǐzi	椅子	椅子	N.	chair	15s
yìdiǎr	一点儿	一點兒		a little	3
yìqǐ	一起	一起	Adv.	together	8
yìxiē	一些	一些	Adj.	some	22
yīnwèi	因为	因為	Conj.	because	22
yínhuīsè	银灰色	銀灰色	Adj.	silver	13s
yīnggāi	应该	應該	Aux.	should	12
Yīngguó	英国	英國	N.	Britain	3
Yīngwén	英文	英文	N.	English (language)	2
Yīngyǔ	英语	英語	N.	English (language)	2s
yìngjiàn (yìngtǐ)	硬件 (硬体)	硬件 (硬體)	N.	hardware	9s
yòng	用	用	V.	to use	12
yóudìyuán (yóuchāi)	邮递员 (邮差)	郵遞員 (郵差)	N.	mailman	6s
yóuyǒng	游泳	游泳	V.O.	to swim	16
			N.	swimming	16s
yóuyǒngchí	游泳池	游泳池	N.	swimming pool	16

yǒu	有	有	V.	to have	5
yǒudiǎr	有点儿	有點兒	Adv.	a little	4s
yǒukòng	有空	有空	V.O.	to have free time	14
yǒushíhou	有时候	有時候	Adv.	sometimes	17
yǒuyìsi	有意思	有意思	Adj.	interesting, enjoyable	21
yòubiān	右边	右邊	N.	on the right	15s
yú	鱼	魚	N.	fish	11s
yúkuài	愉快	愉快	Adj.	happy	21
yǔmáoqiú	羽毛球	羽毛球	N.	badminton	16s
yùfángzhēn	预防针	預防針	N.	immunization shot	19s
yuán	元	元	N.	dollar	13s
yuǎn	远	遠	Adj.	far	18
yuǎnzú	远足	遠足	N.	hiking	16s
yuè	月	月	N.	month	10
yuèyěchē	越野车	越野車	N.	off-road vehicle	18s
yùndòng	运动	運動	N.	sports	16s

Z

zázhì	杂志	雜誌	N.	magazine	15s
zài	在	在	V.	to be at, be in	6
			Prep.	at, in	
zài	再	再	Adv.	again	8
zàijiàn	再见	再見		see you again; goodbye	8
zàixiàn yóuxì (xiànshàng yóuxì)	在线游戏 (线上游戏)	在線遊戲 (線上遊戲)	N.	on-line game	9s
zāng	脏	髒	Adj.	dirty	15s
zǎo	早	早	Adj.	early	10s
zǎofàn	早饭	早飯	N.	breakfast	8s
zěnmeyàng	怎么样	怎麼樣	Pron.	how (used as a predicative or complement)	8
zhāi	摘	摘	V.	to take off (accessories)	13s
zhāixià	摘下	摘下	V.C.	to take off (accessories)	13s
zhànxiàn	占线	佔線	V.O.	to occupy a (phone) line, the line is busy	9s
zhāng	张	張	M.W.	(measure word for piece of paper)	13
zhǎo	找	找	V.	to seek for, look for	21
zhè	这	這	Pron.	this	4
zhècì	这次	這次	Pron.	this time	12
zhèyàng	这样	這樣	Pron.	thus; in this way	12
zhēn	真	真	Adv.	really	15
zhěnsuǒ	诊所	診所	N.	clinic	19s
zhěnglǐ	整理	整理	V.	to arrange, put in order	15s

Each entry lists English meaning, simplified character, traditional character, Pinyin, part of speech, and lesson number.
Note: The letter "s" means that the entry occurs in the supplementary vocabulary to that lesson.

Units of Measurement

10 jiao = 1 yuan	角	角	jiǎo	N.	13s
10 mao = 1 kuai	毛	毛	máo	N.	13s
100 fen = 10 jiao/10 mao = 1 yuan/1 kuai	分	分	fēn	N.	13s

Measure Words (Classifiers) for

books	本	本	běn	M.W.	4
certain animals, boats, or containers, or for one of a pair	只	隻	zhī	M.W.	6
clothes	件	件	jiàn	M.W.	13
company, enterprises, store, etc.	家	家	jiā	M.W.	21
cups, buildings, characters	个	個	gè	M.W.	5
people (polite form)	位	位	wèi	M.W.	9
a piece of paper	张	張	zhāng	M.W.	13
school courses	门	門	mén	M.W.	10
skirt/pants	条	條	tiáo	M.W.	13
telephone conversation	通	通	tōng	M.W.	9s
vehicles	辆	輛	liàng	M.W.	6

A

above, over, on top of	上边	上邊	shàngbiān	N.	15
accessory	饰品	飾品	shìpǐn	N.	13s
accountant	会计师	會計師	kuàijìshī	N.	6s
action	动作	動作	dòngzuò	N.	13s
activity	活动	活動	huódòng	N.	22
address	地址	地址	dìzhǐ	N.	10
after, afterwards, later	以后	以後	yǐhòu	N.	8
afternoon	下午	下午	xiàwǔ	N.	10
again	再	再	zài	*Adv.*	8
age, years old	岁	歲	suì	N.	14
agent	经纪人	經紀人	jīngjìrén	N.	6s
airplane	飞机	飛機	fēijī	N.	12

airport	机场	機場	jīchǎng	*N.*	12
all, everybody	大家	大家	dàjiā	*Pron.*	6
all, both	都	都	dōu	*Adv.*	5
already	已经	已經	yǐjīng	*Adv.*	22
already, as early as	就	就	jiù	*Adv.*	10
also, too	也	也	yě	*Adv.*	1
altogether, in all	一共	一共	yígòng	*Adv.*	18
among (whom, which)	其中	其中	qízhōng		17
and	和	和	hé	*Conj.*	3
apartment	公寓	公寓	gōngyù	*N.*	7s
apple	苹果	蘋果	píngguǒ	*N.*	11s
to apply	申请	申請	shēnqǐng	*V.*	21
architect	建筑师	建築師	jiànzhùshī	*N.*	6s
to arrange, put in order	整理	整理	zhěnglǐ	*V.*	15s
to arrive	到	到	dào	*V.*	12
to ask	问	問	wèn	*V.*	2
at, in	在	在	zài	*Prep.*	6
at the same time	同时	同時	tóngshí	*Adv.*	21
to attend classes, begin class	上课	上課	shàngkè	*V.O.*	8
aunt (father's sister)	姑妈	姑媽	gūmā	*N.*	6s
	姑姑	姑姑	gūgu	*N.*	6s
(mother's sister)	姨妈	姨媽	yímā	*N.*	6s
	阿姨	阿姨	āyí	*N.*	6s
(wife of father's elder brother)	伯母	伯母	bómǔ	*N.*	6s
(wife of father's younger brother)	婶婶	嬸嬸	shěnshen	*N.*	6s
(wife of mother's brother)	舅妈	舅媽	jiùmā	*N.*	6s
automatic transmission	自动排挡 (自排)	自動排擋 (自排)	zìdòngpáidǎng (zìpái)	*Adj.*	12s
autumn	秋	秋	qiū	*N.*	17

B

bachelor's degree	学士	學士	xuéshì	*N.*	21s
badminton	羽毛球	羽毛球	yǔmáoqiú	*N.*	16s
ball game, match	球赛	球賽	qiúsài	*N.*	16
banana	香蕉	香蕉	xiāngjiāo	*N.*	11s
baseball	棒球	棒球	bàngqiú	*N.*	16s
basketball	篮球	籃球	lánqiú	*N.*	16, 16s
to bathe, take a bath	洗澡	洗澡	xǐzǎo	*V.O.*	10s
bathroom, restroom	洗澡间	洗澡間	xǐzǎojiān	*N.*	15
to be all right, okay	行	行	xíng	*V.*	8
to be at, be in,	在	在	zài	*V.*	6
to be like, seem	好像	好像	hǎoxiàng	*V.*	19

bus	公共汽车	公共汽車	gōnggòngqìchē	N.	18
	公车	公車	gōngchē	N.	18s
	(巴士)	(巴士)	(bāshì)		
businessman	商人	商人	shāngrén	N.	6s
busy	忙	忙	máng	Adj.	4s, 9
busy season	旺季	旺季	wàngjì	N.	18s
but	但是	但是	dànshì	Conj.	20
but, however	不过	不過	búguò	Conj.	22
but, yet, however	可是	可是	kěshì	Conj.	4
to buy	买	買	mǎi	V.	13
by the way (a phrase used to start a new topic)	对了	對了	duìle	Conj.	3

C

cake	蛋糕	蛋糕	dàngāo	N.	11s, 14
California State	加州	加州	Jiāzhōu	N.	21
to call	叫	叫	jiào	V.	2
calligraphy	书法	書法	shūfǎ	N.	22
can	能	能	néng	Aux.	12
can, be able to	会	會	huì	Aux.	3
can, may	可以	可以	kěyǐ	Aux.	12
Canada	加拿大	加拿大	Jiānádà	N.	3s
Canadian (people)	加拿大人	加拿大人	Jiānádàrén	N.	3s
candle	蜡烛	蠟燭	làzhú	N.	14s
car	车	車	chē	N.	6
	汽车	汽車	qìchē	N.	18s
cat	猫	貓	māo	N.	6s
to celebrate a birthday	庆生	慶生	qìngshēng	V.O.	14s
cell phone	手机	手機	shǒujī	N.	7
Centigrade	摄氏	攝氏	shèshì	N.	17s
certainly, surely	一定	一定	yídìng	Aux.	14
chair	椅子	椅子	yǐzi	N.	15s
chat room	聊天室	聊天室	liáotiānshì	N.	9s
chicken	鸡肉	雞肉	jīròu	N.	11s
child	孩子	孩子	háizi	N.	6s
China	中国	中國	Zhōngguó	N.	3
Chinese (language)	中文	中文	Zhōngwén	N.	2
	汉语	漢語	Hànyǔ	N.	2s
chopstick	筷子	筷子	kuàizi	N.	11
city	城市	城市	chéngshì	N.	22
class	班	班	bān	N.	21
classmate, student	同学	同學	tóngxué	N.	2
classroom	教室	教室	jiàoshì	N.	15s

clean	干净	乾淨	gānjìng	Adj.	15s
climate	气候	氣候	qìhòu	N.	17
to climb a mountain	爬山	爬山	páshān	V.O.	16s
clinic	医务室	醫務室	yīwùshì	N.	19s
	(医护室)	(醫護室)	(yīhùshì)		
	诊所	診所	zhěnsuǒ	N.	19s
clothes	衣服	衣服	yīfu	N.	13s
clothing (for upper body)	上衣	上衣	shàngyī	N.	13s
club	俱乐部	俱樂部	jùlèbù	N.	16s
coach, trainer	教练	教練	jiàoliàn	N.	16
coat	外套	外套	wàitào	N.	13s
coffee	咖啡	咖啡	kāfēi	N.	11s
cola	可乐	可樂	kělè	N.	11
cold	冷	冷	lěng	Adj.	17
cold, flu	感冒	感冒	gǎnmào	N.	19
colleague	同事	同事	tóngshì	N.	22
college, university	大学	大學	dàxué	N.	10
college student(s)	大学生	大學生	dàxuéshēng	N.	6s, 21s
color	色	色	sè	N.	12
	颜色	顏色	yánsè	N.	13s
to come over	过来	過來	guòlái	V.C.	20
to come (used before a verb to indicate that one is about to do something)	来	來	lái	V.	5
comfortable	舒服	舒服	shūfu	Adj.	19
common	常见	常見	chángjiàn	Adj.	11s
company	公司	公司	gōngsī	N.	21
computer	计算机	計算機	jìsuànjī	N.	4s
	(电脑)	(電腦)	(diànnǎo)	N.	21
computer game	电脑游戏	電腦遊戲	diànnǎo yóuxì	N.	9s
computer programmer	程序员	程序員	chéngxùyuán	N.	6s
	(程式设计师)	(程式設計師)	(chéngshì shèjìshī)		
conscientious, serious	认真	認真	rènzhēn	Adj.	22
consultant	顾问	顧問	gùwèn	N.	6s
to cook	做饭	做飯	zuòfàn	V.O.	20
cool	凉	涼	liáng	Adj.	11s
correct, right	对	對	duì	Adj.	9
to cough	咳嗽	咳嗽	késòu	V.	19
country	国	國	guó	N.	3
cousin (daughter of father's brother)	堂姐	堂姐	tángjiě	N.	6s
	堂妹	堂妹	tángmèi	N.	6s
(daughter of parents' sister or mother's brother)	表姐	表姐	biǎojiě	N.	6s
	表妹	表妹	biǎomèi	N.	6s
(husband of 表姐)	表姐夫	表姐夫	biǎojiěfu	N.	6s

(husband of 表妹)	表妹夫	表妹夫	biǎomèifu	N.	6s
(husband of 堂姐)	堂姐夫	堂姐夫	tángjiěfu	N.	6s
(husband of 堂妹)	堂妹夫	堂妹夫	tángmèifu	N.	6s
(son of father's brother)	堂哥	堂哥	tánggē	N.	6s
	堂弟	堂弟	tángdì	N.	6s
(son of parents' sister or mother's brother)	表哥	表哥	biǎogē	N.	6s
	表弟	表弟	biǎodì	N.	6s
(wife of 表弟)	表弟妹	表弟妹	biǎodìmèi	N.	6s
(wife of 表哥)	表嫂	表嫂	biǎosǎo	N.	6s
(wife of 堂弟)	堂弟妹	堂弟妹	tángdìmèi	N.	6s
(wife of 堂哥)	堂嫂	堂嫂	tángsǎo	N.	6s
cracker	饼干	餅乾	bǐnggān	N.	11s
cup	杯	杯	bēi	M.W.	11
currency	货币	貨幣	huòbì	N.	13s
currency of Hong Kong	港币	港幣	Gǎngbì	N.	13s
currency of the People's Republic of China	人民币	人民幣	Rénmínbì	N.	13s
currency of Taiwan	新台币	新台幣	Xīntáibì	N.	13s
to cycle, to ride a bike	骑自行车	騎自行車	qí zìxíngchē	V.O.	16s

D

dance party	舞会	舞會	wǔhuì	N.	14
dark	深色	深色	shēnsè	Adj.	13s
dark blue	深蓝色	深藍色	shēnlánsè	Adj.	13s
day	日	日	rì	N.	10
to decide	决定	決定	juédìng	V.	21
to decrease	下降	下降	xiàjiàng	V.C.	17s
degree	度	度	dù	N.	17
	学位	學位	xuéwèi	N.	21s
department	系	系	xì	N.	4s
desk	书桌	書桌	shūzhuō	N.	15s
dessert	甜点	甜點	tiándiǎn	N.	11s
to dial a wrong number	打错了	打錯了	dǎcuòle		9s
difficult	难	難	nán	Adj.	4
dining room	餐厅	餐廳	cāntīng	N.	15
dinner	晚饭	晚飯	wǎnfàn	N.	8s
dirty	脏	髒	zāng	Adj.	15s
dish	菜	菜	cài	N.	8
to dive	潜水	潛水	qiánshuǐ	V.O.	16s
to do	做	做	zuò	V.	9
doctor	医生	醫生	yīshēng	N.	6s, 19
doctoral degree	博士	博士	bóshì	N.	21s
doctoral students	博士生	博士生	bóshìshēng	N.	21s
dog	狗	狗	gǒu	N.	6

F

Fahrenheit	华氏	華氏	huáshì	*N.*	17
to fall ill	生病	生病	shēngbìng	*V.O.*	19
far	远	遠	yuǎn	*Adj.*	18
fast	快	快	kuài	*Adj.*	16
father	爸爸	爸爸	bàba	*N.*	6
female	女	女	nǚ	*N.*	6s
fen (RMB unit)	分	分	fēn	*N.*	13s
few, little	少	少	shǎo	*Adj.*	4
first	先	先	xiān	*Adv.*	11, 18
first day	第一天	第一天	dìyītiān	*N.*	20
fish	鱼	魚	yú	*N.*	11s
to fish	钓鱼	釣魚	diàoyú	*V.O.*	16s
five	五/伍	五/伍	wǔ	*Num.*	7
flu	流感 (流行性感冒)	流感 (流行性感冒)	liúgǎn (liúxíngxìng gǎnmào)	*N.*	19s
flu shot	流感疫苗	流感疫苗	liúgǎn yìmiáo	*N.*	19s
food	食品	食品	shípǐn	*N.*	11s
football	橄榄球	橄欖球	gǎnlǎnqiú	*N.*	16s
for a long time	久	久	jiǔ	*Adj.*	17
for example	比如	比如	bǐrú	*Conj.*	22
for public use, communal	公用	公用	gōngyòng	*Adj.*	15
for, to	给	給	gěi	*Prep.*	9
form of address	称谓	稱謂	chēngwèi	*N.*	6s
four	四/肆	四/肆	sì	*Num.*	6
four seasons	四季	四季	sìjì	*N.*	17s
four-wheel drive	四轮驱动 (四轮传动)	四輪驅動 (四輪傳動)	sìlúnqūdòng (sìlúnchuándòng)	*N.*	18s
France	法国	法國	Fǎguó	*N.*	3
French (language)	法文	法文	Fǎwén	*N.*	3
friend	朋友	朋友	péngyou	*N.*	5
from	从	從	cóng	*Prep.*	6

G

German (language)	德语 (德文)	德語 (德文)	Déyǔ (Déwén)	*N.*	3s
(people)	德国人	德國人	Déguórén	*N.*	3s
Germany	德国	德國	Déguó	*N.*	3s
to get up	起床	起床	qǐchuáng	*V.O.*	10
gift	礼物	禮物	lǐwù	*N.*	14s
girlfriend	女朋友	女朋友	nǚpéngyou	*N.*	5s, 6s, 20

to give (as a present)	送(礼)	送(禮)	sòng(lǐ)	*V.O.*	14
give or receive an injection	打针	打針	dǎzhēn	*V.O.*	19s
glasses	眼镜	眼鏡	yǎnjìng	*N.*	13s
gloves	手套	手套	shǒutào	*N.*	13s
to go	去	去	qù	*V.*	8
to go to bed, sleep	睡觉	睡覺	shuìjiào	*V.O.*	9s, 10
to go out	出去	出去	chūqù	*V.C.*	20
gold	金黄色	金黄色	jīnhuángsè	*Adj.*	13s
golf	高尔夫球	高爾夫球	gāo'ěrfūqiú	*N.*	16s
good-looking	好看	好看	hǎokàn	*Adj.*	13
Good luck.	好运	好運	hǎoyùn		21
good, well	好	好	hǎo	*Adj.*	1
goodbye, see you again	再见	再見	zàijiàn		8
government official	官员	官員	guānyuán	*N.*	6s
to graduate	毕业	畢業	bìyè	*V.*	21
graduate school	研究生院	研究生院	yánjiūshēngyuàn	*N.*	21
graduate student	研究生	研究生	yánjiūshēng	*N.*	21s
grandfather	爷爷	爺爺	yéye	*N.*	6s
	祖父	祖父	zǔfù	*N.*	6s
grandmother	奶奶	奶奶	nǎinai	*N.*	6s
	祖母	祖母	zǔmǔ	*N.*	6s
grape	葡萄	葡萄	pútao	*N.*	11s
gray	灰色	灰色	huīsè	*Adj.*	13s
green	绿	綠	lǜ	*Adj.*	11
	绿色	綠色	lǜsè	*Adj.*	13s
gym	健身房	健身房	jiànshēnfáng	*N.*	16
gymnasium	体育馆	體育館	tǐyùguǎn	*N.*	16

H

half	半	半	bàn	*Adj.*	10
handkerchief	手绢	手絹	shǒujuàn	*N.*	13s
happy	愉快	愉快	yúkuài	*Adj.*	21
	高兴	高興	gāoxìng	*Adj.*	22
	开心	開心	kāixīn	*Adj.*	22
Happy birthday to you.	祝你生日快乐	祝你生日快樂	Zhù nǐ shēngrì kuàilè.		14s
hardware	硬件(硬体)	硬件(硬體)	yìngjiàn (yìngtǐ)	*N.*	9s
hat	帽子	帽子	màozi	*N.*	13s
to have	有	有	yǒu	*V.*	5
to have a fever	发烧	發燒	fāshāo	*V.O.*	19
to have a headache	头疼	頭疼	tóuténg	*V.*	19
Have a pleasant journey.	一路平安	一路平安	yílùpíng'ān		21

to have a try, taste	尝尝	嚐嚐	chángchang	*V.*	22
to have free time	有空	有空	yǒukòng	*V.O.*	14
to have or start (a vacation)	放假	放假	fàngjià	*V.O.*	17
he, him	他	他	tā	*Pron.*	1
healthy	健康	健康	jiànkāng	*Adj.*	22s
hello, hey (used in greetings or to attract attention)	喂	喂	wèi (wéi)	*Int.*	9
to help	帮	幫	bāng	*V.*	13
hiking	远足	遠足	yuǎnzú	*N.*	16s
home, family	家	家	jiā	*N.*	6
homework	作业	作業	zuòyè	*N.*	16
homework, assignment	作业	作業	zuòyè	*N.*	4s
	功课	功課	gōngkè	*N.*	4
hospital	医院	醫院	yīyuàn	*N.*	19s
hot	热	熱	rè	*Adj.*	17
hour	点钟	點鐘	diǎnzhōng	*N.*	10s
	钟头	鐘頭	zhōngtóu	*M.W.*	10s
	小时	小時	xiǎoshí	*N.*	10s
house, room	房子	房子	fángzi	*N.*	7s
housewife	家庭主妇	家庭主婦	jiātíng zhǔfù	*N.*	6s
how (used as a predicative or complement)	怎么样	怎麼樣	zěnmeyàng	*Pron.*	8
how many	几	幾	jǐ		5
how many, how much	多少	多少	duōshǎo	*Pron.*	7
how old	多大	多大	duōdà		14
hundred	百	百	bǎi	*Num.*	17
hungry	饿	餓	è	*Adj.*	19

I

I, me	我	我	wǒ	*Pron.*	1
ice	冰	冰	bīng	*N.*	11
ice hockey	冰球	冰球	bīngqiú	*N.*	16s
immediately	马上	馬上	mǎshàng	*Adv.*	20
immunization shot	预防针	預防針	yùfángzhēn	*N.*	19s
to improve	进步	進步	jìnbù	*V.*	12
in front of	前边	前邊	qiánbiān	*N.*	15
in the process of, in the course of (to indicate an action in progress)	正在	正在	zhèngzài	*Adv.*	9
to increase	上升	上升	shàngshēng	*V.C.*	17s
(indicates assumption)	了	了	le	*Part.*	9
(indicates one's act of service)	为	為	wèi	*Prep.*	14
(indicates the superlative degree)	最	最	zuì	*Adv.*	17

inexpensive	便宜	便宜	piányi	*Adj.*	13s
inside	里边	裡邊	lǐbiān	N.	15
interesting, enjoyable	有意思	有意思	yǒuyìsi	*Adj.*	21
international students	留学生	留學生	liúxuéshēng	N.	6s
Internet	网络 (网路)	網絡 (網路)	wǎngluò (wǎnglù)	N.	9s
Internet café	网吧 (网咖)	網吧 (網咖)	wǎngbā (wǎngkā)	N.	9s
internship	实习	實習	shíxí	N.	21
to introduce	介绍	介紹	jièshào	V.	5
to introduce oneself; self-introduction	自我介绍	自我介紹	zìwǒjièshào	V./N.	6s
(introduces the object of a verb)	把	把	bǎ	*Prep.*	20
introduction	介绍	介紹	jièshào	N.	5
it seems	看来	看來	kànlái		22

J

jacket	夹克衫 (夹克)	夾克衫 (夾克)	jiákèshān (jiákè)	N.	13s
Japan	日本	日本	Rìběn	N.	3s, 8
Japanese (language)	日语 (日文)	日語 (日文)	Rìyǔ (Rìwén)	N.	3s
(people)	日本人	日本人	Rìběnrén	N.	3s
jeans	牛仔裤	牛仔褲	niúzǎikù	N.	13s
jeep	吉普车	吉普車	jípǔchē	N.	18s
jiao (RMB unit of 10 cents) 10 fen	角	角	jiǎo	N.	13s
job, to work	工作	工作	gōngzuò	N./V.	6
juice	果汁	果汁	guǒzhī	N.	11s

K

kitchen	厨房	廚房	chúfáng	N.	15
to know	认识	認識	rènshi	V.	5s
to know, recognize	认识	認識	rènshi	V.	8
to know, be aware of, realize	知道	知道	zhīdào	V.	9
Korea	韩国	韓國	Hánguó	N.	3s, 8
Korean (language)	韩语 (韩文)	韓語 (韓文)	Hányǔ (Hánwén)	N.	3s
(people)	韩国人	韓國人	Hánguórén	N.	3s

L

to lack	差	差	chà	V.	10s
landlord	房东	房東	fángdōng	N.	20s
large	大	大	dà	Adj.	13s
late	晚	晚	wǎn	Adj.	10s
lawyer	律师	律師	lǜshī	N.	6s
to learn, to master	学到	學到	xuédào	V.C.	22
leather shoes	皮鞋	皮鞋	píxié	N.	13s
to leave a message	留言 (留话)	留言 (留話)	liúyán (liúhuà)	V.O.	9
to let, allow	让	讓	ràng	V.	13
letter	信	信	xìn	N.	10
library	图书馆	圖書館	túshūguǎn	N.	10
life	生活	生活	shēnghuó	N.	10
to lift weights	举重	舉重	jǔzhòng	V.O.	16s
light	浅色	淺色	qiǎnsè	Adj.	13s
light green	浅绿色	淺綠色	qiǎnlǜsè	Adj.	13s
to like	喜欢	喜歡	xǐhuān	V.	10
literature	文学	文學	wénxué	N.	4
little, a	一点儿	一點兒	yìdiǎr		3
	有点儿	有點兒	yǒudiǎr	Adv.	4s
little steamed buns with stuffing	小笼包	小籠包	xiǎolóngbāo	N.	22
to live	住	住	zhù	V.	7
living room	客厅	客廳	kètīng	N.	15
to look at, see, watch	看	看	kàn	V.	9
long	长	長	cháng	Adj.	17s
long pants	长裤	長褲	chángkù	N.	13s
to love	爱	愛	ài	V.	6
lunch	午饭 (中饭)	午飯 (中飯)	wǔfàn (zhōngfàn)	N.	8s

M

magazine	杂志	雜誌	zázhì	N.	15s
magnetic railway	磁浮铁路	磁浮鐵路	cífú tiělù	N.	18s
mailman	邮递员 (邮差)	郵遞員 (郵差)	yóudìyuán (yóuchāi)	N.	6s
major	专业 (主修)	專業 (主修)	zhuānyè (zhǔxiū)	N.	4s
to make a phone call	打电话	打電話	dǎ diànhuà	V.O.	9
to make, do	做	做	zuò	V.	14
male	男	男	nán	N.	6
manager	经理	經理	jīnglǐ	N.	6s

N

name	名字	名字	míngzi	N.	2
name card	名片	名片	míngpiàn	N.	8s
near	近	近	jìn	Adj.	18
nearby	旁边	旁邊	pángbiān	N.	15
necklace	项链	項鏈	xiàngliàn	N.	13s
necktie	领带	領帶	lǐngdài	N.	13s
nephew (brother's son)	侄子	姪子	zhízi	N.	6s
(sister's son)	外甥	外甥	wàisheng	N.	6s
new	新	新	xīn	Adj.	22
New York	纽约	紐約	Niǔyuē	N.	6
next time	下次	下次	xiàcì		8
niece (brother's daughter)	侄女	姪女	zhínǚ	N.	6s
(sister's daughter)	外甥女	外甥女	wàishengnǚ	N.	6s
nine	九/玖	九/玖	jiǔ	Num.	7
No problem	没关系	沒關係	méiguānxi		20
noble, honored; expensive	贵	貴	guì	Adj.	2
noodle	面	麵	miàn	N.	11
north	北	北	běi	N.	18s
not bad, okay	还好	還好	hái hǎo		4s
not bad, pretty good	不错	不錯	búcuò		13
not, no (used to form negation)	不	不	bù	Adv.	1
notes	笔记	筆記	bǐjì	N.	19
novel	小说	小說	xiǎoshuō	N.	9s
now	现在	現在	xiànzài	Adv.	16
number	号	號	hào	N.	7
	号码	號碼	hàomǎ	N.	7
nurse	护士	護士	hùshi	N.	6s, 19s

O

occupation	职业	職業	zhíyè	N.	6s
to occupy a (phone) line, the line is busy	占线	佔線	zhànxiàn	V.O.	9s
o'clock	点	點	diǎn	M.W.	10
off campus	校外	校外	xiàowài	N.	7
off-road vehicle, jeep	越野车	越野車	yuèyěchē	N.	18s
off-season	淡季	淡季	dànjì	N.	18s
often, frequently	常	常	cháng	Adv.	5
on campus	校内	校內	xiàonèi	N.	7s
on the left	左边	左邊	zuǒbiān	N.	15s
on the right	右边	右邊	yòubiān	N.	15s
one	一/壹	一/壹	yī	Num.	6

oneself	自己	自己	zìjǐ	N.	6s
on-line games	在线游戏 (线上游戏)	在線遊戲 (線上遊戲)	zàixiàn yóuxì (xiànshàng yóuxì)	N.	9s
only	只要	只要	zhǐyào	Adv.	18
opportunity	机会	機會	jīhuì	N.	22
opposite	对面	對面	duìmiàn	N.	15
or	还是	還是	háishì	Conj.	11
or, either . . . or . . .	或者	或者	huòzhě	Conj.	13
orange	橙色 (橘色)	橙色 (橘色)	chéngsè (júsè)	Adj.	13s
orange juice	橙汁	橙汁	chéngzhī	N.	11s
to order food	点菜	點菜	diǎncài	V.O.	11s
organization	社团	社團	shètuán	N.	16s
out, to be	出	出	chū	V.	20
overcoat	大衣	大衣	dàyī	N.	13s
overhead bridge	天桥	天橋	tiānqiáo	N.	18s
overseas, abroad	国外	國外	guówài	N.	21

P

pair	双	雙	shuāng	M.W.	11
pants	裤子	褲子	kùzi	N.	13
to park	停	停	tíng	V.	12
park	公园	公園	gōngyuán	N.	15
parking lot	停车场	停車場	tíngchēchǎng	N.	12
to participate, join	参加	參加	cānjiā	V.	14
to pass	过	過	guò	V.	10s, 17
to pay	付	付	fù	V.	20
to pay the bills	买单	買單	mǎidān	V.O.	11s
peach	桃子	桃子	táozi	N.	11s
pear	梨子	梨子	lízi	N.	11s
Peking Opera	京剧	京劇	jīngjù	N.	22
person	人	人	rén	N.	3
pet	宠物	寵物	chǒngwù	N.	6s
phone	电话	電話	diànhuà	N.	7
to pick up	接	接	jiē	V.	12
pilot	飞行员	飛行員	fēixíngyuán	N.	6s
pink	粉红色	粉紅色	fěnhóngsè	Adj.	13s
place	地方	地方	dìfang	N.	22
plain	清淡	清淡	qīngdàn	Adj.	11s
plate	盘	盤	pán	M.W.	11
to play basketball/badminton/ tennis/table tennis	打球	打球	dǎqiú	V.O.	10
to play, have fun	玩	玩	wán	V.	12

please (polite)	请	請	qǐng	2
pork	猪肉	豬肉	zhūròu	N.	11s
to practice	练习	練習	liànxí	V.	12
to prepare	准备	準備	zhǔnbèi	V.	19
problem, question	问题	問題	wèntí	N.	12
professor	教授	教授	jiàoshòu	N.	6s
purple	紫色	紫色	zǐsè	Adj.	13s
to put on (accessories)	戴上	戴上	dàishàng	V.C.	13s
(clothes)	穿上	穿上	chuānshàng	V.C.	13s

Q

quarter (of an hour)	刻	刻	kè	M.W.	10

R

to rain	下雨	下雨	xiàyǔ	V.O.	17
real estate agent	房地产顾问	房地產顧問	fángdìchǎn gùwèn	N.	6s
really	真	真	zhēn	Adv.	15
to receive	收到	收到	shōudào	V.C.	22
red	红	紅	hóng	Adj.	11
	红色	紅色	hóngsè	Adj.	13s
relatively	比较	比較	bǐjiào	Adv.	13
relatives	亲属	親屬	qīnshǔ	N.	6s
rent	房租	房租	fángzū	N.	20
to rent a house	租屋	租屋	zū wū	V.O.	20s
to rent, hire, lease	租	租	zū	V.	18
to rest	休息	休息	xiūxi	V.	8s, 9s, 19
restaurant	饭馆	飯館	fànguǎn	N.	11s
	餐厅	餐廳	cāntīng	N.	11s
	餐馆	餐館	cānguǎn	N.	11s
	饭店	飯店	fàndiàn	N.	11s
resume	简历	簡歷	jiǎnlì	N.	21s
	(履历表)	(履歷表)	(lǚlìbiǎo)		
(retroflex ending)	儿	兒	ér		3
to return	回	回	huí	V.	8
	回来	回來	huílai	V.C.	9
to review	复习	復習	fùxí	V.	19
rice, meal	饭	飯	fàn	N.	8
to ride	骑	騎	qí	V.	18
ring	戒指	戒指	jièzhi	N.	13s
road, street	马路	馬路	mǎlù	N.	18s
room	房间	房間	fángjiān	N.	7
roommate	室友	室友	shìyǒu	N.	5

to row a boat	划船	划船	huáchuán	*V.O.*	16s
to run	跑步	跑步	pǎobù	*V.O.*	16s

S

salad	沙拉	沙拉	shālā	*N.*	11s
salesman	推销员	推銷員	tuīxiāoyuán	*N.*	6s
salesman, saleswoman	店员	店員	diànyuán	*N.*	13
salty	咸	鹹	xián	*Adj.*	11s
sandals	凉鞋	涼鞋	liángxié	*N.*	13s
scarf	围巾	圍巾	wéijīn	*N.*	13s
scenery	风景	風景	fēngjǐng	*N.*	18
scenery, view	景色	景色	jǐngsè	*N.*	18
school	学校	學校	xuéxiào	*N.*	18
scooter, motorcycle	摩托车 (机车)	摩托車 (機車)	mótuōchē (jīchē)	*N.*	18s
seafood	海鲜	海鮮	hǎixiān	*N.*	11s
seashore	海滩	海灘	hǎitān	*N.*	18s
seaside	海边	海邊	hǎibiān	*N.*	18
season (of sports)	球季	球季	qiújì	*N.*	16s
second	秒	秒	miǎo	*N.*	10s
secretary	秘书	祕書	mìshū	*N.*	6s
to see	见	見	jiàn	*V.*	8
to scck for, to look for	找	找	zhǎo	*V.*	21
to sell	卖	賣	mài	*V.*	13s
to send a short (cell phone) message	发短信 (送简讯)	發短信 (送簡訊)	fā duǎnxìn (sòng jiǎnxùn)	*V.O.*	9s
semester	学期	學期	xuéqī	*N.*	10
to settle the account	结账 (结帐)	結賬 (結帳)	jiézhàng (jiézhàng)	*V.O.*	11s
seven	七/柒	七/柒	qī	*Num.*	7
severe	严重	嚴重	yánzhòng	*Adj.*	19s
severely, very much	厉害	厲害	lìhài	*Adj.*	19s
she, her	她	她	tā	*Pron.*	2
ship	船	船	chuán	*N.*	18
shirt	衬衫	襯衫	chènshān	*N.*	13
shoes	鞋子	鞋子	xiézi	*N.*	13s
short	短	短	duǎn	*Adj.*	17
short pants	短裤	短褲	duǎnkù	*N.*	13s
should	应该	應該	yīnggāi	*Aux.*	12
shrimp	虾	蝦	xiā	*N.*	11s
siblings	兄弟姐妹	兄弟姐妹	xiōngdìjiěmèi	*N.*	6s
to sign a contract	签约	簽約	qiānyuē	*V.O.*	20s

silver	银灰色	銀灰色	yínhuīsè	*Adj.*	13s
to sit	坐	坐	zuò	*V.*	11
six	六/陆	六/陸	liù	*Num.*	7
size	号	號	hào	*N.*	13s
to skate	滑冰	滑冰	huábīng	*V.O.*	16s
skirt	裙子	裙子	qúnzi	*N.*	13
to sleep	睡觉	睡覺	shuìjiào	*V.O.*	9s
slippers	拖鞋	拖鞋	tuōxié	*N.*	13s
slow	慢	慢	màn	*Adj.*	16
small	小	小	xiǎo	*Adj.*	7, 13s
to smoke	吸烟	吸煙	xīyān	*V.O.*	20
smooth	顺利	順利	shùnlì	*Adj.*	22s
sneakers	球鞋	球鞋	qiúxié	*N.*	13s
snow	雪	雪	xuě	*N.*	17
to snow ski	滑雪	滑雪	huáxuě	*V.O.*	16s
soccer	足球	足球	zúqiú	*N.*	16s
socks	袜子	襪子	wàzi	*N.*	13s
software	软件 (软体)	軟件 (軟體)	ruǎnjiàn (ruǎntǐ)	*N.*	9s
some	一些	一些	yìxiē	*Adj.*	22
sometimes	有时候	有時候	yǒushíhou	*Adv.*	17
sorry	对不起	對不起	duìbuqǐ		9
soup	汤	湯	tāng	*N.*	11
sour	酸	酸	suān	*Adj.*	11s
south	南部	南部	nánbù	*N.*	18
Spain	西班牙	西班牙	Xībānyá	*N.*	3s
Spanish (language)	西班牙语 (西班牙文)	西班牙語 (西班牙文)	Xībānyáyǔ (Xibānyáwén)	*N.*	3s
(people)	西班牙人	西班牙人	Xībānyárén	*N.*	3s
to speak	说	說	shuō	*V.*	3
Speaking (phone)	我就是	我就是	Wǒjiùshì		9
to spend (time), celebrate (e.g., birthday), live	过	過	guò	*V.*	14
spicy	辣	辣	là	*Adj.*	11s
sports	运动	運動	yùndòng	*N.*	16s
sports car	跑车	跑車	pǎochē	*N.*	18s
spring	春天	春天	chūntiān	*N.*	17
spring break	春假	春假	chūnjià	*N.*	17
spring roll	春卷	春捲	chūnjuǎn	*N.*	11s
staff	职员	職員	zhíyuán	*N.*	6s
to start, begin	开始	開始	kāishǐ	*V.*	22
to starve, hungry	饿	餓	è	*V.*	19
steamed rice	白饭	白飯	báifàn	*N.*	11s
to stir fry	炒	炒	chǎo	*V.*	11

stop, station	车站	車站	chēzhàn	N.	18s
strawberry	草莓	草莓	cǎoméi	N.	11s
structural particle	的	的	de	*Part.*	2
student	学生	學生	xuésheng	N.	1
to study abroad	留学	留學	liúxué	*V.O.*	21
to study, to learn	学	學	xué	*V.*	1
subway	地铁	地鐵	dìtiě	N.	18s
suit	西装	西裝	xīzhuāng	N.	13s
summer	夏	夏	xià	N.	17
	暑期	暑期	shǔqī	N.	21
summer vacation	暑假	暑假	shǔjià	N.	17s, 21
surname, family name	姓	姓	xìng	N.	2
sweater	毛衣	毛衣	máoyī	N.	13s
sweet	甜	甜	tián	*Adj.*	11s
to swim; swimming	游泳	游泳	yóuyǒng	*V.O./N.*	16
swimming pool	游泳池	游泳池	yóuyǒngchí	N.	16

T

table	桌子	桌子	zhuōzi	N.	15
to take medicine	吃药	吃藥	chīyào	*V.O.*	19
Take care	保重	保重	bǎozhòng		22s
to take off (accessories)	摘	摘	zhāi	*V.*	13s
	摘下	摘下	zhāixià	*V.C.*	13s
(clothes)	脱	脱	tuō	*V.*	13s
	脱下	脱下	tuōxià	*V.C.*	13s
tall building	大楼	大樓	dàlóu	N.	22
tangerine juice	柳橙汁	柳橙汁	liǔchéngzhī	N.	11s
	(柳丁汁)	(柳丁汁)	(liǔdīngzhī)		
taxi	出租汽车	出租汽車	chūzūqìchē	N.	18s
	(计程车)	(計程車)	(jìchéngchē)		
tea	茶	茶	chá	N.	11
to teach, coach	教	教	jiāo	*V.*	16
teacher	老师	老師	lǎoshī	N.	1, 6s
T-shirt	T-恤衫	T-恤衫	tīxùshān	N.	13s
	(T-恤)	(T-恤)	(tīxù)		
television	电视	電視	diànshì	N.	9
temperature	气温	氣溫	qìwēn	N.	17s
ten	十/拾	十/拾	shí	*Num.*	7s, 11
tenant	房客	房客	fángkè	N.	20s
tennis	网球	網球	wǎngqiú	N.	16s
Thai (language)	泰语	泰語	Tàiyǔ	N.	3s
	(泰文)	(泰文)	(Tàiwén)		
(people)	泰国人	泰國人	Tàiguórén	N.	3s

Thailand	泰国	泰國	Tàiguó	N.	3s
to thank, be grateful for	感谢	感謝	gǎnxiè	V.	19
Thank you, Thanks.	谢谢	謝謝	xièxie		9
that	那	那	nà	Pron.	4
then, after that, afterwards	然后	然後	ránhòu	Adv.	10
therefore	就	就	jiù	Adv.	12
therefore, consequently	所以	所以	suǒyǐ	Conj.	19
they, them	他们	他們	tāmen	Pron.	5
thing	东西	東西	dōngxi	N.	22
to think, feel	觉得	覺得	juéde	V.	13
this	这	這	zhè	Pron.	4
this time	这次	這次	zhècì	Pron.	12
three	三/叁	三/叁	sān	Num.	7
thus, in this way	这样	這樣	zhèyàng	Pron.	12
ticket	票	票	piào	N.	13
tidy	整齐	整齊	zhěngqí	Adj.	15s
time	时间	時間	shíjiān	N.	17
(duration of point in)	时候	時候	shíhou	N.	9
tip	小费	小費	xiǎofèi	N.	11s
tired	累	累	lèi	Adj.	4s
today	今天	今天	jīntiān	N.	8
together	一起	一起	yìqǐ	Adv.	8
tomorrow	明天	明天	míngtiān	N.	12
too	太	太	tài	Adv.	4
tourist guide	导游	導遊	dǎoyóu	N.	6s
train	火车	火車	huǒchē	N.	18, 18s
to travel	旅行	旅行	lǚxíng	V.	18
truck	大货车	大貨車	dàhuòchē	N.	18s
to try	试试	試試	shìshi	V.	13
tunnel	隧道	隧道	suìdào	N.	18s
two	两	兩	liǎng	Num.	5
	二/贰	二/貳	èr	Num.	7
two people (colloquial)	俩	倆	liǎ		16

U

uncle (father's elder brother)	伯伯	伯伯	bóbo	N.	6s
(father's younger brother)	叔叔	叔叔	shūshu	N.	6s
(husband of father's sister)	姑父	姑父	gūfù	N.	6s
	姑丈	姑丈	gūzhàng	N.	6s
(husband of mother's sister)	姨丈	姨丈	yízhàng	N.	6s
	姨父	姨父	yífù	N.	6s
(mother's brother)	舅舅	舅舅	jiùjiu	N.	6s

underground passage	地下道	地下道	dìxiàdào	N.	18s
underpants	内裤	內褲	nèikù	N.	13s
underwear	内衣	內衣	nèiyī	N.	13s
United States of America, the	美国	美國	Měiguó	N.	3
upstairs	楼上	樓上	lóushàng	N.	20
to use	用	用	yòng	V.	12
(used after a personal pronoun or noun to show plural number)	们	們	men		4
(used after a verb to indicate a brief action)	一下	一下	yíxià		5
(used at the end of a sentence to indicate surprise)	啊	啊	a	*Int.*	20
(used at the end of a sentence to transform it into a question)	吗	嗎	ma	*Part.*	1
(used at the end of an interrogative sentence)	呢	呢	ne	*Part.*	1
(to indicate an assumption or a suggestion)	吧	吧	ba	*Part.*	9
(used before a verb to indicate that something is rather late)	才	才	cái	*Adv.*	10
(used between a verb or an adjective and its complement to indicate result, possibility or degree)	得	得	de	*Part.*	16

V

vacation	假期	假期	jiàqī	N.	17s
vegetable	青菜	青菜	qīngcài	N.	11s
very	非常	非常	fēicháng	*Adv.*	16
very, quite	很	很	hěn	*Adv.*	3
vest	背心	背心	bèixīn	N.	13s
virus	病毒	病毒	bìngdú	N.	9s
to visit	参观	參觀	cānguān	V.	15
volleyball	排球	排球	páiqiú	N.	16s

W

English	Simplified	Traditional	Pinyin	Type	Lesson
to wait	等	等	děng	V.	9
to wait for a moment	等一下儿	等一下兒	děng yíxiàr		9
waiter/waitress	服务员	服務員	fúwùyuán	N.	11
to walk	走	走	zǒu	V.	15
	走路	走路	zǒulù	V.O.	18
to want	想	想	xiǎng	V.	8
to want, desire	要	要	yào	V.	9
wardrobe	衣橱	衣櫥	yīchú	N.	15s
warm	暖和	暖和	nuǎnhuo	Adj.	17
warmhearted	热心	熱心	rèxīn	Adj.	22
to wash one's face	洗脸	洗臉	xǐliǎn	V.O.	10s
watch	手表	手錶	shǒubiǎo	N.	13s
watermelon	西瓜	西瓜	xīguā	N.	11s
we, us	我们	我們	wǒmen	Pron.	4
wear, put on (accessories)	戴	戴	dài	V.	13s
(clothes)	穿	穿	chuān	V.	13s
to wear	穿	穿	chuān	V.	13
weather	天气	天氣	tiānqì	N.	17s
Web page	网页	網頁	wǎngyè	N.	9s
Web site	网站	網站	wǎngzhàn	N.	9s
week	星期	星期	xīngqī	N.	14
to welcome	欢迎	歡迎	huānyíng	V.	15
west	西部	西部	xībù	N.	18
wharf, dock, pier	码头	碼頭	mǎtóu	N.	18s
what	什么	什麼	shénme	Pron.	2
where	哪儿	哪兒	nǎr	Pron.	7
which	哪	哪	nǎ	Pron.	3
what size	几号	幾號	jǐ hào		13s
white	白	白	bái	Adj.	12
	白色	白色	báisè	Adj.	13s
who, whom	谁	誰	shéi	Pron.	2
window	窗户	窗戶	chuānghu	N.	15s
winter	冬	冬	dōng	N.	17
winter vacation	寒假	寒假	hánjià	N.	17s
to wish	祝	祝	zhù	V.	10
with	跟	跟	gēn	Prep.	5
wonderful	棒	棒	bàng	Adj.	14
wonton	馄饨	餛飩	húntun	N.	11s
to work for others	打工	打工	dǎgōng	V.O.	21
to wrap	包	包	bāo	V.	16
to write	写	寫	xiě	V.	10
to write a letter (to the speaker)	来信	來信	láixìn	V.O.	22

Y

year	年	年	nián	N.	10
yellow	黄	黃	huáng	*Adj.*	13
	黄色	黃色	huángsè	*Adj.*	13s
yesterday	昨天	昨天	zuótiān	N.	16
you	你	你	nǐ	*Pron.*	1
you (polite)	您	您	nín	*Pron.*	2
You're welcome.	不客气	不客氣	Búkèqi		9s, 14
(in reply to thank you)	不谢	不謝	Búxiè		9s
younger brother	弟弟	弟弟	dìdi	N.	6s
younger sister	妹妹	妹妹	mèimei	N.	6s, 12

Z

| zero | ○/零 | ○/零 | líng | *Num.* | 7s |

The following list shows the 432 characters that appear in the Character Book, grouped by the lesson in which they are first introduced. Students are required to memorize how to read and write these key characters to build up their literacy skills. The number of new characters introduced in each lesson is carefully controlled, and is provided in the list.

(1) 第一课　你好！ (13 characters)
你 好 是 学 生 吗 我 呢 也 他 不 老 师

(2) 第二课　您贵姓？ (17 characters)
您 贵 姓 请 问 的 英 文 名 字 中 叫 什 么 她 谁 同

(3) 第三课　你是哪国人？ (14 characters)
哪 国 人 很 对 了 法 美 说 会 一 点 儿 和

(4) 第四课　你学什么？ (14 characters)
那 书 这 本 工 程 难 太 可 功 课 多 们 少

(5) 第五课　这是我朋友 (14 characters)
朋 友 来 介 绍 下 室 有 几 两 个 都 常 跟

(6) 第六课　我的家 (16 characters)
家 大 从 在 四 爸 妈 姐 作 男 没 辆 车 只 狗 爱

(7) 第七课　你住哪儿？ (21 characters)
住 宿 舍 号 房 间 电 话 小 码 二 三 五 六 七 八 九 手 机 校 外

(8) 第八课　你认识不认识他？ (21 characters)
认 识 去 上 以 后 事 想 回 起 吃 饭 菜 今 天 次 怎 样 行 再 见

(9) 第九课　他正在打电话 (22 characters)
打 喂 等 知 道 谢 吧 忙 正 看 视 做 网 就 位 留 言 时 候 晚 要 给

(10) 第十课　我每天七点半起床 (29 characters)
活 期 门 每 床 睡 觉 半 才 刻 分 然 图 馆 午 喜 欢 球 写 信 子 邮 件 地 址 祝 年 月 日

(11) 第十一课　你要红茶还是绿茶？ (25 characters)
红 茶 还 绿 服 务 员 坐 先 喝 杯 冰 乐 瓶 啤 酒 面 饺 盘 炒 十 碗 汤 双 筷

(12) 第十二课　我可以借你的车吗? (25 characters)
借明用得场接妹飞玩到排挡开应该题白色停到习练能进步

(13) 第十三课　我想买一件衬衫 (23 characters)
买衬衫店条裙或者裤黄错比较穿黑试帮让钱块张影票

(14) 第十四课　我今年二十岁 (15 characters)
岁空星过为舞参加定蛋糕送棒客气

(15) 第十五课　图书馆在宿舍前边 (18 characters)
前边迎观里厨公旁走厅面餐洗澡卧桌园真

(16) 第十六课　她打篮球打得很好 (20 characters)
篮俩教游泳非快体育池健身锻炼现昨赛业包慢

(17) 第十七课　春天就要来了 (22 characters)
春久放假夏秋冬其最暖短热华氏百度极刮风雨冷雪

(18) 第十八课　我们要坐火车去旅行 (20 characters)
火旅离远只钟骑自共汽路近西部景船南听海租

(19) 第十九课　我感冒了 (23 characters)
感冒饿像舒头疼发烧咳嗽病考复所医药休息准备笔记

(20) 第二十课　我把小谢带来了 . . . (17 characters)
把带啊搬出吸烟关系但女必须第付楼马

(21) 第二十一课　暑假你要做什么? (18 characters)
暑毕决申研究院找司实脑班意思愉平安运

(22) 第二十二课　我到上海了 (25 characters)
因已经丽城市处新些方动如京剧东笼尝始高兴收心板保重